the Pacific Crest

Volume 2: Oregon & Washington

Trail

by Jeff Schaffer
and
Bev & Fred Hartline

Acknowledgments

The authors are indebted to numerous individuals who contributed time and effort that aided us in the completion of this guide. Thomas Winnett, editor-in-chief of Wilderness Press, contributed his usual wise counsel and gave over-all guidance to the project.

Lee Corbin of the U.S. Forest Service Region 6 provided us with insight on Pacific Crest Trail design and specs. Data on trail segments under construction were supplied by Howard Rondthaler, Earl E. Nichols and James P. Wiggins.

Ken Ng provided a three-month shuttle taxi service together with great outdoor meals while back in Berkeley Bill Hicks watched the house and fed the cat. Other shuttling assistance was provided by Bob and Hilary Straub, Earl Davis, Donna Lamb, Sandy Frost and Fred Rigby.

The trail company of Eugene Young, Ken Ng and Mike Schaffer made the sometimes-lonely task of trail mapping more enjoyable.

Jeff Schaffer
Berkeley, California

Bev & Fred Hartline
Seattle, Washington

January 1974

All maps and photos by Jeff Schaffer, except as noted.

Title page: Mt. Rainier, from near Chinook Pass.
Photo by Bev Hartline.

Typesetting by Lehmann Graphics.
Printed by Hooper Printing and Lithograph.

Contents

Chapter

the Pacific Crest Trail in the Northwest

1

History of the Trail

The idea of a Pacific Crest Trail originated in the early 1930s, in the mind of Clinton C. Clarke of Pasadena, California, who was then chairman of the Executive Committee of the Mountain League of Los Angeles County. "In March 1932," wrote Clarke in *The Pacific Crest Trailway* (out of print), he "proposed to the United States Forest and National Park Services the project of a continuous wilderness trail across the United States from Canada to Mexico . . . . The plan was to build a trail along the summit divides of the mountain ranges of these states [Washington, Oregon and California], traversing the best scenic areas and maintaining an absolute wilderness character."

The proposal included formation of additional Mountain Leagues in Seattle, Portland and San Francisco by representatives of youth organizations and hiking and mountaineering clubs similar to the one in Los Angeles. These Mountain Leagues would then take the lead in promoting the extension of the John Muir Trail northward and southward to complete a pathway from border to border. When it became evident that more than Mountain Leagues were needed for such a major undertaking, Clarke took the lead in forming the Pacific Crest Trail System Conference, with representatives from the three Pacific Coast states. He served as its President for 25 years.

As early as January 1935 Clarke published a handbook-guide to the PCT, giving the route in rather sketchy terms ("the Trail goes east of Heart Lake, then south across granite fields to the junction of Piute and Evolution Creeks"—this covers about nine miles).

In the summer of 1935—and again the next three summers—groups of boys under the sponsorship of the YMCA explored the route in relays, proceeding from Mexico on June 15, 1935, to Canada on August 12, 1938. This exploration was under the guidance of a YMCA secretary, Warren L. Rogers, who served as Executive Secretary of the Pacific Crest Trail System Conference from 1932 to 1957.

As early as 1920 the Forest Service had located and posted a trail from Crater Lake to Mt. Hood in Oregon, named the Oregon Skyline Trail. In 1928 the Forest Service began to study a high mountain route across Washington, and the reconnaisance of this trail, later called the Cascade Crest Trail, was completed in 1935. In 1937, Region Six (Oregon and Washington) of the Forest Service developed a design for PCT trail markers and posted them from the Canadian border to the California border. These green-and-white "Pacific Crest Trail System" diamonds can still be seen today from just north of Copco Reservoir, near the southern Oregon border, to the North Cascades, near the northern Washington border.

Region Five (California) did not follow this lead. In 1935, Clarke suggested to the Department of the Interior that the National Park Service construct the trail as a pathway connecting the state's national parks. Because so much of the land to be traversed was outside national parks, the Department declined. Nothing beyond Clarke's rough description and generalized maps, published in hardback in 1945, appeared until the late 1960s, and anyone who wanted to walk or ride the PCT from Mexico to Oregon—or vice versa—was pretty much on his own for large portions of the 1600-mile distance. Clarke died in 1957, at the age of 84, confident that his dream would one day be fulfilled.

In 1965 the Bureau of Outdoor Recreation, a Federal agency, appointed a commission to make a nationwide trails study. The Commission, noting that walking for pleasure was second only to driving for pleasure as the most popular recreation in America, recommended establishing a national system of trails, of two kinds—long National Scenic Trails in the hinterlands, and shorter National Recreation Trails in and near metropolitan areas. The commission recommended that Congress establish four Scenic Trails—the already existing Appalachian Trail, the partly existing Pacific Crest Trail, a Potomac Heritage Trail and a Continental Divide Trail. Congress responded by passing, in 1968, the National Trails System Act, which set the framework for a system of trails and specifically made the Appalachian and the Pacific Crest trails the first two National Scenic Trails.

Congress, in a 1968 law, created a citizens' Advisory Council for the PCT which was to decide all the details of the final route; the Forest Service said it would adopt whatever the citizens wanted. The Advisory Council was also to concern itself with standards for the physical nature of the trail, markers to be erected along the trail, and the administration of the trail and its use.

In 1972 the Advisory Council agreed upon a route, and the Forest Service put it onto maps for use inside the Service. These were sent to planners of the various national forests along the route, for them to mark a temporary route in the places where no trail yet existed along the final PCT route. Less than half of the final California PCT route existed, so roads and alternate trails had to be selected for its incomplete stretches. In Oregon and Washington, the PCT was in considerably better shape: Oregon had the Oregon Skyline Trail, complete from Lake of the Woods north to the Columbia River; Washington had the Cascade Crest Trail, almost complete from border to border.

The final proposed route was sent to Washington, D.C., where, on January 30, 1973, it was published in the Federal Register. Accompanying the maps that depicted the final route was a verbal description of it. The material in the register, however, does not give a center line which can be precisely and unambiguously followed; it is only a *route,* and the details in some areas remain to be settled. Furthermore, private land in southern Oregon and southern Washington must be acquired, or at least an easement secured for using it. It will be years before this is done, and in our opinion decades before the final Pacific Crest Trail becomes a continuous, walkable, maintained trail from Mexico to Canada. Where the trail is poor or it does not exist, this guidebook provides you with an alternate route.

In a sense, the Pacific Crest Trail will never be completed—it is constantly undergoing change. If a trail segment attracts more backpackers to an area than it can withstand, the trail segment must be rerouted. A conspicuous example of such rerouting is the 1972 trail detour above North Matthieu Lake in Oregon's Three Sisters Wilderness. This lake, near the McKenzie Highway, was too easily accessible to backpackers, day hikers, mountaineers and fishermen. Sometimes a section of trail should be rerouted but can't be due to the nature of the terrain it crosses. This is true at Shoe Lake, in Washington's Goat Rocks Wilderness, which has received too much use. Now the lake is closed to overnight camping. As with lakes, meadows—particularly soggy ones—suffer from the hiker's tread. Today the PCT generally skirts meadows rather than cutting directly across them.

The Pacific Crest Trail tends to increase in length yearly. Old trail segments are being lengthened, since one of the criteria for the PCT is that, as a general rule, the trail should not be steeper than 15 percent (a 15-foot rise in 100 horizontal feet). Many segments of the Oregon Skyline and Cascade Crest trails, constructed decades ago, are considerably steeper. If you're hiking the OST, you'll find that the segment from Mt. Thielsen north to Windigo Pass is longer than the mileage signs indicate: the switchbacks have been stretched out to reduce the gradient. In 1973 a hiker on the CCT could see the comparison between the old and new trail standards. Starting east from the Suiattle River, he would hike up the lazy new switchbacks to a crossing of Miners Creek, then he would labor pantingly on an old trail segment that climbed almost straight up a slope to a junction with the Suiattle Trail. We're sure you'll notice the difference between the old and the new segments and that you'll appreciate the improvement.

Stuart Falls, along the old PCT

2

Getting Ready to Hike the Trail

What to Expect

Of the thousands of backpackers who will taste wilderness along the Pacific Crest Trail each year, probably less than a hundred will complete the Oregon-Washington section and hardly any will complete the entire tri-state route. Probably the vast majority of the trail's travelers will be confining their wilderness visit to less than two and one half weeks and therefore will be able to carry all their needs on their backs without having to use resupply points.

We hope some readers will walk the whole trail, Mexico to Canada. That would take more than five months, and few people could do it all in the same year. You would have to start in early April. The California section would take you three months or more. If you were on schedule, you would celebrate your arrival at the Oregon border on or around the Fourth of July, and if you were really covering ground, you might even make it to Ashland's fireworks display at nearby Emigrant Lake. Five weeks later would see you setting foot on Washington soil, and perhaps by Labor Day your labor of wilderness love would be consummated in British Columbia's Ernest C. Manning Provincial Park.

If you are planning a short stretch and expect to encounter snow, hike from south to north. This way you'll encounter more downhill snow slopes than uphill ones, since snow lingers longer on north slopes—the ones you'll be descending. It's more fun to slide down a snowbank than to climb up one.

If the Cascade Range in Oregon and Washington were a uniform, continuous range, you could expect the snowpack to retreat uniformly northward as the summer wore on, and you could plan a month-long trek north so that you would always have a dry trail yet always have an adequate water source. However, this plan could have an undesired effect if you began at the height of the mosquito season: you'd have a continuous cloud of mosquitoes accompanying you north. The Cascade Range, however, is far from uniform, and often you will find yourself descending a snowbound pass into a warm, soothing, lake-dotted basin. If you are hiking the entire PCT, you are bound to encounter both pleasant and adverse trail conditions. If you want to avoid snow-clad trails, incessant mosquitoes and severe water shortages, then hike the following segments at these recommended times (remembering, of course, that weather patterns vary considerably from year to year), south to north:

Seiad Valley, Siskiyou Mountains, southern Oregon
    mid-May through mid-June

Mt. McLoughlin, Sky Lakes basin, Seven Lakes basin
    mid-July through late Ausust

Crater Lake
    July

Mt. Thielsen, Windigo Pass, Odell Lake
    mid-July through late August

Three Sisters
    late July through early August

Mt. Washington, Three Fingered Jack
    late June through mid-July

Mt. Jefferson
    mid-July through late August

Mt. Hood
    late July through mid-August

Columbia River gorge
    early June through early August

Southern Washington, Mt. Adams
    mid-July through mid-August

Goat Rocks
    late July through mid-August

White Pass, Mt. Rainier, Stampede Pass, Snoqualmie Pass, Stevens Pass
    mid-July through mid-August

Glacier Peak, North Cascades, Manning Provincial Park
    late July through early August.

There are, of course, advantages and disadvantages to hiking in any season. In the North Cascades, for example,

● early June will present you with spectacular snow-clad alpine scenery—but also soft-snow walking and a slight avalanche hazard;

- early July will present you with a riotous display of wildflowers—plus sucking mosquitoes and biting flies;
- early August will present you with the best trail conditions—and lots of backpackers;
- early September will present you with fall colors and ripe huckleberries—but also nippy nights and sudden snow storms.

Weather

By now you should be forming in your mind a vague idea of where and how long you expect to hike. Let's sharpen that idea by looking at the weather. The warmest temperatures are in mid-July through early August; they can vary from the 90s in southern Oregon to the 70s in the North Cascades. During this period night temperatures for the entire two-state route rarely drop below 50°F—you'll swelter if you're cooped up in a down mummy bag.

In late June, with its long daylight hours, the maximum and minimum temperatures are almost as high as those in midsummer. In addition, you can expect to be plagued with mosquitoes through early August. A *tent is a necessity*–preferably one large enough for you and your friends to prepare meals in. During these warm summer nights, you'll want to sleep *atop* your sleeping bag, and although the mosquitoes abate somewhat after dark, without a tent you won't get a mosquito-free sleep until later on in the season when the nights are cooler. Only when the wind picks up (late morning through late afternoon) or when a storm sets in are you afforded partial relief from these cursed insects. In Washington you will also be exposed to at least three species of biting flies—Ouch! But they are slower and easier to swat.

By late August the days have got considerably shorter and the temperatures lower. The evenings and nights in southern Oregon are comfortable but those in northern Washington are nippy, if not freezing. Expect to see morning frost on your tent and prepare for brisk, "autumn" days. Too, there's likely to be a water shortage, particularly in most of Oregon. The national forests may be closed to backpacking or they may require the backpacker to refrain from building campfires and use only a stove. A stove is also useful for boiling stagnant water and for melting snow. An advantage of a hike at this time, however, is that both Oregon and Washington will have a variety of berries ready for picking.

Another consideration is storms. Storm frequencies increase northward. Northern California is virtually storm-free from mid-June through early September. In central Oregon the period of good weather is only July through August, and even then occasional storms may be expected. If you visit southern Washington, be prepared for bad weather, even though you might get to hike a week or two at a time in beautiful midsummer weather. Expect bad or threatening weather in northern Washington. It is possible to hike two solid weeks in the North Cascades without receiving a drop of precipitation, but don't count on it—you might just receive two solid weeks of rain. Here, a tent is necessary to keep out the rain as well as to keep out the seasonal mosquitoes and flies.

As with storm frequencies, lake temperatures are influenced by the sun's apparent seasonal migratory pattern. Lakes are generally at their warmest in late July through early August. Also affecting a lake's temperature are its latitude, elevation, size, depth, inflow source and the side of the mountain, if any, that it is on. Below are some representative *maximum* temperatures you can expect to find at certain lakes and rivers, south to north.

Klamath River, northern California	80°F
Emigrant Lake, near Ashland	78
Margurette Lake, Sky Lakes Area	75
Dumbbell Lake, Three Sisters Wilderness	73
Scout Lake, Mt. Jefferson Wilderness	67
Wahtum Lake, northern Oregon	65
Eagle Creek, Columbia River gorge	57
Columbia River	65
Shoe Lake, Goat Rocks Wilderness	65
Pear Lake, north of Stevens Pass	63
Lake Janus, north of Stevens Pass	72
Mica Lake, Glacier Peak Wilderness	33
Stehekin River, North Cascades National Park	50

Planning and Preparation

After you decide which segment of the PCT you want to do, based on scenery, climate, available time or whatever, next comes the question of transportation. In California, buses stop at many towns near the PCT route, but in Oregon and Washington, they only speed along the major highways that cross our route. You may choose to hitchhike. Or you might possibly take a car. A list of highways that cross or come close to the PCT appears later in this chapter. You can begin your hike at any of them.

Unlike round trips and loop trips, a hike along part of the PCT does not take you back to where you started. So if you take a car and leave it at the trailhead, you have a transportation problem. The solution may be any of several:

- walk back to where you started
- hitchhike back to where you started
- arrange for someone to drop you off and pick you up
- arrange with another group to meet halfway along the trail and exchange car keys
- take at least two people and two cars, and leave one car at each end of your trek
- take a bicycle in your car, ride it to your trailhead, and after walking your section pick it up with the car.

If you are going to be on the trail for more than a couple of weeks, you will want to have supplies waiting for you somewhere along the route. On the following pages is a list of places on or near the route where you can mail a package to yourself. Alternatively, you can drive there and leave the package with someone, if you can assure yourself that the person will watch over it.

The main thing to mail yourself, of course, is food—nourishing, lightweight, backpacking food. You can also make a hidden cache along the trail, but that entails some risk. In addition, depending on the length of your trek, you may mail clothing, flashlight batteries, medicine and other consumable items. Then, if you are doing the whole trail from Mexico to Canada, you will use up about four pairs of boot soles, and unless you are a good cobbler, that will require mailing three pairs of boots to yourself. As for fuel, do not mail white gas, but you may mail butane or propane cartridges.

Hikers who are used to the High Sierra or the North Cascades may be out of the habit of worrying about water, since in those mountains it is seldom far away, even in late summer. But dehydration can be a problem along parts of the PCT. The trail description mentions every place where you will have to hike more than five miles between watering spots. Of course, some years are wetter than others, and, moreover, if you are hiking in early summer, you can probably ignore most of these warnings. The trail description also mentions the distances between supply points on or near the route.

Hiking Hints

1. Enjoy the adventures of a wilderness experience, but do not take unnecessary chances. An illness which is normally minor

can become serious in high elevations. If you get sick, try to get out of the mountains, or at least to a lower elevation, while you can still travel.

2. Leave word with friends where you are going and when you expect to return.

3. If you think you are lost, take it easy, keep calm and don't panic. Sit down and figure out where you are—that's one thing this book's *topographic* maps are for. Use your head, not your legs.

4. In a storm, or before sunset on a good day, stop and make camp in a sheltered place. Hypothermia can kill. Don't get caught unprepared in cold, wind-driven rain. Pack along a change of woolen clothing and a tent. A lightweight ground cloth is recommended even on overnight hikes. It can be used as a tarp if a perfectly clear, cloudless morning is followed by a cold, rainy night.

5. If you are making a long-distance backpacking trip, you might stop in midafternoon every few days to wash your clothes. String them up on a line and they will dry by sunset.

6. Three of anything (shouts, whistles, flags, smokes) are a sign of distress. If they are seen or heard, help will soon be on the way. (Use these "three signals" only in emergencies.)

7. Bring sunburn lotion, insect repellent and lip balm. If you intend to climb any mountain or if you expect to encounter a lot of snow, bring dark glasses or mountaineering goggles.

8. Be alert. Poison oak grows in the Columbia River gorge and on the lower slopes in southern Oregon and northern California. Rattlesnakes may also be found in these areas.

9. Sign all trail registers. The register will help others find you if you become lost. These trail registers are also used to determine which trails receive the most use and should have priority for maintenance.

10. If you must ford a raging stream, take off your socks, then put your boots back on. If there's any possibility of drowning, keep your pack's waist strap loose so you can get the pack off quickly. Otherwise keep the pack relatively tight so it does not sway and throw you off balance. Cross the stream, quickly drain your boots and wipe out the insides.

Land-use Regulations

The Oregon and Washington portions of the PCT pass through national parks, national forests, Bureau of Land Management land and private land. All these areas have their own regulations, which you ignore only at your own risk—risk of physical difficulty as well as possibility of being cited for violations.

On private land, of course, the regulations are what the owner says they are. The same is true on Indian lands, which are closely approached by the PCT in several localities. Some of the national forest lands are still used by Indians.

Regulations on Bureau of Land Management land are not of major consequence since only the old Oregon Skyline "trail" in southern Oregon passes through such lands.

You will be concerned primarily with Forest Service and Park Service regulations. What follows is a list of the *more important* ones.

1. *Wilderness permits* are required for entry in all Wilderness areas. They may be obtained free on application from an area's headquarters or its ranger stations. If you intend to hike through several areas, write the Forest or Park in which you plan to start and request a National Park Service-U.S. Forest Service Joint-Use Wilderness Permit. If you are hiking the entire PCT, write the Cleveland National Forest, 3211 5th Avenue, San Diego, CA 92103. The permit will be valid for the entire stretch. (See the list of headquarters at the end of this chapter.)

2. If you are backpacking only in non-Wilderness and non-Park areas, you may still need a *campfire permit*. Check with the Forest Service headquarters or one of its ranger stations for the forest you intend to visit. Campfire permits may require each party to carry a shovel. If you don't build any fires but only use gas stoves, you can leave the shovel behind. A stove is particularly recommended since dead and down wood may be scarce at some popular subalpine campsites. Rotting wood should be preserved, since it enriches the soil and hosts organisms which larger animals feed on.

3. A *fishing license* is required for all who fish. Both Oregon and Washington have a variety of fishing licenses (and fees) based on your age, state of residency and length of fishing excursion. For further information, write:

Oregon State Game Commission
1634 S. W. Alder St. — P.O. Box 3503
Portland, OR 97208

    or

Washington State Department of Game
600 North Capitol Way
Olympia, WA 98504

4. *Destruction,* injury, defacement, removal or disturbance in any manner of any natural feature or public property is prohibited. This includes:

    a. Molesting any animal, picking flowers or other plants;

    b. Cutting, blazing, marking, driving nails in, or otherwise damaging growing trees or standing snags;

    c. Writing, carving or painting of names or other inscriptions anywhere;

    d. Destruction, defacement or moving of signs or other structures.

5. *Collecting specimens* of minerals, plants, animals or historical objects is prohibited without written authorization, obtained in advance, from the Park Service or Forest Service. Permits are not issued for personal collections.

6. *Smoking* is not permitted while traveling through vegetated areas. You may stop and smoke in a safe place.

7. Pack and saddle *animals* have the right-of-way on trails. Hikers should get completely off the trail, on the downhill side if possible, and remain quiet until the stock has passed.

8. It is illegal to cut *switchbacks.* This leads to trail erosion.

9. Use *existing campsites* if there are any. If not, camp away from the trail and at least 100 feet from lakes and streams, on mineral soil or unvegetated forest floor—never in meadows or other soft, vegetated spots. Stock animals must be kept at least 200 feet from lakes and their inlet streams.

10. *Construction* of improvements such as rock walls, large fireplaces, bough beds, tables, and rock-and-log stream crossings is prohibited.

11. *Soap* and other pollutants should be kept out of lakes and streams. Use of detergents is not recommended, since they affect the water detrimentally.

12. *Toilets* should be in soft soil away from camps and water. Dig a shallow hole and bury all.

13. You are required to *clean up* your camp before you leave. Tin cans, foil, glass, worn-out or useless gear, and other unburnables must be carried out.

14. *National Parks* but not National Forests prohibit dogs and cats on the trail and prohibit carrying or using firearms.

Border Crossing

U.S. to Canada via PCT

Hikers planning to enter Canada on the PCT should consider the legal requirements as falling into two phases: entering Canada, and returning to the U.S. Furthermore, it should be remembered that there are two separate bureaucracies in each of the two countries: Customs/Excise (objects) and Immigration (people).

Citizens or permanent residents of the U.S. may cross the border in either direction without passport or visa. However, they should carry papers establishing their citizenship and residency. Birth, baptismal or voter's certificates are acceptable. A naturalization certificate or Alien Registration Receipt card is required if applicable. People (other than Canadian citizens) who are only temporarily in the U.S. should check with Canadian and U.S. officials to ensure that they have the proper documents. Minors should carry a letter from parent or guardian authorizing the trip.

There is no provision whereby persons may legally enter Canada without first reporting to Canadian Customs and Immigration at an authorized port of entry—Osoyoos or Huntington B.C. for hikers on the PCT. The Collector of Customs at either of these ports of entry may "at his discretion" authorize by telephone. It is recommended that such authorization be obtained in advance. You will probably have to specify a *date of entry* as accurately as possible, and the Collector of Customs may direct you to meet the Royal Canadian Mounted Police at some specified location in order that he may perform an after-the-fact border-crossing inspection. If you need to contact the R.C.M.P. about this, write to

Officer Commanding
R.C.M. Police
Hope, B.C., Canada

For Canadian Customs purposes, a person must be 16 years old to import tobacco products, and 19 to import alcoholic beverages. Personal gear not for resale and reasonable quantities of consumables are not dutiable; however, legally one is limited to two days' worth of food. If you plan to carry any firearms into Canada, check in advance with Canadian Customs: handguns and automatic firearms are expressly prohibited; all other guns must be cleared by Customs. Fishing tackle is not restricted. Dogs must have been vaccinated against rabies within one year. A document certifying this, signed by a licensed veterinarian of the U.S. or Canada, and bearing an adequate, legible description of the dog, must be carried. Cats hiking across the border are not restricted, but horses are subject to inspection by a Canadian Department of Agriculture veterinarian.

To minimize hassles when returning to the U.S. after entering Canada on the PCT, we recommend that the hiker limit his purchases to food to be consumed in transit and items of slight value such as books or magazines. He should also have some definitive evidence of his citizenship and identification (see above).

Canada to the U.S. via PCT

In addition to the general information in the previous section, hikers should have the following details in mind.

Persons expecting to cross the U.S. border hiking north to south on the PCT may request to be inspected in advance for immigration purposes. Presumably this inspection would take place at a U.S. port of entry, where the hiker should be issued a Form I-94. Upon re-entry into the U.S. on the PCT one should surrender this form to a Border Patrol Officer or mail it to the office that issued it.

The U.S. Bureau of Customs inflexibly requires that "any person importing or bringing merchandise into the United States from a contiguous country other than in a vessel or vehicle shall immediately report his arrival to the customs officer at the port of entry nearest to the place at which he shall cross the boundary line and shall present such merchandise to such customs officer for inspection" [19 U.S.C. 1459]. For the PCT, the nearest port of entry is either Sumas or Oroville, Washington, and the hiker would be required by law to go to one of these stations as soon as possible after crossing the border. The obvious legal solution is *do not import any merchandise*. Then you need only satisfy the Immigration requirements detailed above.

Border Monument 78

Fred Hartline

Further Information

We recommend that the hiker begin his border-crossing hassles several months in advance of renouncing civilization for the high trails of the PCT. Further information may be obtained from any of the following agencies. You probably will not be able to get all the information you need from any one of these agencies, so you might write several of them.

Canadian Government
Travel Bureau
Ottawa, Canada
: Sends pamphlet entitled "Canada Border Crossing Information," which covers general requirements for crossing from the U.S. to Canada.

Department of Nat. Revenue
Customs and Excise
Pacific Region
Box 1200, Postal Terminal "A"
Vancouver 1, B.C.
: Should be able to answer specific questions on border crossing from U.S. to Canada on the PCT.

District Director of Customs
Seattle, Washington 98104
: Should be able to answer specific questions pertaining to Customs regulations for crossing from Canada to the U.S. on the PCT.

District Director
Immigration and Naturalization
815 Airport Way, South
Seattle, Washington 98134
: Should be able to answer specific questions pertaining to Immigration regulations for crossing from Canada to the U.S. on the PCT.

Highways That Cross or Touch the Route
South to North

California State 96 at Seiad Valley
Interstate 5 at Siskiyou Summit, Oregon
Dead Indian Road—part of the Temporary Route
Oregon State 140 between Fish Lake and Lake of the Woods
Oregon State 62 in southern Crater Lake National Park
Oregon State 138 just north of Crater Lake National Park
Oregon State 58 at Willamette Pass
Oregon State 242 at McKenzie Pass
Oregon State 20 at Santiam Pass
U.S. 26 at Wapinitia Pass

Oregon State 35 at Barlow Pass
Interstate 80N near Cascade Locks
Washington State 14 east of Stevenson
U.S. 12 at White Pass
Washington State 410 at Chinook Pass
Interstate 90 at Snoqualmie Pass
U.S. 2 at Stevens Pass
Washington State 20 at Rainy Pass
British Columbia 3 in Manning Provincial Park

Post Offices Along or Near the Route
South to North

If you are planning to hike a segment several hundred miles long, you may wish to mail supply packages to yourself. If you are hiking the entire three-state route, you should enclose shoes, clothes and other items in your "CARE" food packages. Address them to

Yourself
General Delivery
P.O., State ZIP
HOLD UNTIL (date)

Only the larger post offices are listed below. There are additional ones at Timberline Lodge, Lake of the Woods Resort and most of the other resorts on or near your route, but due to the trail's increased popularity, they no longer have space to store packages for every hiker. Please don't burden them. Rather, send your packages to the following post offices:

Seiad Valley, CA 96086
Horse Creek, CA 96045
Klamath River, CA 96050
Hornbrook, CA 96044

Ashland, OR 97520
Crater Lake National Park, OR 97604
Diamond Lake Lodge, OR 97731
Government Camp, OR 97028
Cascade Locks, OR 97014

Stevenson, WA 98648
Mt. Rainier National Park, WA 98397
Chelan, WA 98816
    (take shuttle bus to Stehekin, then the relaxing, leisurely,
    46-mile ferry boat ride along sinuous Lake Chelan to this
    resort town)

Manning Provincial Park, British Columbia, Canada

Government Administrative Headquarters

General

Regional Forester
  California Region
  630 Sansome Street
  San Francisco, CA 94111

Regional Forester
  Pacific Northwest Region
  P.O. Box 3623
  Portland, OR 97208

Bureau of Land Management
  710 N. E. Holladay
  Portland, OR 97232

Specific, South to North

Klamath National Forest
  1215 South Main
  Yreka, CA 96097

Rogue River National Forest
  Box 520
  Medford, OR 97501

Winema National Forest
  Klamath Falls, OR 97601

Sky Lakes Area: see Rogue
  River and Winema N.F.'s

Crater Lake National Park
  Crater Lake, OR 97604

Umpqua National Forest
  P. O. Box 1008
  Roseburg, OR 97470

Deschutes National Forest
  211 East Revere
  Bend, OR 97701

Willamette National Forest
  P. O. Box 1271
  Eugene, OR 97401

Diamond Peak Wilderness: see
  Deschutes, Willamette N.F.'s

Three Sisters Wilderness: see
  Deschutes, Willamette N.F.'s

Mt. Washington Wilderness: see
  Deschutes, Willamette N.F.'s

Mt. Hood National Forest
  P.O. Box 16040
  Protland, OR 97216

Mt. Jefferson Wilderness: see
  Deschutes, Willamette and
  Mt. Hood N.F.'s

Mt. Hood Wilderness: see
  Mt. Hood N.F.

Gifford Pinchot N.F.
  P. O. Box 449
  Vancouver, WA 98660

Mt. Adams Wilderness: see
  Gifford Pinchot N.F.

Snoqualmie—Mt. Baker
  National Forest
  Seattle, WA 98104

Goat Rocks Wilderness: see
  Gifford Pinchot and
  Snoqualmie N.F.'s

Mt. Rainier National Park
  Longmire, WA 98397

Wenatchee National Forest
  Wenatchee, WA 98801

Glacier Peak Wilderness: see
  Wenatchee, Mt. Baker N.F.'s

North Cascades National Park
  Sedro Woolley, WA 98284

Lake Chelan Natl. Rec. Area:
  see North Cascades N.P.

Okanogan National Forest
  Okanogan, WA 98840

Pasayten Wilderness: see
  Okanogan N.F.

Manning Provincial Park
  British Columbia, Canada

Forgotten Anything?

Here is a checklist of items we feel you should consider bringing along. You might prefer to bring other things too.

this guidebook
nature guides
wilderness permit
fishing permit

pack
tent
nylon cord
ground cloth
ensolite pad
sleeping bag
stuff sack

cap or hat
dark glasses
poncho
parka or jacket
change of clothes
change of underwear
swimsuit
wool socks
gaiters
boots
boot laces
sewing kit

stove
fuel
matches
flashlight
cooking gear

can opener
pocket knife
food
salt & pepper
water bottles
   (½ gal. total cap.)
halazone tablets
aspirin
first-aid kit
snakebite kit
insect repellent
   (lots of it)
suntan lotion
lip balm
toothbrush
toothpaste
soap
washcloth
towel
toilet paper

pencil and note pad
postage stamps
wallet
camera
film
mountaineering gear

high hopes
conservation ethic

3

Getting Ready to Appreciate
the Trail

Introduction

The California section of the Pacific Crest Trail is noted for its great diversity of plants and animals, minerals and rocks, climates and landscapes. The Oregon section of the PCT provides quite a contrast, having the most homogeneous vegetation and landscape of this tri-state route. The Washington section falls between these two extremes. Along the route covered by this volume, certain rocks, plants and animals appear time and time again. The most common entities appear to be

    rock: andesite, basalt
    flower: lupine
    shrub: huckleberry
    tree: mountain hemlock
    invertebrate: mosquito
    fish: trout
    amphibian: western toad, tree frog
    reptile: garter snake
    bird: Oregon junco
    mammal,
        small: chipmunk, golden-mantled ground squirrel
        large: man, deer.

The average elevation of Oregon's section of PCT is 5118 feet, whereas Washington's section is 4549 feet—lower in part because the weathering and erosional processes farther north are more intense (contrast Washington's 4549 to California's 6115). Not only is the average trail elevation different between these two northwest states, so too is the typical terrain that the trail traverses. The Oregon section is flatter, drier, more volcanic and less glaciated than Washington's section. In Oregon, a typical hike is through a mountain-hemlock forest while traversing rolling ridges and crossing lake-bound basins. In Washington, a typical hike is through alternating forests of mountain hemlock and subalpine species while climbing over passes and dropping somewhat into glaciated canyons. Both states, of course, have many distinctive features worth investigating.

Geology

Near the western edge of the North American continent, the Cascade Range is also near the western edge of the huge crustal North American plate that extends eastward to the largely submerged mid-Atlantic ridge. Along this ridge, molten volcanic products from beneath the earth's crust are ejected onto the ocean floor. However, the deposits along this north-south trending ridge generally are transported away from it before they can accumulate to a thickness that would reach sea level. A notable exception is fiery Iceland, where the volcanic deposits have succeeded. The North American plate is moving westward from the mid-Atlantic ridge at such a rate that it is overtaking and overriding the Pacific plate, which extends from the Oregon-Washington coast west to the Japanese Islands. As the North American plate overrides the Pacific plate, it buckles, and it also forces that plate down to such depths and pressures that it disintegrates and melts. Geophysicists theorize that some of the molten residue from this disintegrated plate migrates to the earth's surface to form volcanoes and lava flows—which brings us back to the subject of the Cascade Range.

The Cascade Range has probably experienced eruptions for the last 30 million years at a rate comparable to that of today—a minor eruption every few tens of years, a major eruption every few hundred years. Just how long the Cascades have existed is questionable, for the earliest volcanic deposits have either been eroded away or else they remain buried under the depths of newer deposits. The western edge of North America has been around—in one form or another—since the Paleozoic era (see GEOLOGIC TIME TABLE), for we can find nonmarine rocks of this age or older in the Siskiyou Mountains of northern California and in the North Cascades of northern Washington.

The geologic history of the Cascades is fairly well known from the mid-Tertiary period onward. In the late Eocene and early Miocene epochs, deposits from the ancient Cascade Range reached a thickness of six miles in some places. For such an accumulation to occur, the regional crust must have been relatively stable for some time. By the mid-Miocene, the range experienced folding, faulting and, in the north, intrusion by granitic batholiths, plutons, stocks, and dikes. (These intrusive masses are distinguished by their relative size; a batholith may be tens of miles across, whereas a dike may be only a few feet or a few inches across.) During the mid-Miocene, linear vents east of the Cascades opened and poured forth the very fluid Columbia River basalts, which flooded much of the terrain of southern Washington and northern Oregon. The many flows from the fiery episodes are best seen by the hiker as he descends north toward the Columbia River along the lower half of the Eagle Creek Trail.

Plant fossils collected east of the Cascades indicate the environment was considerably more humid than it is today. From this knowledge the paleobotanist infers that the Cascades were lower in elevation, since there was no evidence of a rain shadow

GEOLOGIC TIME TABLE

Era	Period	Epoch	Began (years ago)	Duration (years)
	Quaternary	Holocene	12,000	12,000
		Pleistocene	2,000,000	2,000,000
Cenozoic		Pliocene	11,000,000	8,000,000
		Miocene	25,000,000	14,000,000
	Tertiary	Oligocene	40,000,000	15,000,000
		Eocene	60,000,000	20,000,000
		Paleocene	70,000,000	10,000,000
	Cretaceous	*Numerous*	135,000,000	65,000,000
Mesozoic	Jurassic	*epochs*	180,000,000	45,000,000
	Triassic	*recognized*	225,000,000	45,000,000
	Permian	*Numerous*	280,000,000	55,000,000
	Carboniferous		345,000,000	65,000,000
Paleozoic	Devonian	*epochs*	400,000,000	55,000,000
	Silurian		440,000,000	40,000,000
	Ordovician	*recognized*	500,000,000	60,000,000
	Cambrian		570,000,000	70,000,000
Pre-cambrian	No formally accepted chronostratigraphic units; oldest rocks are about 3 billion years old; Earth is about 4½ billion years old.			

Goat Rocks: glacial striations on volcanic rocks

that would be created if they were as high as today's crests. One need only drive to Sisters or Wenatchee to notice how much drier the east slopes of today's Cascades are compared to their west slopes.

After the partial flooding of the range by the Columbia River basalts, the earth's internal forces, quite likely due to the interaction between the North American and Pacific plates, uplifted the range and initiated a series of erupting volcanoes. Uplift and eruptions continued during the Quaternary, but in this epoch, the higher peaks were subjected to repeated glaciations brought on by changes in the world-wide climatic pattern. Some paleoclimatologists have speculated that the moving plates have rearranged the ocean basins, thereby affecting ocean currents and also major weather patterns, but the influences that initiated the Ice Age (the Pleistocene epoch) are still hotly debated.

The same processes at work in the past are at work today. Volcanoes attempt to grow ever upward, but they are checked by the forces of gravity, weathering and erosion. The higher a peak grows, the more it is attacked by the icy fingers of glaciers. Gravity pulls loose particles downward; the right snow conditions initiate avalanches; minor eruptions and near-surface intrusions melt snowpacks, thereby creating enormous mudflows. Particularly good examples of the destructive power of such mudflows may be seen in the Mt. Rainier environs.

The major volcanoes we see today are quite young—definitely late Quaternary. Many of them have erupted in geologically recent times, and there is every reason to believe they will erupt again. The Pacific Crest Trail traverses most of these "dormant" volcanoes, including, south to north: Mt. McLoughlin (9495), Crater Lake (12,000-foot-high Mt. Mazama until 6600 years ago), the Three Sisters (10,358, 10,047, 10,085), Mt. Jefferson (10,497), Mt. Hood (11,235), Mt. Adams (12,276), Mt. Rainier (14,410) and Glacier Peak (10,541). Geologic vignettes of these and other summits are included in our trail descriptions.

Recommended Reading

American Geological Institute, *Dictionary of Geological Terms*. Garden City: Doubleday, 1962.

Baldwin, Ewart M., *Geology of Oregon,* 2nd ed. Eugene: University of Oregon, 1964. Available from its Cooperative Book Store.

Crandell, Dwight R., *The Geologic Story of Mount Rainier.* (U.S. Geological Survey Bulletin 1292) Washington: U.S. Government Printing Office, 1969.

——, *Surficial Geology of Mount Rainier National Park, Washington.* (U.S. Geological Survey Bulletin 1288) Washington: U.S. Government Printing Office, 1969.

Dole, Hollis M., ed., *Andesite Conference Guidebook.* (Oregon Dept. of Geology and Mineral Industries Bulletin 62) Portland: Oregon Dept. of Geology, 1968.

Huntting, Marshall T., et al., *Geologic Map of Washington* (1:500,000). Olympia: Washington Dept. of Conservation, 1961.

McKee, Bates, *Cascadia: The Geologic Evolution of the Pacific Northwest.* New York: McGraw-Hill, 1972.

Pough, Frederick H., *A Field Guide to Rocks and Minerals,* 3rd ed. Boston: Houghton Mifflin, 1960.

Putnam, William C., *Geology,* 2nd ed. New York: Oxford University Press, 1971.

Shelton, John S., *Geology Illustrated.* San Francisco: W.H. Freeman, 1966.

Staatz, Mortimer H., et al., *Geology and Mineral Resources of the Northern Part of the North Cascades National Park, Washington.* (U.S. Geological Survey Bulletin 1359) Washington: U.S. Government Printing Office, 1972.

Tabor, R.W., and D.F. Crowder, *On Batholiths and Volcanoes . . . North Cascades, Washington.* (U.S. Geological Survey Professional Paper 604) Washington: U.S. Government Printing Office, 1969.

Wells, Francis G., and Dallas L. Peck, *Geologic Map of Oregon West of the 121st Meridian.* (U.S. Geological Survey Misc. Geol. Investig. Map I-325, 1:500,000) Washington: U.S. Government Printing Office, 1961.

Biology

One's first guess about the Pacific Crest Trail — a high adventure rich in magnificent alpine scenery and sweeping panoramas —turns out to be incorrect along some parts of the trail. The real-life trail hike will sometimes seem to consist of enduring many repetitious miles through viewless forests, battling hordes of mosquitoes, or even hiking up to a whole day at a time without reaching fresh water. If you get bogged down in such unpleasant impressions, it may be because you haven't developed an appreciation of the natural history of this remarkable route. There is a great variety of plants and animals, rocks and minerals, landscapes and climates along the PCT, and the more you know about each, the more you will enjoy your trek.

FLORA

A backpacker who has just completed the California section of the PCT might conclude that southern Oregon's forests form a more integrated "neighborhood" of species than California's forests did. Passing through different environments of the Sierra Nevada, he may have noticed the segregation of tree species and concluded that as he ascends toward the range's crest, he passes through a sequence of forests: Douglas-fir, white fir, red fir, mountain hemlock. Near the Oregon border, however, he discovers that these four species—and others—reside together. Certainly, this aggregation would never be seen in the Sierra. The great diversity of environments found within that range has allowed each species to adapt to the environment most suitable for it.

Southern Oregon is much more uniform in its topography. Competition, nevertheless, is still present, and the discerning hiker soon learns what species to expect around the next bend. Ponderosa pines thrive in the drier southern Oregon forests, yet they are nonexistent in the dry pumice soils of the Crater Lake vicinity. Here you'll find lodgepole pines which, ironically, are water-loving trees. These are usually seen growing in boggy soils near lakes, creeks and wet meadows, where they often edge out the mountain hemlocks, which are by far the most common tree you'll see along the PCT in Oregon and Washington. The most suitable habitat for hemlocks appears to be shady north slopes, on which pure stands of tall, straight specimens grow. At lower elevations, mountain hemlocks give way to western hemlocks and Douglas-firs, and, as the environment becomes drier south-

---

From top, left to right: fireweed, paintbrush, tiger lily; Newberry knotweed, corn lily, pasqueflower; pearly everlasting, phlox, Sitka valerian

ward and eastward, these two species yield to ponderosa pines. The harder one looks at a forest—even a small piece of it—the more he realizes that this seemingly uniform stand of trees is in fact a complex assemblage of particular plants, animals, soils, rocks and microclimates all influencing each other.

Our trail description commences at Seiad Valley, a man-made ranchland carved from a Douglas-fir forest. Near the end of our odyssey, along Agnes Creek and the Stehekin River, we also encounter a Douglas-fir forest. The two are hardly alike. The Douglas-fir forest of northern California and southern Oregon contains, among other trees, incense-cedar, ponderosa pine, white fir, Oregon oak and madrone. Its counterpart in northern Washington contains, among others, western redcedar, western white pine, grand fir, vine maple and Engelmann spruce.

The two forests vary considerably in the density of their vegetation. Not only does the rain-laden northern forest have a denser stand of taller conifers, but it also has a denser understory. Its huckleberries, thimbleberries, Devil's club and other moisture-loving shrubs are quite a contrast to the stiff, dry manzanita, ceanothus and scrub oaks seen in the southern forest. Wildflowers in the northern forest are more abundant than their counterparts to the south. During rainstorms, they are too abundant, for their thick growth along the trail ensures that you'll be soaked by them from as high as your waist on down. Both forests have quite a number of species in common, but from central Oregon northward, the moisture-oriented species become prominent. Now we find bunchberry dogwood, Oregon grape, Lewis monkey flower and other species growing on the dark, damp forest floor.

In contrast to trees, which are quite specific in their habitat selection, flowers can tolerate a broad range of environments. You'll find, for example, the Lewis monkey flower at timberline on the slopes of Mt. Hood and also on the Douglas-fir forest floor that borders the southern shore of the Columbia River. Both environments are moist, but the Mt. Hood alpine meadows, at 6000 feet above the bottom of the Columbia River gorge, are a considerably harsher environment.

Some flowers prefer open meadows to shady forests; others prefer dry environments. Thistle, lupine and phlox are found along the sunnier portions of the trail. Growing from crevices among rocks are the aptly named stonecrops, and on the pumice flats too dry for even the lodgepole pines to pioneer, the Newberry knotweed thrives.

From top, left to right: Oregon grape, columbine, ligusticum; vanilla leaf, lupine, bistort; yarrow, thistle, beargrass

In addition to adapting to specific climatic conditions, a plant may also adapt to a specific soil condition. Thus we see on the otherwise barren mica schist slopes of Condrey Mountain, near the southern Oregon border, acre after acre of pink, prostrate pussy paws.

Lastly, a species may have a distribution governed by the presence of other species. Corn lilies thrive in wet meadows, but lodgepoles invade these lands and shade them out. Mountain hemlocks may soon follow and eventually achieve dominance over the lodgepoles. Then the careless camper comes along, lets his campfire escape, and the forest burns. Among the charred stumps of the desolate ruins rises the tall, blazing magenta fireweed, and Nature, once again, strives to transform this landscape back into a mature forest.

FAUNA

We have seen that plants adapt to a variety of conditions imposed by the environment and by other species. Animals, like plants, are also subject to a variety of conditions, but they have the added advantage of mobility. On a hot summer day, a beetle under a scant forest cover can escape the merciless sun by seeking protection under a loose stone or under a mat of dry needles.

Larger animals, of course, have greater mobility and therefore can better overcome the difficulties of the environment. Amphibians, reptiles, birds and mammals may frequent the trail, but they scamper away when you—the intruder—approach. At popular campsites, however, the animals come out to meet you, or more exactly, to obtain your food. Of course, almost anywhere along the trail you may encounter the ubiquitous mosquito, always looking for a free meal. But in popular campsites you'll meet the robin, the gray jay, the Clark nutcracker, the Townsend and yellow-pine chipmunks, the golden-mantled ground squirrel, and at night, mice and black bears. You may be tempted to feed them, or they may try to help themselves, but please protect them from your food—they will survive better on the "real, organic" food Mother Nature produces. Furthermore, an artificially large population supported by generous summer backpackers may in winter overgraze the vegetation. In the following paragraphs we'll take a closer look at three species.

Mule deer. Two subspecies of this large mammal can be found along much of the Oregon-Washington PCT. Mule deer, like other herbivores, do not eat every type of plant they encounter, but tend to be quite specific in their search for food. Their

primary browse is new growth on huckleberry, salal, blackberry, bitterbrush and snowbrush, although they also eat certain grasses and forbs. Together with other herbivores, parasites and saprophytes (organisms feeding on decaying organic matter), they consume a small portion of the 100 billion tons of organic matter produced annually on the earth by plants.

Mule deer face a considerable population problem because some of their predators have disappeared. After the arrival of "civilized" man, the wolves and grizzly bears were exterminated except in some remote areas of northern Washington. In their places, coyotes and black bears have increased in numbers. Coyotes, however, feed principally on rabbits and rodents, and only occasionally attack a fawn or a sick deer. Black bears occasionally kill fawns. The mountain lion, a true specialist in feeding habits, preys mainly on deer and may kill 50 of them a year. This magnificent mammal, unfortunately, has been unjustly persecuted by man, and many deer that are saved from the big cat are lost to starvation and disease. Increasing human population compounds the problem. The expansion of settlements causes the big cats to retreat farther, which leaves them farther from the suburban deer. Forests must be logged to feed this expansion of settlements, and then the logged-over areas sprout an assemblage of shrubs that are a feast for deer. The deer population responds to this new food supply by increasing in number. Then the shrubs mature or the forest grows back, and there is less food for the larger deer population, which is now faced with starvation. Forest fires produce the same feast-followed-by-famine effect.

Golden-mantled ground squirrel. There are two species of these ground squirrels, the Sierra Nevada golden-mantled ground squirrel, which ranges from the southern Sierra north to the Columbia River, and the Cascades golden-mantled ground squirrel, which ranges from the Columbia River north into British Columbia. On the eastern Cascade slopes of Washington, the Cascades golden-mantled ground squirrel lives in the same habitat as the yellow-pine chipmunk, but they have slightly different niches, or roles, to carry out in their pine-and-fir-forest environment. Both have the same food and the same burrowing habits, but the ground squirrel obtains nuts and seeds that have fallen to the forest floor, whereas the chipmunk obtains these morsels by extracting them from their source. The ground squirrel, like its distant cousin the marmot, puts on a think layer of fat to provide it with enough energy to last through winter hibernation. The chipmunk, like the black bear, only partly hibernates. During the winter, it awakens periodically to feed on the nuts and seeds it has stored in its ground burrow.

Western toad. Every Westerner is familiar with this drab, chunky amphibian. Along the Oregon-Washington PCT, we encounter its subspecies known as the boreal toad. This cold-blooded animal is amazingly adaptable, being found among rock crevices in dry, desolate lava flows as well as in subalpine wildflower gardens in the North Cascades. Its main environmental requirement appears to be the presence of at least one early-summer seasonal pond in which it can breed and lay eggs.

Although you may encounter dozens of boreal toads along a stretch of trail in one day (they occur in clusters), they prefer to actively hop or crawl about at night. Should you bed down near one of their breeding ponds, you may hear the weak chirps (they have no "croaking" vocal sacs) from dozens of males. Moreover, these toads may swarm all over you in their search for meals. Rolling over on one won't give you warts, but later you might feel the puncture, bite or sting of a mosquito, ant or yellow jacket that otherwise would have made a tasty meal for the toad.

In each of the three short studies above, an animal has a specific role to perform in its community. A fluctuation in its population will cause a fluctuation in the numbers of the other species that it usually feeds upon or that feed upon it. Man's presence, in some cases, has upset the complex interspecific relationships that have evolved over the millennia. Even as man increasingly asserts his influence over nature, he will have to learn to live within its framework, for he, like any other species, is an integral part of the natural world.

Recommended Reading

Burt, William H., and Richard P. Grossenheider, *A Field Guide to the Mammals,* 2nd ed. Boston: Houghton Mifflin, 1964.

Henderson, Jan, *Flowers of the Parks: Mount Rainier National Park, North Cascades National Park.* Longmire, Washington: Mt. Rainier Natural History Association, 1972.

Horn, Elizabeth L., *Wildflowers 1: The Cascades.* Beaverton, Oregon: Touchstone Press, 1972.

Ingles, Lloyd G., *Mammals of the Pacific States.* Stanford: Stanford University Press, 1965.

McMinn, Howard E., and Evelyn Maino, *An Illustrated Manual of Pacific Coast Trees,* 2nd ed. Berkeley: University of California Press, 1963.

Murie, Olaus J., *A Field Guide to Animal Tracks.* Boston: Houghton Mifflin, 1954.

Odum, Eugene P., *Fundamentals of Ecology,* 3rd ed. Philadelphia: W. B. Saunders, 1971.

Peterson, Roger T., *A Field Guide to Western Birds.* Boston: Houghton Mifflin, 1972.

Sharpe, Grant and Wenonah, *101 Wildflowers of Crater Lake National Park.* Seattle: University of Washington Press, 1959.

Stebbins, Robert C., *A Field Guide to Western Reptiles and Amphibians.* Boston: Houghton Mifflin, 1966.

Sudworth, George B., *Forest Trees of the Pacific Slope.* New York: Dover, 1967.

4

Hiking the Trail

Our Route Description and Maps

The heart of this book is the words and maps that describe the route of the Pacific Crest Trail from Seiad Valley, California to Manning Provincial Park, British Columbia. South of Oregon's State Highway 140, the final PCT is largely incomplete. This guide offers three choices for getting to that highway from Highway 96 in northern California. North of 140, the Pacific Crest Trail generally coincides with Oregon's Oregon Skyline Trail and Washington's Cascade Crest Trail. Where the PCT differs from either the OST or the CCT, both the PCT and the alternate route along one of the others are described. In some places we describe alternate routes that we think are preferable to the PCT and alternate routes that provide the hiker with access to a resort where he can resupply. In the trail description, these route descriptions are easily distinguished from the PCT route description because they have shorter lines of type. We also give brief descriptions of ascents of the major peaks along or near the route.

The 140 topographic maps in this guidebook show the Pacific Crest Trail as it existed in 1973. All but two are at a scale of 1:50,000, or about 0.8 inch per mile. You might notice that our route differs in places from the routes shown on Forest Service and U.S. Geological Survey maps. This is because we *surveyed* the complete route during the summer of 1973. In addition to mapping the new trail segments, we corrected the many minor mistakes found on topographic maps, added roads and reservoirs, and tried to draw in every switchback leg over 100 feet long. At times, we must admit, incessant mosquitoes, driving rains or inadequate topographic control points hampered our efforts. Nevertheless, we feel confident we mapped *at least* 90% of them.

We believe our set of maps are the most accurate maps of the Oregon-Washington PCT available, because we covered every inch of the route. Why such a concern for accuracy? Well, if you're hiking in early June, you may tred miles of snowfields and scarcely see the trail. Under such circumstances, you may get off route. Or you may sometime decide to go cross-country. In either case, when you try to find the trail again, you'll want a map that shows the trail and topography accurately. In the trail description, numbers in the margin indicate what maps the text refers to.

The verbal description of the route from northern California to southern British Columbia first of all tells you how to find your way. There are hundreds of choice points en route, and although most of them are well signed, a few are deceptive and many give inaccurate mileages. At every choice point we tell you which compass direction to head. We also name the trails and roads at every junction and give the elevation of the junction. Where the trails and roads have numbers, we give those too. For junctions near settlements, we give the distance to the settlement, and we tell you how far it is to the *next* settlement. Between junctions, our description tells whether you will be ascending or descending, and how steeply. It gives your compass heading and the elevations of features you cross, such as creeks, roads and passes. We give the distance between two consecutive points on the route to the nearest tenth of one mile. These do not always agree with Forest Service Wilderness map mileages partly because our route does not always coincide with theirs. Along the alternate routes we also include a running total of miles. A separate table at the end of this chapter gives the cumulative distance from Seiad Valley to Manning Provincial Park and vice versa, including the major points encountered along the way.

Our verbal description of the route also tells something about the country you are walking through—the landmarks, the geology, the biology (plants and animals), the geography, and sometimes a bit of history. After all, you're not hiking the Pacific Crest Trail just to rack up the miles/make your pedometer click/prove your man(woman)(child)hood.

Following the Trail

The "Pacific Crest Trail" is usually a trail, sometimes a road and—in certain places or at certain times—a snowfield. Quite naturally, you'll want to stay on route. For that purpose, we recommend relying on the route description and maps in this book. To be sure, there are various markers along the route—

Goat Rocks: duck, post and plastic streamer

trail signs, PCT emblems (blue and white), PCT road signs (brown and white), PCTS diamonds (green and white), gray diamonds, tree branches with plastic streamers, plus posts, blazes and ducks. (A blaze is a place on a tree trunk where man has carved away a patch of bark to leave a conspicuous scar. A duck is a man-made pile of rocks that is obviously unnatural.) Since all these markers can be ephemeral, our route descriptions do not emphasize them.

For short horizontal distances, we have used yards because one yard approximates the length of one long stride. (We give vertical distances in feet.) If you are concerned about reaching a particular junction, you can pace off the distance. Alternatively, you can develop a sense of your ground speed. Then, if it is 1½ miles to the next junction and your speed is 2 miles an hour, you should reach it in ¾ hour, or 45 minutes. Be suspicious if you reach an unmarked junction sooner or later than you had expected. Fortunately, most junctions are signed.

Oregon-Washington Pacific Crest Trail—Cumulative Mileage

	South to North	Miles between points	North to South
State Highway 96 at Seiad Valley	0.0		972.0
		13.9	
Road 48N20 at Cook and Green Pass	13.9		958.1
		12.8	
Alex Hole spur road	26.7		945.3
		8.6	
California-Oregon State Line	35.3		936.7
		18.3	
Mt. Ashland Ski Area	53.6		918.4
		9.9	
Interstate 5	63.5		908.5
		11.4	
Ashland	74.9		897.1
		10.6	
Hooper Springs Wayside	85.5		886.5
		13.0	
Beaver Dam Campground	98.5		873.5
		10.0	
State 140 at PCT trailhead	108.5		863.5
		27.5	
Devils Peak/Lee Peak saddle	136.0		836.0
		16.7	
Stuart Falls Campground	152.7		819.3
		8.2	
State Highway 62	160.9		811.1
		15.3	
Red Cone Spring	176.2		795.8
		10.7	
State Highway 138	186.9		785.1
		13.0	
PCT high point in Oregon	199.9		772.1
		15.8	
Cascade Lakes Road at Windigo Pass	215.7		756.3
		10.3	
Summit Lake Road	226.0		746.0
		14.2	
State Highway 58 at Willamette Summit	240.2		731.8
		21.4	
Road 2049 at Irish Lake	261.6		710.4
		13.7	
Cliff Lake	275.3		696.7
		14.8	
Sisters Mirror Lake	290.1		681.9
		14.5	
Glacier Way Trail	304.6		667.4
		10.3	
State Highway 242 at McKenzie Pass	314.9		657.1
		10.0	
Coldwater Spring	324.9		647.1
		7.6	
State Highway 20 at Santiam Pass	332.5		639.5
		13.9	
Rockpile Lake	346.4		625.6
		19.4	
Scout Lake, Jefferson Park	365.8		606.2
		14.6	
Skyline Road near Olallie Lake	380.4		591.6
		20.8	
Warm Springs River	401.2		570.8
		23.7	
U.S. Highway 26 at Wapinitia Pass	424.9		547.1
		6.3	
State Highway 35 at Barlow Pass	431.2		540.8
		5.3	
Timberline Lodge	436.5		535.5
		17.3	
Road N12/N18 at Lolo Pass	453.8		518.2
		17.2	
Wahtum Lake	471.0		501.0
		15.9	
Oregon-Washington State Line	486.9		485.1
		12.7	
Cascade Crest trailhead	499.6		472.4
		18.7	
Cold Spring	518.3		453.7
		8.0	
Carson-Guler Road N60	526.3		445.7
		17.7	

Cumulative Mileage — Concluded

	South to North	Miles between points	North to South
Road 123 at Sawtooth Huckleberry Field	544.0		428.0
Roads N84/85 intersection	558.0	14.0	414.0
Road 1011	579.3	21.3	392.7
Walupt Lake Trail	593.5	14.2	378.5
PCT high point in Washington	607.4	13.9	364.6
U.S. Highway 12 near White Pass	623.7	16.3	348.3
Bumping Lake Trail	636.7	13.0	335.3
State Highway 410 at Chinook Pass	652.1	15.4	319.9
Barnard Saddle	663.6	11.5	308.4
Government Meadow	675.6	12.0	296.4
Tacoma Pass	693.0	17.4	279.0
Road 212 at Stampede Pass	703.5	10.5	268.5
Interstate 90 at Snoqualmie Pass	721.7	18.2	250.3
Pedro Camp	743.0	21.3	229.0
Deep Lake	755.0	12.0	217.0
Deception Pass	767.8	12.8	204.2
U.S. Highway 2 at Stevens Pass	787.0	19.2	185.0
Pear Lake	805.2	18.2	166.8
White Pass	823.7	18.5	148.3
Fire Creek Pass	841.7	18.0	130.3
Suiattle River	858.5	16.8	113.5
Suiattle Pass	866.6	8.1	105.4
Stehekin River at High Bridge	884.0	17.4	88.0
State Highway 20 at Rainy Pass	903.1	19.1	68.9
Methow Pass	913.7	10.6	58.3
Harts Pass	933.6	19.9	38.4
Holman Pass	947.6	14.0	24.4
United States-Canada Border	964.7	17.1	7.3
Highway 3 in Manning Park	972.0	7.3	0.0

5

The Trail

Nestled in an alluvial valley below the Siskiyou Mountains to the north and the Marble Mountains to the south is the sleepy little community of Seiad Valley. Located on State Highway 96 midway between popular Klamath River towns and campgrounds downstream and bustling Interstate 5 upstream, this western Shangri La is the perfect place for us to commence our journey. This guidebook offers you two route descriptions that start from this settlement. The first one follows the Rogue River National Forest planner's recommended temporary route, which traverses the crest of the Siskiyou Mountains, descends to Ashland, and then climbs northeast to the Fish Lake area. The second, the Wilderness Press "late summer" alternate route, heads east on roads to the old Oregon Skyline route, then follows that route north to the Lake of the Woods Recreation Area. Both routes are predominantly along either dirt or paved roads. We'll describe the Forest Service route first.

See map 1

This route begins at the **Seiad Store** and post office (elev. 1375), which has a Pacific Crest Trail register for hikers to sign. Because *Ashland, our next supply point, is a distant 74 miles away,* we purchase our last-minute supplies here. Now burdened down with heavy packs yet high in anticipation of the upcoming adventure, we strike west along the highway, immediately crossing Seiad Creek and passing the Seiad Valley Road, which heads northeast up to Horse Tail Falls and to Cook and Green Pass. Wildwood Tavern is soon reached, opposite School House Gulch (1380-0.5), from where the old trail once started. Following the road as it curves west, we quickly reach the new trailhead for the

Lower Devils Peak Lookout Trail (#12W04) (1380-0.3). Since it is an exhausting 4600-foot ascent to the Kangaroo Mountain meadows, one is prudent to start this strenuous trek in the cool

Left: North Sister, from South Matthieu Lake

Seiad Valley, view east up the Klamath River

shade of the morning. Under a cover of madrone, Douglas-fir, incense-cedar and Oregon oak, our trail quickly reaches a jeep road, which we follow up for 100 feet, to where the trail re-appears and then climbs moderately west alongside two sets of powerlines that parallel the highway below. The trail turns northeast into a shaded gully with its accompanying poison oak, and we soon reach a junction with the original trail, now aban-doned. Switchbacking upward, we reach Fern Spring (2140-1.3), a small seep trickling from a pipe into a concrete cistern. As our well-engineered trail climbs high on the ridge of pre-Cretaceous schist, it provides changing panoramas of the surrounding coun-try. A final half mile of switchbacks up a moderate slope brings us to just below the crest and to a spur trail that drops 200 feet in its 250-yard descent northwest to a pipe spring. Returning to the route well-slaked, we climb gently southeast 0.1 mile to a saddle on

Lower Devils Peak (5050-4.1). One hundred yards farther is a fire lookout, now abandoned and scheduled to be dismantled. Its concrete first story, however, will remain as a shelter for hikers. From the saddle we head north to the east ridge of Middle Devils Peak and a junction with the unsigned **Darkey Creek trail (5170-0.7)**, which descends southeast to Seiad Valley. After an initial steep climb up the east ridge, our trail eases off slightly up the northeast slope to a saddle, where we pause for a view of snow-capped Mt. Shasta (14,162). The gradient doesn't improve as we perspiringly climb up the south ridge of Upper Devils Peak to its western arm. Here we encounter another spur trail, which descends 330 steep yards past silver pines to a seeping spring amid a cluster of alders. Our trail now makes a traverse north, and along it we observe specimens of the quite rare weeping spruce, with their drooping branches and scaly bark. Along its open stretches, the trail is adorned with phlox and wild parsley. Descending to a saddle, we reach a junction with the faint **Portuguese Creek trail (#12W03) (5760-1.2)**, which descends west, but we climb north up the ridge to the

Rattlesnake Mountain trail (5980-0.3), which makes an obvious contour northwest across the slopes. We veer northeast across the south buttress of Kangaroo Mountain and spy a creek disappearing behind some rocks near the trail below us. Hurrying down the semi-obscure but well-ducked trail, we discover that the creek really does disappear—into a sinkhole dissolved from a moderately dipping layer of gray marble that contrasts strongly with the orange Mesozoic ultrabasic intrusives of this area. Noting that cattle also use this area, we carefully search for an unpolluted water source. Heading east, we reach a meadow containing good campsites and a small lily-pad pond fed by the Kangaroo Springs. Below the springs, the trail leaves the wet meadow, crosses to a dry one, and then reaches a southeast slope, where it makes an initial steep descent before climbing steadily to the east ridge of Kangaroo Mountain. From this ridge we can gaze down at Lily Pad Lake (5750-1.2) with its poor campsites and its hundreds of frogs. Beyond it we see our trail climbing north to a **jeep road (5900-0.2)**. We follow this path east across chaparral-mantled slopes and past outcrops of dark blue-green serpentine as we descend to

Cook and Green Pass (4750-4.1) and a junction with Klamath National Forest Road 48N20; an unsigned Rogue River National Forest road descends gently northeast. Here there is a spacious, but dry, roadside campsite. Water may be obtained by hiking northwest 0.6 mile on a trail to Bear Gulch, or in late season by descending Road 48N20 southeast 1.6 miles along a 700-foot descent to Horse Tail Falls. From this pass we follow an obvious trail east up the ridge toward Copper Butte. Scattered knobcone pines in a vegetative cover that includes manzanita and western serviceberry give way to a forest of red fir, mountain hemlock and western white pine. Like tombstones, slabs of greenish-gray, foliated mica schist stand erect along the trail and, in the morning light, reflect the sun's rays as glacially polished rocks do. Our trail switchbacks up to point 5845, descends slightly eastward, then continues its switchbacks up Copper Butte (6194-2.0), which it traverses high on the north slope before descending to the ridge and a junction with

Trail 11W02 (6070-0.3), which ascends north from Seiad Creek, Salt Gulch and Low Gap. In about 0.1 mile our now-ducked trail diagonals northeast steeply down a barren northwest slope that is bisected by an old logging road. Our trail passes between two small stands of conifers just before reaching the road, where it curves right and begins to descend steeply. We follow this road 100 yards down to a large red-fir stump with a rock pile atop it. The trail recommences here, amid a dense patch of gooseberries (no place for wearing shorts), and follows old blazes up toward a ridge that we cross just before reaching Peak 6185. Our trail now stays close to the crest as it descends to a saddle and a junction with the **Lowdens Cabin trail (6050-2.2),** which we can see contouring northeast. From the saddle, the route south-southeast is hard to follow, due to a multitude of cattle paths. Our trail descends south along the break in slope just east of the prominent gully below us. Near a small, lone incense-cedar it curves southeast to a seasonal spring immediately below the obvious descending row of conifers, then drops steeply to a meadow called

3
4

Johnsons Dairy (5720-0.4), where level but dry and windy campsites can be found. More protected campsites are found at a flat 0.1 mile southwest down the unsigned Horse Creek trail. From Johnsons Dairy, cattle paths once more hamper our progress east; the true trail stays level across a boggy field of corn lilies that lies above a thicket of scrubby alders. If the trail is too overgrown to follow, head toward a conspicuous gap in the trees near the edge of the forest. Once within the forest we follow our trail down a pleasant gully containing a trickling creek, but all too soon we leave this verdant sanctuary as we climb steeply toward White Mountain. En route we encounter the lower end of a small, flowery meadow, up which we diagonal northeast for 30 yards in order to find the trail again at the forest's edge. Shortly beyond, a small hillside meadow is reached that has a seeping spring 40 feet below the trail. Our trail now contours the south slope of White Mountain before reaching a wet meadow where the unmaintained **Selby's Cabin trail (5900-2.0)** once began its half-mile descent to the cabin. Soon a saddle is reached that gives us good views north and south, plus a view of the steep ascent ahead—old trails tend to go directly over summits rather than contour around them. With the sun's rays beating down on us, we climb with heavy packs steeply up the ridge, only to descend eventually to a level, unused road. This we follow for a half mile southeast to a saddle, and find the signed trailhead at a sharp curve where Road 47N63 becomes

Road 47N81 (6300-2.6). From this point east, we will follow a temporary route that stays on roads all the way to the trailhead along Oregon State Highway 140 just east of Fish Lake. By hiking south along level Road 47N63 for 0.4 mile, then descending a short distance downslope, we can obtain water from any of the Reeves Ranch Springs. Our route proceeds south up Road 47N81 through a burned-over area from which we can look back and trace most of our semicircular route out of Seiad Valley. Acres of pussypaws grow on this open slope, and also on the mica-rich soils of nearby summits. Our road curves east to open Middle Creek Ridge (6640-1.7), with jeep tracks leading southeast down it, then heads northeast up toward Condrey Mountain (7112) before descending moderately east to a saddle and the Buckhorn Camp spur road. This spur descends west-southwest 0.3 mile to a poor campsite beside a trickling spring. Two hundred feet farther east, our road is joined by the **Alex Hole spur road (6630-1.6),** which descends northwest one-quarter mile to the delightful Alex Hole campsite, located between a willow-lined spring and a Swiss-chalet-styled outhouse. Here, where your far-reaching view north is framed by cliffs of mica schist, your only neighbors may be the animals, such as deer, chipmunks and mountain bluebirds. Back at our road, we continue southeast up to a junction with

Road 40S01 (6740-0.2). We turn sharply left and head north on it out of the forest up to the open slopes of Peak 7043, from where we can view a panorama extending east beyond Pilot Knob, a prominent butte that lies close to one of our proposed alternate routes. We now descend to just below the crest of a broad saddle, where we meet the **Mud Spring spur road (6700-2.1),** which heads north-northwest over the saddle, then down. Mud Spring, 0.2 mile along this spur, is really several very refreshing clear-water springs. From this junction our road continues its descent, traversing the barren and logged-over slopes of Big Rock (6852) before reaching the Miller Glade spur road (6143-1.8), which ascends north slightly before making its descent. The waterless Miller Glade Picnic Area, with its picnic table and chalet outhouse, lies one-quarter mile along this spur. Our road curves east and descends to a junction with **Road 48N19 (5960-0.3).** We can obtain water if we follow this road 0.3 mile gently down to a sloping meadow where Bearground Spring emanates from a cluster of alders a short distance above the road. Dropping even more, our road passes a dead-end spur that heads west (5750-0.5) before our route descends a ridge to a

Five-way junction (5317-1.2) at a saddle that separates a large western area of bluish-gray mica schist from an eastern band of greenish-gray actinolite-chlorite schist. Here Road 193 descends west to Elliot Creek; Road 47N01 heads south on the level, then descends to Beaver Creek; and Road 48N13 climbs east 1.5 miles before switchbacking northwest to our ridge route as Road 4135. Our road, still 40S01, starts north, then makes short switchbacks up a ridge where a **spur road (5760-0.9)** forks left (east), then curves north. We stay right as our road first climbs southeast along the ridge, then gradually curves northeast to a junction with **Road 4135.** This road is followed northeast for 70 yards to where it curves right and around a southeast slope. We get back on **Road 40S01 (5840-0.2),** which starts northeast up a ridge but then cuts across a northwest slope and meets Road 4135 again at a **saddle (6150-0.8).** The broad Road 4135 is followed only 35 yards, to where it curves northwest in its descent toward Medford. Our road, as before, climbs directly up a ridge as it leads north-northeast to the **California-Oregon State Line (6500-0.6).** Just beyond the border, small springs can be found above the roadside as our route curves east. It momentarily touches the border again, then turns north and traverses a slope of Triassic metasediments before reaching a junction with Road 41S15 (6670-1.9), which descends toward Beaver Creek and Interstate 5. Our road, now signed *41S01.1,* turns sharply left and climbs steadily west toward Observation Peak (7430), then passes roadside springs as it curves north to Observation Gap. Traversing the west slope of Peak 7273, we soon reach

6

7

Jackson Gap (7061-2.7), where we get an unobstructed view east-northeast of Mt. McLoughlin (9495), Oregon's southernmost volcano. Giant Mt. Shasta, as usual, dominates the southeast horizon. We turn onto Road 392, which to the west curves down to the Applegate River, and follow it northeast to the **Sheep Camp Spring spur road (6950-0.5),** on our right. This spur descends 200 yards southwest to several seeping springs and a possible campsite. Our route now stays on or close to the open crest as it descends to **Wrangle Gap (6496-2.1).** Here a spur road descends steeply west to Wrangle Campground—the answer to an exhausted hiker's prayer. This little-used recreation site, nestled among red firs, has a large stone shelter complete with fireplace, two stoves, tables and even a sink with running water! This is indeed a welcome side trip, and it may be your last chance to obtain water before Ashland. Road 392 (concurrently signed road *41S01.1*) now heads east across open slopes to the seeping springs of Wymer Glade, then descends across forested slopes to

Siskiyou Gap (5879-3.2), a zone of greater erodability that separates the metamorphic rocks on the west from the granitic rocks on the east. We continue on Road 392 as it traverses a northwest slope and descends slightly to a saddle with a **five-way junction (5860-0.7).** Three roads descend from the saddle, but our road climbs north up a ridge, then winds east up a slope beneath Siskiyou Peak (7147), from where Road 3962A (6838-2.6) descends north toward Wagner Gap and Talent. We continue northeast on our open ridge route, which eventually descends to a saddle (6620-2.3), from which the now-closed Mt. Ashland Trail once descended north. Our road begins to climb east toward Mt. Ashland, then contours the slopes clockwise to the Mt. Ashland summit road (6760-0.9). This switchbacks 1.3 miles up the granitic hulk to its summit (7533), which has a weather radar site, the top of a ski lift and big views. Our road contours south, then descends east to the dry **Mt. Ashland Picnic Area,** with tables, outhouses and a red-fir-framed view. Curving northeast, our road soon reaches the **Mt. Ashland Ski Area (6600-1.4),** with a "Skihaus" that is open only during ski season.

If you are short on supplies, you can head down to Ashland along the Ashland Loop Road. This starts out as our Road 392 and descends northeast to **Bull Gap (5500-2.5).** From here we take Road 3963 north along the ridge, crossing **Road 3903 (4350-3.9)** about midway down the increasingly open forest route to **Glenview Drive (2200-4.6).** Descend this north, then descend Fork Street. Pioneer Street is quickly reached, and is followed for two blocks to C Street. The Ashland Post Office is one block southeast, at the corner of **First and C Streets (1920-1.1-12.1).** To return to the temporary route, head southeast along this one-way street until it becomes **Siskiyou Boulevard (1950-0.2),** then follow it southeast to its junction with **State Highway 66 (Ashland Street) (2010-1.1).** Follow this highway past the Ashland Shopping Center and the **Ashland Ranger Station (2000-0.9),** then over Interstate 5 and southeast down to the junction with **Dead Indian Road (1920-1.1-15.4),** where you rejoin the temporary route.

8
9
10
13
14
11

From the Mt. Ashland Ski Area the temporary route follows paved Road 4059 down the dry ridge to a junction with old **U.S. Highway 99 (4240-9.1),** just 40 yards north of the Interstate 5 overpass. The Mesozoic granitic rocks are now overlaid by mid-Tertiary, thick, basaltic andesite flows; the red firs and mountain hemlocks have yielded to Douglas-firs and orange-barked madrones. From this junction a desirable alternate route starts south along Highway 99 before curving north through the "mountain lakes" area to Dead Indian Road. It has the advantages of running water, campsites, crest views and solitude. It also closely approximates the proposed Pacific Crest Trail. This **recommended route** is described below immediately after the Old Oregon Skyline route description.

Following the temporary route suggested by the Forest Service trail planners, we turn north, head down 99, turn east on State Highway 273 and cross under Interstate 5 before reaching **Callahan's (3950-0.9)**. This restaurant, which opens at 5 p.m., is the *best* dining place along or near the entire tri-state Pacific Crest Trail. If you've been starving these last few miles, you'll be glad to know that (when this was written) each of their dinners included all the salad, soup and spaghetti you could eat. After a hearty meal, it is a chore to don our packs once more and tread down State 273. Nevertheless, we must continue, and in the twilight hours we may sight a porcupine or two ambling across the road. The Southern Pacific railroad tracks and several creeks are crossed as we descend to wild-rose-lined ranch fences and a junction with

11
12
13

State Highway 66 (2290-6.7). Just east of it is the shallow upper end of Emigrant Lake, a popular fishing area; the deeper parts are relegated to water skiers and swimmers. To reach a campsite before dark, we increase our pace along the highway as it makes a broad curve away from the reservoir's west shore. We reach the entrance to the **Emigrant Lake Recreation Area (2150-1.8)**, a paved road that heads southeast 0.4 mile up to a lateral dam, then curves north 0.6 mile to a public campground with cold pay showers. Rather than face up to the noise and congestion of this populated campground, we push on just a bit farther to the

Glenyan KOA (2140-0.2). This campground not only has friendly hosts, hot showers, food, a laundromat and a lounge, it also has secluded campsites for backpackers, located on the west side of Neil Creek, away from the car campers. This is an excellent place for a layover day, for the route ahead is mainly hot, dry and up. *Fish Lake Resort, 36 miles farther,* will be our next supply center. Bearing in mind that it is 13.2 miles uphill to the Hooper Springs Wayside, we start off early in the morning with a generous supply of water. After our road crosses questionably pure Neil Creek three times, we arrive at a junction with

Dead Indian Road (363) (1920-2.6), which is the terminal point of the Ashland Loop Road alternate route. The Ashland Ranger Station is 1.1 miles northwest on Highway 66; the Ashland Shopping Center is 0.6 mile farther. Our road heads north past the Ashland Municipal Airport and curves northeast past a small knoll with a roadcut that has exposed alternating layers of volcanically derived siltstone and sandstone from the upper Eocene epoch. Our road crosses Bear Creek (1870-0.9) and parallels its tributary, seasonal Walker Creek, up past rocky, open pastures, which begin to lose their radiant green by early June. We cross Walker Creek (2420-4.1) and climb a broad, sloping ridge that slowly curves east toward the forested highlands. The grazing cattle and horses, together with the rustling blackbirds, trilling meadowlarks and circling hawks, lend an air of tranquility to this rustic land. With increasing elevation comes cooler air and the appearance of scattered Oregon oaks, incense-cedars, ponderosa pines and Douglas-firs. By the time we arrive at the headwaters of Frog Creek (4300-5.2), our open woodland has—or had—transformed into a mature forest. In midsummer 1973, a raging fire, probably started by a tossed cigarette from a careless motorist, spread north up these slopes. Our road makes a hairpin turn, then a stiff climb to desolate

13
15
16

Hooper Springs Wayside (4430-0.4), once adorned with dogwoods and western chokecherries. About this time, you perhaps begin to suspect a major shortcoming of this temporary route:

Emigrant Lake

there isn't a single campsite or campground along Dead Indian Road. The first real campsite you'll encounter en route is 13.0 miles away—the Beaver Dam Campground along Road 3706. After refilling water bottles at the drinking fountain, we continue upward and finally reach the edge of the highlands at a junction with **Buck Prairie Road (5220-2.6)**, which contours southeast. The temporary route before us is now a leisurely walk as we follow Dead Indian Road down to a wide, open flat and a junction with the **Howard Prairie-Hyatt road (4535-4.2)**. This paved road curves southeast 2.0 miles along Howard Prairie Lake to Grizzly Campground and continues 2.4 miles farther to the restaurant and general store of the Howard Prairie Lake Resort. At this reservoir, foot-long rainbow trout seem to be caught almost every day—reason enough for anglers to make this side trip. Our route passes the reservoir's shallow northwest arm, which becomes a grassy meadow by late summer, and then arrives at a junction with the **Keno Access Road (4540-1.4)**, a paved shortcut to Klamath Falls. We now make a gradual, forested climb to a low saddle before descending to

16
17
18B
19
20

Deadwood Junction (4638-3.3) and brick-red Road 3706. This dirt road we follow north through a forest of lodgepole pine that changes to shady woods of Douglas-fir, flowered with columbine and bleeding heart, as we descend to **Beaver Dam Campground (4530-1.5)**, a full 26.2 miles beyond the Glenyan KOA. This lovely campground is little-used despite its accessibility; car campers evidently prefer trout-stocked reservoirs to willow-and-aspen-lined creeks such as Beaver Dam Creek. We cross this creek and arrive at Daley Creek Campground, which is under a lodgepole cover near the confluence of Daley, Deadwood and Beaver Dam creeks. From here our road climbs moderately northeast before it descends gently north toward Highway 140. Western hemlock and western white pine put in their appearance with the Douglas-fir before we reach the South Fork Little Butte Creek (4650-3.7). As in most of Oregon's Douglas-fir forests, huckleberry, gooseberry, currant and Oregon grape thrive beneath the shady canopy. Continuing north, our route reaches and then parallels the terminus of a late Quaternary basalt flow from Brown Mountain to the east. We now descend to wide, deep North Fork Little Butte Creek (4550-2.5). The North Fork Campground beside its north bank is probably popular because of the brook trout that inhabit its waters. We reach a junction with Road 3720 (4600-0.1), but keep right as we head northeast on Road 3706 past the Fish Lake Summer Homes spur road and arrive at a junction with

State Highway 140 (4660-0.9). With the Pacific Crest Trail only a few miles away, we progress east on 140 toward our last contact with "civilization"—the Fish Lake area. The lake was formed by a basalt flow that descended west from Brown Mountain and dammed North Fork Little Butte Creek. The lake's level has since been raised by a man-made dam, and is kept high by spring-fed water gushing from the base of the lava flow at the lake's east end and by water transported down the Cascade Canal. This canal, crossed by the Pacific Crest, Mt. McLoughlin and Oregon Skyline trails, originates at Fourmile Lake, a reservoir *east* of the Little Butte Creek drainage divide.

The highway passes the Doe Point Campground spur road (4680-1.0) and then reaches the **Fish Lake spur road (4740-0.5).** This spur descends to Fish Lake Campground and **Fish Lake Resort,** where you can purchase limited supplies and test your skill at catching rainbow and eastern brook trout. Not until we reach *the south rim of Crater Lake, 59 miles distant,* will we see another store. Ready for adventure, we now stride east on Highway 140, which after an initial climb descends to a broad gully, then in 0.1 mile crosses the Cascade Canal. Forty yards farther, beside a spur road that goes north to a parking area, is the trailhead of the **Pacific Crest Trail (#2000) (4980-1.3).** The proposed trail south, which has been under construction since 1972, should be completed all the way to the Old Baldy trail segment and the Keno Access Road by late 1974.

20
21
22

Before describing the route north along the Pacific Crest Trail, we will now describe a "late summer" **alternate route** that starts in Seiad Valley, heads east toward Copco Reservoir and then climbs north through southern Oregon along the old **Oregon Skyline Trail** (really a system of roads—the trail was never built).

By late July, the water supply along the Siskiyou crest temporary route has become quite precarious, but this stretch can be bypassed if you head east up **California State Highway 96** alongside the Klamath River. A series of dams upstream guarantees that you'll always find running water in its channel. This route is also recommended for those who enjoy swimming holes or who have descended north from the Marble Mountains and would like a flat stretch with settlements. Fishing for salmon during the June run and sighting majestic great blue herons are two more incentives to head east. On the negative side, the route is hot and it mostly follows paved and dirt roads—as does the temporary route. One can also expect to encounter many

speeding lumber trucks (except on Sundays) along shoul-
derless Highway 96. The Klamath River, being pleasantly
warm, is also disturbingly polluted. Purify the water if you
intend to drink it; better yet, obtain water at settlements,
campgrounds and creeks.

This route begins at the Seiad Store and heads southeast, crossing the Klamath River (1430-1.0), then reaching
a junction with Road 46N46 (1430-0.5) 40 yards shy of
Walker Creek. If you are traveling *south* along the PCT,
follow this road 40 yards south, then turn right and follow
paved Road 8D001 along the Klamath River to a fork
(1440-2.4) where the pavement ends. Veer left on Road
46N66, which climbs slightly and curves south, and follow
it across Grider Creek (1520-1.5), then upstream to where
the road makes a hairpin turn (1750-0.9) and a spur
road descends south to the Grider Creek trailhead
(1720-0.2-6.5). From here Volume 1 of **The Pacific Crest
Trail** will guide you faithfully south to the Mexican border.

Our alternate northbound route continues east along
Douglas-fir-shaded Highway 96 past verdant O'Neil
Creek Campground (1500-3.7) and a general store at a
gasoline station. Eventually we reach the quiet summer
22 resort of **Hamburg (1560-3.8),** with a cafe and a general
store. Just out of town we come across Sarah Totten
Campground (1560-0.9). Here you'll notice a drier, more
open vegetative cover than at O'Neil Creek Campground.
Besides Douglas-fir, madrone, ponderosa pine and
incense-cedar, you'll also find canyon live oak (maul oak),
manzanita and ceanothus. Beyond this campground the
alternate route crosses the Scott River just before reaching
a junction with the Scott Bar road (1560-1.4) and curving
northeast. Up the next stretch of highway the vegetation
changes from a thinning forest to an Oregon-oak woodland. The route curves east and we reach the hamlet of
Horse Creek (1650-4.7), which has a cafe, general store and
post office. Continuing east, we cross to the north side of
the Klamath River and follow it upstream to the
Oak Knoll Ranger Station (1708-6.7), operated by the
Klamath National Forest, where water, advice and fire
permits are available. Approximately halfway to Interstate 5, we trek east to the community of **Klamath River
(1750-4.9),** with its saloon, general store, post office and
trees of heaven, these native to China. After curving
north up to Beaver Creek (1772-0.7), our route bears east
and makes no pretense about shade; indeed, it can get

blistering hot. Temporary relief is found when you reach
envigorating Lumgrey and Empire creeks (1850-4.8), but
your day's goal should be the **Tree of Heaven Campground
(2140-5.9),** where a spur road descends 0.3 mile to the river
bank. In addition to several specimens of the walnutlike
tree of heaven near campsites 16-18, the campground also
has juniper, willow and Oregon ash. Here tap water flows
freely, fishing is fair, and the river's midsummer temperature approaches 80°F. In this drier landscape, the
canyon's metamorphic rocks stand out more boldly than
farther west. Hillsides are now chaparral-covered as we
continue our journey east and arrive at a junction with
State Highway 263 (2040-4.5), which heads south up the
Shasta River eight miles to Yreka. As your road curves
north, you reach the Swallows Cafe (2040-0.3), which is
worth a rest and liquid stop before you continue north and
cross over the river to the

Interstate 5 Randolph Collier Rest Area (2056-2.0). This
suburban transplant of picnic tables, spacious restrooms,
pet areas and neatly trimmed lawns was obviously constructed to impress incoming out-of-state travelers. For
you, it's a great place to relax, fish or toss a frisbee, if you
have packed one along. Moving again, we cross east under
Interstate 5 to the old, one-lane **Anderson Grade Road
(2060-0.1)** and start north up it beside the Klamath River.
Along this ash-and-oak-lined stretch of river can be found
some of its better swimming holes. The river curves east,
and so does our dirt road as it crosses straight Hornbrook
Valley, which is composed of easily erodable Cretaceous
marine sediments. On the northwest horizon we see Mt.
Ashland and the evenly graded Road 4059, along which the
temporary route descends. Where the Southern Pacific
railroad tracks cross over the river toward our road, we
enter the realm of Vulcan: from here to mid-Washington
we'll tread along volcanic rocks of a mid-Tertiary age or
younger. With this profound thought in mind, we continue
east along the river to an unsigned **paved road (2116-5.0)**
that crosses it over to a junction with the

Copco Lake Road (2115-0.1). Three miles west on this
road, you will find that the Hornbrook Market and post
office are about all that remains in this once-lively settlement. The route east takes you past private riverside de-
velopments to Dry Creek and "R" Fishhook Cafe and
Tavern (2160-3.6), which is your last source of food until
Lake of the Woods Resort 54 miles farther. The road

23

continues along the river to a junction (2200-1.5), where a road crosses the river to the Iron Gate Fish Hatchery. (If you are traveling south, you can raft down the Klamath from here all the way to Seiad Valley.) Our road crosses Brush Creek, a shady ribbon of green, then climbs to a saddle (2520-1.1) before winding slowly down to Pacific Power and Light Company's Iron Gate Reservoir. As we contour along its west shore, we pass the Mirror Cove (2370-1.9) and Juniper Point (2380-1.0) picnic areas before reaching the Camp Creek Recreation Area (2360-0.9). The road curves southeast to a saddle, passes an exposure of massive boulder conglomerate in the cliffs above, and arrives at **Wanaka Spring (2440-1.4),** a roadside faucet with an unimproved, unsigned camping area below. In 0.1 mile we pass a junction with the spur road that descends to this area, and then bear east as late-Tertiary lava flows loom above us. Our road now descends to and crosses a shallow bay, where we find the unsigned but well-used **Jenny Creek camping area (2360-1.3).** A short walk north brings us to fresh water from Jenny Creek. Another possible campsite along this alternate route is on a forty-yard-long peninsula (2360-1.2) of columnar basalt that juts south into the reservoir, coming within 40 yards of the opposite shore. The columns at its point are great for diving into the warm lake water—when the water level is high! Moving along, we pass the Fall Creek Picnic Area (2360-1.1), under a large, solitary ponderosa pine, and 40 yards later head left as our road forks north away from the reservoir. It follows, then crosses, Oregon-oak-lined Fall Creek (2490-0.9). Soon we reach the run-down shacks of Copco and arrive at a junction with

Copco Road (2620-0.3), up which we climb earnestly north. As our road reaches the edge of the flat highland, we encounter a narrow spur road (3300-1.4) heading west. Now under the welcome cover of a sparse forest of ponderosa pine, incense-cedar and Oregon oak, we follow our road northeast to the **California-Oregon State Line (3310-0.8).** In summer the heat has cost us a great deal of sweat on this ascent, but now it brings out the tantalizing aromas of the pines and ceanothus bushes. The road is now graded red, and shortly we encounter our first "Pacific Crest Trail System" green-and-white diamond nailed to a tree. We cross upper Fall Creek (3320-1.2) and pass several ranch houses at the edge of an open flat as our road heads north within the forest's edge to a junction with

23

24

a **road (3308-0.6)** signed *Agate Flat* and *Jenny Creek*. If you're worried by a route with a large number of junctions, you can play it safe and stick to Copco Road, ascending northeast, and follow it north 8.0 miles to a junction with State Highway 66 just 0.9 mile west of the Oregon Skyline route junction. The OST route veers left (northwest), stays right at a junction (3315-0.2), curves north and climbs up to a ford of Shoat Springs creek (3340-0.5). Next, you make a short, moderate ascent to where your road bifurcates. Follow either branch, since they rejoin in 0.3 mile, and head north-northwest to a junction with a curving, **unsigned road (3430-0.8)**. We follow this northeast to an intersection with

Copco Road (3540-0.5) once again. Hikers headed south should know that the road we were just on is signed *Johnson Ranch* and *Box-O*. We head north 70 yards on Copco Road, then fork right (north-northeast) on a peaceful, little-used road. We follow this dry, well-forested, winding route until it finally veers north-northeast and intersects **Road W50 (3740-4.0)**, which heads north-northwest. This we take for 15 yards, to where Road W62 forks west, then go 30 yards more to **Road W61**, which heads north-northeast. We hike along this wider road as it curves northwest past a fork with Road W61.2 (3730-1.4) to a junction with an **unsigned road (3730-0.2)** just before ours turns quickly west. We now head north-northeast on this road and cross abandoned South Parker Road as our road curves east and heads gently up to a fork (3730-0.4). We veer left (northeast) onto a one-lane road and go north to another **fork (3725-0.5)** just south of State Highway 66. Here we angle right (northeast) and curve east to yet another fork almost within a stone's throw of the highway. Heading north about 80 yards, we reach

24

25

26

State Highway 66 (3385-0.5) halfway between its mileposts 25 and 26. Should you decide to head west 6.6 miles along 66 toward our recommended route (to be described immediately after this OST description), you would pass the following points of interest: Copco Road, Jenny Creek and the Pinehurst site, Mountain View Inn Cafe, shady Tubb Springs Wayside, the new, paved Hyatt Lake Road, Keene Creek Reservoir and Green Springs Summit (4551), from which the Ashland Flat road—on our recommended route—starts north.

From State Highway 66 the Oregon Skyline route starts gently north up **Road W47 (Moon Prairie Road)**, which is signed with PCTS diamonds. This we follow religiously, ignoring all other tempting roads, as it curves gradually northeast up to a ridge (4130-2.0) and then descends to a wooden bridge over **Johnson Creek (3810-1.3)**, which in late summer may be your last source of water until the Lake of the Woods area about 22 miles farther. Here is one of the better campsites that you'll find along this section of the alternate route, despite the slightly polluted nature of the creek. Our road quickly tops a saddle in a forest of ponderosa pine, descends gently north-northeast and crosses a long, golden meadow, then intersects broad Road 100 (3940-1.3). Upon reaching the edge of Johnson Prairie, we get a good view of Old Baldy (6340), north of us, upon whose shoulders winds the only stretch of trail along this route to Highway 140. We follow the meadow's edge, cross a seasonal creek, and head north-northwest past an outhouse (shown on the map) and a spur road that bears west. Just beyond it we reach a junction with

Road W46 (4002-1.3), along which Moon Prairie Road continues southeast. We turn north and follow the curving path northeast past a good campsite at the meadow's north end, then head southeast to meet **Road W45 (3980-0.3)**, which we follow north to a fork with **Road 45-3 (4030-0.4)**. This road we take east, then northeast, to a fork with **Road 45-5 (4060-0.8)**. Here Road 45-3 curves east and we start north up rocky Road 45-5. Climbing moderately, we pass Road 45-6, which forks left, then reach another **fork (4560-1.1)** just as our road eases off and curves west toward the ridge crest. We take the narrow road branching right and follow it north past a spur right, then a spur left, before it veers northeast. Leaving the forest of sugar pine, white fir, Douglas-fir and incense-cedar behind, we bear east-southeast almost level to an abrupt roadend, from where a **jeep road (4950-1.2)** climbs north. This we follow steeply up to an abandoned road that parallels the paved Keno Access Road above it, then go 120 yards east on it to a large rock pile beside a PCTS diamond. Here we take a faint trail 50 yards up to a junction with

Keno Access Road (5170-0.2) at the *Kent Peak* sign. We follow this road as it contours northeast into Klamath County (5080-0.5), past a fork with County Line Road (5080-0.4), round a big gully (5160-1.3), and finally to the cryptic start of the

Old Baldy trail (5150-0.5). For those having trouble finding its trailhead, about 20 feet in from the road, search in an area 0.15 mile (264 yards) southwest of the West Fork Johnson Creek gully, which in turn is 0.3 mile northwest of the Johnson Creek road junction. The first half of this trail, up to the Old Baldy summit, is on Bureau of Land Management land, and as of 1973, it was an unmaintained, hard-to-follow route. About every hundred yards or less along it, however, are blazes, ducks and plastic streamers; if you progress 200 yards without seeing any markers, you're probably on the wrong path. The trail starts west through a forest of ponderosa and sugar pine up to a gully, where it switchbacks east, then climbs northeast, and nearly tops a broad, grassy saddle (5770-1.4). From here it strikes southwest to another clearing before turning west-northwest toward the summit. Upon reaching the upper slopes of Old Baldy, the trail steepens and climbs directly up to its northeast ridge (6190-1.0), on which snow patches may linger through mid-June. After a short 50-yard descent, our trail reaches the Rogue River National Forest boundary and suddenly is transformed into a well graded, maintained route. Now it ascends gently to a poorly marked junction with the

Old Baldy summit trail (6190-0.2). This ducked path climbs 0.1 mile up to a jeep road that we follow 0.15 mile to the rocky, open summit. Abandoned by fire lookouts, it is now under the watchful eye of turkey vultures. From it we see Mt. Shasta (bearing 176°), Yreka (185°), Soda Mountain (217°), Hyatt Reservoir and Mt. Ashland (242°) and Mt. McLoughlin (354°). With these landmarks identified, a careful observer should be able to trace the temporary PCT, the Oregon Skyline Trail and the recommended route. Back at the junction, our trail turns north, descends a ridge and switchbacks at times before reaching **Road 3802 (5390-2.5).** We follow this one-third mile northeast to a union with a major logging road coming from the south, then go north to

Dead Indian Road (#363) (5310-1.8). The temporary route up Road 3706 from Deadwood Junction lies 5.4 miles west on this highway, which twice crosses Beaver Dam Creek. The Oregon Skyline route heads east up the highway and quickly reaches a saddle before curving northeast and descending to a junction with Lake of the Woods' **West Shore Road (#3701) (4974-4.9).** You can take this road north to a junction with State Highway 140 (4995-3.5), from which the **Mt. McLoughlin Trail (#3716)** climbs up a ridge to a junction with the **Pacific Crest Trail (#2000)**

27
28
29
30

(6260-4.1). If you would rather take the PCT north from its trailhead at 140, then follow this highway west 3.6 miles. At the junction with 140, you can also head east, quickly passing the Lake of the Woods Ranger Station, Spruce Campground and Billie Creek and then reaching the southern terminus of the trail portion of the **Oregon Skyline "Trail" (4980-0.7-8.3).**

From the West Shore Road junction, our route bears east, then curves north and passes the Winema National Forest East Side Recreation Residences below us before reaching the entrance to **Sunset Campground (4990-2.2),** which in the summer is crowded with water skiers, swimmers, campers and fishermen. You'll find the lake's waters are stocked with rainbow, Kokanee and eastern brook. Continuing north, you reach a junction with Road 3704 (4954-1.0), along which you trek northwest to a **spur road (5000-0.3)** that heads a quarter mile southwest down to the lakeshore and the Lake of the Woods Resort. Here you can restock on supplies and obtain a good meal. Back on Road 3704, continue northwest past the entrance to **Aspen Point Campground (4970-0.4)** and reach **State Highway 140,** which we take 0.15 mile (264 yards) southwest to the southern terminus of the **Oregon Skyline Trail (4980-0.8-109.3).** This trail is described immediately after the PCT description from Highway 140 north to Devils Peak, where the two trail segments finally merge.

**29
30
11
31**

Between the temporary PCT and the Oregon Skyline routes lies our **recommended crest route,** which starts along old U.S. Highway 99 and progresses northwest past lakes to the Old Baldy trail. From the **Mt. Ashland Ski Area road (#4059)** junction, we head south on 99 and immediately cross under Interstate 5, then hike up through a sixty-foot roadcut of massive basaltic andesite. We soon reach the road's summit at Siskiyou Pass (4466), where we obtain good views west up the temporary route and south down toward the summer alternate route. A quarter mile farther we reach a junction with **Pilot Rock Road (4420-1.3),** up which we hike east to an intersection on a **saddle (4805-1.0).** Our route follows the road that heads southeast up the ridge, then curves east around a summit and angles toward Pilot Rock. It then descends to a **fork (4800-1.1),** where the main road veers up and right (southeast), but we go left (east) and switchback down to a creek (4640-0.4).

Mt. McLoughlin above Lake of the Woods

After a short drink, we contour east around imposing Pilot Rock, which is a remnant of massive lava flows, then reach the Pilot Rock Jeep Road 35 yards before crossing a small creek. You could follow this steep road up to a saddle, but, it is much easier to stay on the present road as it winds across north slopes up to the saddle and this ridge crest **jeep road (4960-1.0).** This we follow up nearly to the top of Porcupine Mountain (5306), then past two road junctions and two closed gates as our route traverses flowery meadows containing dozens of species which in early June are a riotous display of color. We now descend to a spring by an abandoned mile-high cabin (5280-2.9) that makes a very good campsite. Continuing down to a saddle, we reach an **intersection (5160-0.4),** where we meet two roads that descend and two roads that ascend. We take the road that parallels a fence on its right as it climbs straight up the ridge crest to the shoulder of Little Pilot Peak, then angles east to a junction with another **jeep road (5760-1.2),** below which lies a small pond 100 yards northwest. Our road now heads northeast, passing several small roadside springs and a pond below us, to a junction with the

    Soda Mountain Fire Lookout Road (5760-0.4). If you would like to survey your route or the adjacent countryside, there's hardly a better spot to do it from than the fire lookout atop Soda Mountain (6091), one-half mile up the road. Our route descends moderately along the ridge road to a saddle, where a road from the southeast merges with ours, then we continue down to a junction with the **Soda Mountain Road (5360-0.9),** 0.1 mile south of some power lines. We head north down it and cross under the power lines three times before curving toward Hobart Bluff, a vertically jointed lava flow 400 feet thick. At its base lies Hobart Lake (4770-1.9), a willow-lined, over-sized lily pond 0.1 mile east of the road. Its water is drinkable when purified, and adequate campsites lie along its shore. With constant views to the west, we continue to descend gradually north until just before a knoll, which we climb up to and then shortly reach

32

33

Highway 66 (4545-2.4). Forty yards east on it at **Green Springs Summit (4551)** is a junction with the **Ashland Flat Road**—the old Hyatt Lake road. Since the opening of the new, paved road to Hyatt Lake, this dirt road now sees little use except by those who know its attributes and delights. We start gently north up it, then descend through an open forest of Douglas-fir, ponderosa pine, white fir and Oregon oak to Ashland Flat, a large cattle pasture delimited by a rustic wood-plank fence. We follow the fence-lined route as it curves around the pasture to the forest's edge, where our road veers north and crosses Keene

Little Hyatt Reservoir

Creek. Now on the east side of the creek, our route passes through a grassy meadow just before reaching **Little Hyatt Reservoir (4620-3.0)**, a beautiful gem that outshines its two larger sisters. Under the ponderosa pines along its shoreline, you can fish or just stretch out and relax. Swimming is best near the dam, from which you can dive off. It is a great place for a layover day. Moving along, we parallel willow-lined Keene Creek to where the road crosses it and the smaller Burnt Creek, then climbs to a junction with the Burnt Creek road (4740-0.8). We continue up our road, which climbs moderately as it curves east through a pleasant forest to a junction with paved

Howard Prairie-Hyatt road (5020-0.7). Starting northeast on it, in 0.1 mile we reach a spur road that heads southeast another 0.1 mile to **Hyatt Lake Resort,** which houses a cafe and a small store. At this lake you can swim or fish for rainbow and eastern brook trout without worrying about speeding motorboats—a ghost forest of bleached-white snags occupies its shallow waters. Evidently, at the time of the dam's construction, the planners felt it too costly to remove the trees that would be flooded. We continue north along the lake's west shore and reach Camper's Cove Cafe and Store (5020-0.5), which sells mostly fishing tackle. Beyond it our road passes many lakeside campsites—and some places used by spotted sandpipers for nesting—then curves northwest up to trickling Cottonwood Creek (5060-1.8) before winding east gradually down to a junction with paved

33

18A

Hyatt Lake Road (5020-1.3). This road climbs above the lake's east shore and passes summer cabins before starting its descent south to Highway 66, 7.3 miles from our junction. Our road now heads northeast across a broad, level divide, then descends, crossing Willow Creek (4740-1.3) before reaching a junction with the **south-shore access road (4640-0.5).** Here you can head 1.4 miles north to **Howard Prairie Lake Resort,** where meals and supplies may be obtained, and then continue onward to the temporary PCT route along Dead Indian Road, 5.0 miles from this junction. Our recommended route turns right (east) and parallels Willow Creek down to the often-crowded **Willow Point Campground (4560-0.7)** along the shore of Howard Prairie Lake. This reservoir, though shallower than Hyatt, is considerably better in appearance, since all the trees were removed before its basin was flooded. Our road continues east to a point, from where Mt. McLoughlin projects

above the distant lakeshore, then it climbs southeast above
the lake's south shore to a saddle (4616-1.7) at a junction
with Jenny Creek Road. Continuing east, we soon start a
contour northeast to the Klum Landing Campground
(4570-1.0), which sees less use than the lake's other
campgrounds. The pavement stops for a short stretch as
our road descends to **Grizzly Creek (4450-0.6),** which is our
last source of water until the Lake of the Woods area,
about 21 miles farther. We then make a moderate ascent,
reach renewed pavement, and follow our road as it parallels Moon Prairie Road a short distance before reaching a
junction with

Keno Access Road (4649-1.0). Moon Prairie Road (#386)
can be taken north 4.2 miles to Deadwood Junction, along
Dead Indian Road, from which the temporary PCT starts
north on Road 3706. At our junction there is a large sign
with a map of the resort area we have just hiked through.
We head east along the paved forest highway until we
reach a clearing with a *Mt. Shasta* sign pointing south
toward that majestic peak. This alerts us that in 0.3 mile we
will reach the *Kent Peak* sign, where we will join the
Oregon Skyline route (5170-4.4-34.2), which follows the
highway 2.7 miles east to the Old Baldy trailhead. To
follow this route north, consult the Oregon Skyline route
description, which appears just before this recom-
mended-route description.

18A
34
21

As of September 1973, the southernmost Oregon trailhead of
the much-publicized **Pacific Crest Trail (#2000) (4980-0.0)** lay
along Highway 140 just 0.2 mile west of the Jackson/Klamath
county line and 40 yards east of the Cascade Canal. Beside the
trailhead, a small parking lot is used by car campers as well as
backpackers. If you intend to camp in this vicinity, you might
pick a spot alongside the Cascade Canal, a short way up the trail.
Just after we start up this trail, we cross this canal, then parallel it
northeast. The trail almost touches the canal before it angles
away and up open slopes that provide a view south of Brown
Mountain and its basalt flows. As the PCT climbs, it too crosses
lava flows; then it enters a white-fir forest and continues up to a
switchback just 30 yards west of the unseen Mt. McLoughlin
Trail. We now feel the weight of our packs as we climb moderately northwest to a junction with the

Mt. McLoughlin Trail (#3716) (6250-4.7) in a forest of red fir
and mountain hemlock, where, atop the fresh snow of a late
spring snow flurry, the chickenlike tracks of the blue grouse may

be seen. From this ridge point, the Mt. McLoughlin Trail climbs about four miles, switchbacking steeply up much of the distance to the summit. We'll pass higher mountains before our odyssey is completed, but few that so dominate a landscape as andesitic Mt. McLoughlin (9495) does. It stands alone. From its summit you can see south to Mt. Shasta, north past Crater Lake to the "matterhorn" of Mt. Thielsen and beyond to the snow-clad Three Sisters. About one-quarter mile east, Trail 3716 reaches the Freye Lake spur trail, which descends northwest 250 yards to forested campsites beside shallow, tranquil Freye Lake. Over the next 0.9 mile east, Trail 3716 descends steeply, then moderately, passing a trailside spring before reaching a trailhead at a parking loop along the old Fourmile Lake Road, which is blocked off to the west. Most hikers climbing the mountain start from here, but this ridge trail extends 3.0 miles farther down to another trailhead across from a junction of Road 3701 with Highway 140.

Back at the Mt. McLoughlin Trail junction, the Pacific Crest Trail quickly tops the ridge, then winds slowly down through the forest, not once offering us a view, and reaches a junction with the **Twin Ponds Trail (#3715) (5840-3.7).** This junction lies between two shallow ponds that by late summer are no more than dry, grassy meadows. Small campsites may be found at Summit Lake, 0.4 mile northwest down Trail 3715. Its trailhead lies 2.3 miles southeast, down at the west end of Fourmile Lake Campground. From the junction our trail starts northeast, quickly veers north past a stagnant pond, climbs steadily up a ridge, and descends slightly to a junction with the

21
30
35
36

Blue Rock Trail (#3737) (6120-1.6), which has ascended 2.0 miles from the Twin Ponds Trail junction at Squaw Lake. Our trail heads north to a gully that is snowbound until late June, then veers east up to a gentle slope before curving northeast and climbing to a broad saddle (6300-1.6). Our route now contours across a slope forested with mountain hemlock, red fir and western white pine. Some deer and coyote tracks in patches of snow here may invite an interpretation in tracking. We round a north ridge, descend southeast to another saddle (6240-1.2), then bear northeast down toward a saddle and meet our first of several junctions with the

Oregon Skyline Trail, here signed the **Badger Lake Trail (#3759) (6010-1.1).** The OST is described from Highway 140 north to Devils Peak immediately after this PCT description to that peak. The Oregon Skyline Trail descends into the basin, but the Pacific Crest Trail takes to the ridge as it contours almost directly north along it to our second junction, unsigned, with the

Oregon Skyline Trail (6070-2.6). The two trails become one, which leaves the ridge, crosses a trickling outlet from a pond, then angles northeast gently up to a junction with the

Sky Lakes Trail (#3762) (6130-0.9). The OST route follows this trail to an escarpment and drops into the popular, easily accessible Sky Lakes Area. Our route heads north-northwest in a forest of lodgepole pine and mountain hemlock, ascends a gentle slope past several nearby ponds, then reaches an open forest as it approaches a cliff above the Dwarf Lakes Area. Glaciated Pelican Butte (8036) is the prominent summit in the southeast; the more subdued Cherry Peak (6623) is directly east. We can't see the lakes below us, because the area is so forested. Our trail switchbacks slightly up to avoid the cliff, switchbacks slightly down the west side, and soon encounters an unsigned 100-yard spur trail (6600-2.5), which takes us to an overlook with a view that encompasses most of the rolling hills to the west. We now switchback several times up to a small summit before descending the ridgeline to a saddle and a junction with the

Wickiup Trail (#3728) (6585-1.0). This lateral descends east past more than a dozen stagnant ponds before reaching the OST 70 yards south of Lake Land (5990-2.0). The PCT now takes us northeast up to a ridge where the views east of the Sky Lakes Area really begin to open up. Along the trail segment that crosses a barren slope of volcanic blocks, you are likely to find, sprouting in the thin volcanic soil, numerous creamy-white western pasqueflowers (also called anemones), which are readily identified by their finely dissected leaves, hairy stems and dozens of stamens. By late August, their flowers are transformed into balls of silky plumes. Our trail contours north-northeast to the west edge of a saddle and reaches the

Luther Mountain trail (6840-1.2) at an unsigned junction that is easy to miss in early summer, for the PCT here is then buried under a thick snowpatch. The 2.6-mile Luther Mountain trail strikes due east across the rocky slopes of this peak (7153), makes ten switchbacks down to three presentable ponds, and then winds gradually down to the OST junction at Margurette Lake (6010), but not before passing virtually every body of water in the vicinity. This is quite a lovely side trip to take if you are not in a hurry. From the Luther Mountain trail junction, we descend moderately to a ridge and follow it north as it gradually levels off, to a junction with the

Hemlock Lake Trail (#985) (6600-0.9), which descends west about one mile to Hemlock Lake (6100), then continues beyond to a trailhead. We climb again, straight up a ridge, and obtain views south of Mt. McLoughlin as we round the west slope of Shale Butte (7367)—really a highly fractured lava flow—then traverse the east slope of Lucifer (7481) to a saddle and a junction with the

Devils Peak Trail (#984) (7230-1.9), which descends northwest about a mile to a junction with the Seven Lakes Trail (#981). Trail 984 coincides with ours as we veer northeast across the saddle to a junction (7240-0.2). From here it climbs 600 yards moderately up the southwest ridge to Devils Peak (7582), then descends steeply east to the Devils Peak/Lee Peak saddle. The PCT traverses the south slope and meets the steeply ascending **Oregon Skyline Trail (7300-0.4)** just 20 yards southwest of this saddle. Since Devils Peak offers you the best panorama you will have seen so far along the entire route, you shouldn't pass up the opportunity to scale its summit. Leave your backpack behind, but bring your camera and climb the steep ridge trail 400 yards west to the broken-down stone-and-cement shelter atop the peak. The peaks you see to the north make up the southern rim of Crater Lake; beyond them protrudes the summit needle of Mt. Thielsen (9182). To the southeast lies the vast expanse of Upper Klamath Lake (4140); to the south stands our ever-guiding beacon, Mt. McLoughlin (9495). Back at the saddle, our route descends north, and it will be described immediately after the following description of the Oregon Skyline Trail.

38

30

The **Oregon Skyline Trail** provides you with a lower, lake-dotted alternate route from Highway 140 north to Devils Peak. By late July the mosquitoes have abated, yet the lake levels are still high enough to make this hike north a memorable trip. The clearly signed trailhead, at Highway 140, is about 0.2 mile east of Spruce Campground, which is on the north shore of Lake of the Woods. From this trailhead we walk west-southwest for 80 yards and reach a *Skyline Trail* sign at the start of the **Rye Spur Trail (#3771).** This we follow west, then northwest up to an intersection with a short **nature trail (#3735) (5000-0.2)** that descends one-quarter mile east to the highway. Our trail now switchbacks steeply up a moderate slope, then climbs north to **Road 3633 (5360-0.7),** which we follow 130 yards west to a resumption of the trail north. As you climb up it, you might notice diminutive tree frogs hopping across the path ahead; they definitely prefer the ground to the trees, and you'll see hundreds of them before you reach the Canadian border. At last our trail reaches water at the swiftly flowing

Cascade Canal (5701-0.6), and, like every hiker who crosses it in early summer, you'll think what great fun it

would be to raft down its smooth seven miles from Fourmile Lake around this ridge to the Fourmile Lake road.
But this doesn't get you to Devils Peak, so, after taking a
long drink, start up the dry trail once again. Douglas-fir
and ponderosa pine give way to white fir and red fir as the
trail climbs high on the southeast slope of Rye Spur. Near
some volcanic masses (6200-1.3) just east of the summit,
the trail reaches its zenith, from where we are presented
with an unobstructed panorama east to the country beyond
Upper Klamath Lake. Our trail now makes a long,
gradual, shaded descent north to a crossing of the **Cascade
Canal (5730-3.3)** on an obvious concrete slab. If we hike a
short way west up the road alongside the canal, we will
reach a lakeside parking lot at the end of the Fourmile
Lake road (#350). Before reaching the parking lot, however, we will reach a junction with the

   Badger Lake Trail (#3759) (5750-0.1), just east of the
twenty-foot-high dam. We start up it north-northeast, pass
a small auxiliary dam, then parallel Fourmile Lake's east
shore for about half a mile through a dense lodgepole forest
before the trail snakes northeast up to Woodpecker Lake
(5910-1.2), then Badger Lake (5910-0.2), neither too impressive. There is, nevertheless, a fairly nice campsite at
the northeast edge of Badger Lake, and the incoming water
from Lilly Pond does *look* drinkable—if you judge water
by its clearness. We cross this inlet creek and reach the
murky, one-foot deep Lilly Pond (5915-0.3), and then
wonder if one can really judge water by its looks. If you
want fresh water to drink, continue uptrail 150 yards past
the pond to where a signed spur trail leads 24 yards east to a
seeping spring. Our trail heads north through flat, wet
country, winds northeast up past a junction with the
Long Lake Trail (6060-1.3), heading east-northeast, then
reaches Long Lake (6080-0.3). On the map, this lake looks
quite inviting, but in reality it is just as murky as Lilly Pond
and almost as shallow. At its north end is an unsigned spur
trail (6083-0.4) that heads east 200 yards to the unde-
veloped site of Long Lake Camp—spacious enough for
group camping, but don't forget to treat the lake water.
North of Long Lake, our trail crosses an unnoticeable
gentle divide west of Lost Peak (6761), then descends past
a pond on its way down to a junction with the

   Lost Creek Trail (#3712) (5960-1.0), which is a short
lateral ascending east from Road 3561. One reason this
"lakes region" is so popular is that there are about two

30

36

Mt. McLoughlin beyond Island Lake

dozen half-day trails leading into it. Center Lake, lying just below us, is a good place to make camp. Our trail now angles northwest over a low divide and descends slightly to an intersection with the

Pacific Crest Trail (#2000) (6010-0.2). Whereas the PCT clings to the ridge, our trail descends northwest into a basin and passes a junction with the **Blue Canyon Trail (#982) (5930-0.3),** which heads west, then reaches a campsite beside scenic Island Lake (5960-0.4). Gorgeous early-summer sunsets can be captured at this lake as cloudy skies and snow-clad Mt. McLoughlin are reflected in the tranquil evening waters that surround a silhouetted, tree-covered island. Our route passes several more lakes, which are generally bordered with thick stands of water-loving, mosquito-sheltering mountain hemlock and lodgepole pine, and then reaches the east shore of Red Lake (5835-1.0). The trail follows the shoreline a quarter mile, then leaves the lake, continues north and reaches a junction, where the

Red Lake Trail (#987) (5870-0.8) ascends north. Our trail climbs east-northeast, winding up to our second intersection with the **Pacific Crest Trail (#2000) (6070-0.7),** on which we hike northeast a short distance up to a junction with the

Sky Lakes Trail (#3762) (6130-0.9). The PCT climbs north back to the ridge again, but our route heads northeast gently up to an escarpment, only to descend to Deer Lake (6060-0.6), on the flat basin floor. Shallow enough for a warm summer swim, yet deep enough to be minimally fit for drinking, this lake typifies many that we'll see in the Sky Lakes basin. Curving east, our trail passes a large pond on its way to a junction with the

Cold Spring Trail (#3710) (6050-0.4), which is the shortest and easiest lateral into the Sky Lakes area. We now head northeast, descend to the dry outlet of Lake Notasha, and immediately reach a junction with the **Isherwood Trail** (#3729) (5980-0.3), which makes a 1.2-mile loop north past lakes Notasha, Elizabeth and Liza, then curves east around Isherwood Lake and north Heavenly Twin Lake before it reaches the OST again. This loop is a great one for hikers who like maximum exposure to lakes and campsite possibilities. The OST continues northeast, passes between the two Heavenly Twin Lakes (5975) and leads past campsites to a junction with unsigned **Trail 3709** (5980-0.3), which descends southeast. We now head north alongside north Heavenly Twin Lake, cross its outlet, and reach a reunion with the **Isherwood Trail** (#3729) (5980-0.4), curving toward us from the northwest. Passing by ponds as usual, we hike north and reach a junction with the

37   **Wickiup Trail** (#3728) (6004-0.6), which winds 2.0 miles past numerous ponds as it climbs up to the crest and the PCT. Our trail descends to Lake Land (5990) in 70 yards, progresses north through the Sky Lakes area past small lakes, then descends to a pleasant lakeside campsite at Horseshoe Lake (5938—named Trappers Lake on the map) before reaching a junction with the **Cherry Creek Trail** (#3708) (5940-1.3), which follows the lake's outlet creek east. In 130 yards our trail turns west; from here an unsigned 0.9-mile loop trail makes an initial ascent northeast before curving around past Donna and Deep lakes, then climbing back up to the OST. Our route climbs west up a slope above Horseshoe Lake and reaches a truly excellent campsite at

Margurette Lake (6010-0.4). With a prominent cliff for a tapestry and Luther Mountain for a crown, this deep lake reigns as queen of the Sky Lakes. Near the campsite, the unsigned **Luther Mountain trail** contours around the lake's east side before climbing lazily past lakes up to a pond-studded bench. Striations on its rocks indicate that its ponds may have been carved by glacial ice. In contrast, the ponds and lakes of the Sky Lakes basin below appear to be the products of irregularities on the surface of old lava flows. This lateral trail now switchbacks up the southeast ridge of Luther Mountain before traversing across its south face to the western edge of a saddle and a junction with the **Pacific Crest Trail (#2000) (6840-2.6)**. We recommend that you take this trail up to Devils Peak rather than tackle the steep OST route that lies ahead. The Oregon Skyline Trail heads north alongside Margurette Lake, crosses its outlet, and reaches the unsigned reunion (6040-0.4) of the loop trail ascending moderately southwest from Deep Lake, 100 feet below us. Our trail now climbs up past unseen Tsuga Lake, on our left, then descends slightly to the Snow Lakes (6080), nestled at the foot of the vertically fractured northeast face of Luther Mountain (7153). Just beyond them, we reach tiny Martin Lake and climb gently before contouring north to the

Nannie Creek Trail (#3707) (6050-1.3), which continues east up to the Puck Lakes. Our route turns left and begins a steep climb up a gully—just a taste of what's to come —then temporarily eases off to a moderate gradient. The slope's gradient increases as we approach Devils Peak, but the trail, with snow patches lasting through early July, makes little attempt to switchback. Finally, just before leaving the forest of mountain hemlock, the trail makes short, steep switchbacks up to a reunion with the **Pacific Crest Trail (#2000) (7300-1.9-25.5)**, just 20 yards southwest of the Devils Peak/Lee Peak saddle.

37
38

The north slope down which the **Pacific Crest Trail** descends from the Devils Peak/Lee Peak saddle is usually snowbound through late July. Early-summer backpackers generally slide or run down the snowpack until they pick up the trail in the mountain-hemlock forest below. Those ascending this north slope will find the ascent strenuous but safe. The trail switchbacks down this slope, crosses a cascading, bubbling creek, then makes a gradual descent north past smaller creeks to a switchback before it descends to a flat above the Seven Lakes Basin and reaches **Spur Trail 981A (6220-2.9)**. This trail climbs southeast one-half mile to Cliff Lake (6260) and goes on over the crest. Our trail now descends gently northeast, crosses several creeks, then reaches a junction with the

Seven Lakes Trail (#981) (6150-0.7), which descends half a mile southwest to shallow Grass Lake (6020). We continue level northeast around a corner, then wind across gentle, usually dry,

forested slopes to a ridge and down it to a junction with the
Sevenmile Trail (#3703) (5860-2.7). This is the shortest and
easiest trail into the Seven Lakes Basin. From here it descends
gently northeast 1.9 miles to a trailhead at the Sevenmile Marsh
Campground, at the end of Road 334. The PCT descends quickly
to a flat, broad saddle and the **Middle Fork Basin Trail** (#1077)
(5790-0.2), which strikes west about a mile gradually down to
Ranger Spring at the headwaters of the Middle Fork Rogue
River. Our route continues north across the dry flat and begins
an ascent up the southeast flank of Big Bunchgrass hill (6631). It
then follows a forested gully, where snowpatches linger through
early July, up to an open meadow and a junction with the

Bunchgrass Trail (#1089) (6330-2.1), which heads west-
northwest straight ahead and down a gully. Our route starts
north up toward Maude Mountain (7184), but quickly curves
northwest and climbs to its west spur, where it contours north
along west slopes past Ethel Mountain (6998), then descends
past Ruth Mountain (6845) to a saddle (6340-2.0) just east of
Lone Wolf (6676). We now start east, but immediately switchback northwest and descend through a forest of red fir and
38 mountain hemlock before curving north to a flat. The trail climbs
39 to a low saddle, then meanders down to the west side of a
40 pumice-filled flat known as the Oregon Desert. In a strict sense,
it is not a desert, for it is covered with an open stand of evenly
spaced lodgepole pines. Nevertheless, you'd be hard pressed to
find even a drop of water on the surface—the ground water lies
sufficiently far beneath it that only the pines that tap this source
can survive. The even, low-density spacing of the pines indicates
that there isn't enough water to go around. Shrubs and
wildflowers are virtually nonexistent here. Not until a rich,
water-absorbing layer of soil humus develops, which might take
thousands of years, can we expect this forest really to flourish.
Leaving this "desert" behind, we top a low saddle, from where
an abandoned trail once went southeast, then cross another flat
and reach a junction with the

McKie Camp Trail (#1094) (6040-2.6), which descends southwest. We head north, shortly begin a descent, and, after half a
mile from the last junction, pass by an enormous five-
foot-diameter mountain hemlock. Soon our trail begins to
descend moderately toward a gulch, which it crosses; then it
heads north past another gulch to a ridge that we descend steeply
to a flat. From here, we continue our journey northwest to a
junction with the **Lucky Camp Trail** (#1083) (5430-2.5). In a
hundred yards we reach a well-used campsite beside a welcome,
refreshing, ten-foot-wide creek—your first trailside water since

the creeks in the Seven Lakes area, about 12.5 miles back. But don't camp here, the real treat is yet to come! Under a stately Douglas-fir forest, we round a ridge and shortly reach a bridge over Red Blanket Creek, then in 25 yards meet the **Upper Red Blanket Trail (#1090) (5450-0.7)**, which heads down along this vibrant creek. Following the creek upstream, we soon reach the **Stuart Falls Campground (5588-0.3)** and the joyfully cascading Stuart Falls. Unquestionably one of the best campsites along the PCT, this spacious flat, under the protective cover of a tall-conifer forest, has tables and a four-man shelter beside a singing creek, our last permanent source of water until Castle Creek, 9.6 miles ahead. Here, one would like to postpone his trek indefinitely, but we must move on, so we say goodbye to this beautiful setting and begin a short, moderate ascent that quickly brings us to the **Crater Lake National Park south boundary.** Just beyond it we cross a dry gulch and climb up to the terminus of **Road 27 (5590-0.2).** The designated PCT route through this park mostly follows dirt roads such as this one, but fortunately *all* of them are closed to motor vehicles. Only a few miles of the route within the park are actually along trails. We start up this closed road, with Bald Top (6220) on our left, and cross several seasonal creeks as our road winds up to a saddle and a junction with

Road 26 (6291-2.3). (Several months after the author surveyed **40** the trail segment from the saddle north of the Oregon Desert to this junction, a new trail segment was completed. This new, five-mile segment, shown as a dotted line on maps 39 and 40, climbs northeast from the saddle, rounds the Goose Egg, then follows the ridge north to this junction.) To the east lies forested Pumice Flat, which, like the Oregon Desert, was filled with dacite pumice falling from the skies when Mt. Mazama—once reigning over the site of Crater Lake—collapsed after a quick series of catastrophic eruptions that occurred about 6600 years ago. We turn left (west) and follow Road 26 as it curves north toward a cliff-bounded swale that is a pleasant spot to camp in when there are still snow patches for water. Our road tops a saddle, then descends to a junction with **Road 25 (6379-1.0),** which ascends from the west to this junction and then turns north. We now follow this road north to a large, open flat that is being invaded by lodgepole pines. From here, we can see Union Peak (7698) off to the west, which is all that's left of an ancient, gentle-sloped "shield" volcano built up by very fluid lava flows. Its last upwelling was of viscous magma, which cooled in the volcano's throat to form a resistant plug that stands today as Union Peak. Our route soon makes a moderate descent north down a large, forested gully that remains snowbound well into

July, then curves northeast and climbs a low ridge before descending to the blocked roadend just before paved

Crater Lake Highway (State 62) (6180-4.7). The PCT route, which begins as a trail on the other side of the highway, makes a long arc around the lake's west rim, generally staying two to three miles away from it and 1000 to 2500 feet below it. The route avoids the lake's rim because one of the criteria for the PCT is that it bypass heavily traveled routes—and the Rim Drive surely is one of them. But since we know that you're not going to hike past the lake without seeing it, we'll now describe a road route that takes you up and along the rim before it descends to a reunion with the PCT.

From the closed-Road 25 junction with Highway 62 at a level stretch, start due east on the highway, which then curves down to a junction with the **south rim access road (6020-0.8),** on your left. Head north along this paved road as it passes the entrance to **Mazama Campground (6020-0.2),** then contours east before climbing north to the park headquarters and post office (6479-3.7). These are immediately north of a junction where the clockwise, one-way Rim Drive terminates at our road. Having obtained at least a drink of water, if not a self-mailed "care" package, you now continue up the moderately steep road and pass several springs before you crest Munson Ridge and ascend gently north to the

41
42

Crater Lake rim (7100-2.9). Your first view of this 1932-foot deep lake, like a view down into the Grand Canyon, is one of disbelief—your memory tries to recollect a similar feature. As the deepest lake in the United States, and seventh deepest in the world, Crater Lake is a pristine ultramarine blue on a sunny day, and the 900-foot height of our vantage point deepens the color. The lake's size is also impressive. Although there are much larger lakes in the United States, few its size are located in an alpine setting, which transforms it into a beautiful fantasyland in winter. The roundness of the lake is also striking, since most large lakes tend to be considerably more asymmetrical.

It was the distinct manner of formation that gave Crater Lake its roundness. Not really a "crater" lake as is seen atop some cinder cones, this lake is actually a *caldera* lake, a body of water occupying a basin that formed when some material lying within a circular ring of faults was explosively thrown out and the remainder collapsed within the ring. A true crater lake is much smaller, and it occupies a basin that is formed by an accumulation of volcanic ejecta rather than by collapse along faults. Crater Lake is not Oregon's only caldera lake. Seventy miles northeast of it are the relatively obscure Paulina and East lakes, about 6340 feet in elevation, which occupy Newberry caldera.

The sequence of events that led up to the formation of Crater Lake was probably as follows. During the last glacial stage of the Pleistocene epoch, Mt. Mazama, its summit towering 12,000 feet above sea level, reigned as monarch above all the other Oregon stratovolcanoes. (Perhaps 100,000 years earlier, Mt. Hood in northern Oregon also achieved this height.) Mazama was almost the size of Mt. Adams, in southern Washington, but it differed considerably in shape. Rather than having a conical or a dome form, it had an irregular form, with perhaps two or three subsidiary summits in addition to dacite domes and basalt cinder cones lower down on its flanks. Deep, glaciated canyons also disrupted its symmetry. Large glaciers, fed by the mountain's ice fields, ground their way down these canyons as far as 17 miles from the mountain's summit. The peak had steep southern slopes compared to

42

Wizard Island in Crater Lake

the northern ones, and therefore the summit lay above a point approximately midway between the lake's south shore and its center. Late in the mountain's history, an arc of vents developed, which essentially followed the northern half of today's rim, and from the vents spewed thick flows of andesite and dacite. You can easily delineate the bottom of the porphyritic andesite flow that composes the Watchman (8056), on the rim two-and-one-half miles northwest of us. After a period of relative quiescence, the mountain erupted in its final death-throes, expelling approximately 15 *cubic miles* of ash and ejecta. About half of the ash was deposited beyond a 60-mile radius from the source; a three-inch deposit built up on the slopes of Mt. Rainier, and trace amounts reached hundreds of miles into British Columbia and Alberta. (Where the ash fell in lakes, it is possible to determine how much sediment has been deposited in them over the last 6600 years.) What was left of the mountain's rubble apparently collapsed into the mountain's emptied magma chamber. In its dying gasp, the chamber erupted a small amount of andesite that poured out on the floor of the caldera and built up a cone whose top is seen today as forested Wizard Island. Crater Lake reminds us that a volcano which for thousands of years appears dead can suddenly come to life and unleash its devastating forces. Man has conquered the summits of the Cascades' volcanoes, but he has yet to conquer the energy within them.

Turning toward a more pragmatic subject, food, we obtain meals and purchase some limited supplies at the building just east of the road junction, which houses a cafeteria, a coffee shop, a restaurant and a store that sells mainly souvenirs. Beyond it is towering Crater Lake Lodge, which serves elegant meals at prices to match. The next resort we'll pass near is the very complete *Diamond Lake Resort, about six miles off route and about 22 more miles ahead of us. The Cascade Summit store, on the west shore of Odell Lake, is just off the trail, but a full 67 miles ahead.* Except for snow patches lasting through August, our route ahead is dry until Thielsen Creek, 24 miles distant.

When we leave this Rim Village behind, we can take either the Rim Road or the short **Discovery Point Trail.** Your choice will depend upon the size of pack you're carrying, for although the rim trail is much preferred, it climbs quite steeply. From the Rim Village road intersection, you can pick up the Discovery Point Trail by walking just a few steps north. You'll probably be greeted by Clark's nutcrackers—raucous fellows who make it well known that they are proud members of the crow family. More discreet are mountain bluebirds, western tanagers and Oregon juncos. Also looking for handouts are golden-mantled ground squirrels, seemingly present wherever park tourists can be found. Our trail takes us up the rim through a forest of mountain hemlock, lodgepole pine and a few specimens of the five-needled, characteristically alpine whitebark pine. After obtaining some tree-framed views of the lake, as well as some close views of the pinnacles below, we descend this trail to a large

Parking lot and turnaround point (7090-0.9); the road beyond it becomes one way. A sign informs us that on June 12,1853, a prospector named John Wesley Hillman discovered "Deep Blue Lake" at a point about a mile northwest of here. Sixteen years later, the lake was given its present name by visitors from Jacksonville, a town just west of Medford. The local Indians, of course, discovered the lake eons ago, and, if their legends can be believed, their early ancestors probably witnessed the destruction of Mt. Mazama. Since the trail up to Discovery Point dies out on a slope, we now follow Rim Drive. This road rounds a low summit, then returns to the rim and the Wizard Island Overlook. Just beyond it, our road reaches a junction with

42
43

Road 31 (7172-1.3), a closed fire road. If you've tired of the traffic, you can retreat 4.4 miles down this road to the little used PCT route along Road 30. Otherwise, continue your climb up and around The Watchman to The Watchman Overlook (7590-1.4), where an excellent perspective of Wizard Island is obtained. The andesite flow emanating from its cone reaches the lake's western edge just under the shallow, brilliant emerald-green water. At this overlook, a popular, short trail climbs up to the summit of The Watchman, where a truly rewarding view of the lake is obtained as well as a panorama of much of southern Oregon. Also at this overlook you'll find a snowpack that remains through late July. Our road now curves around Hillman Peak, which is an andesite flow like The Watchman, then descends to a junction with the

North rim access road (7253-2.3), ascending south from the Diamond Lake area. From this point you can make an easy cross-country descent three miles northwest directly down the slope and reach Road 30 about a half mile west of

Red Cone Spring. Our alternate route follows the paved access road down along the contact with the Llao Rock dacite plug dome until just before reaching an unmarked junction with **Road 30 (6501-2.5)**. The PCT route is 0.8 mile west along this road. Continuing our descent, we head toward Mt. Thielsen before reaching the barren flats of the Pumice Desert—a valley drowned in the fatal dacite ash-, pumice-, and bomb-falls of the erupting Mt. Mazama. We head north, enter lodgepole forest, and in 0.7 mile reach a reunion with the **Pacific Crest Trail (#2000) (6029-3.8-19.8)**, which bears north-northeast along a dirt road. From this junction, supplies may be obtained by heading north along the paved road to South Store, 7.0 miles distant, located on the southeast shore of Diamond Lake. From the store, you can follow our "business loop" route description back up to the PCT.

From the **Crater Lake Highway,** the Pacific Crest Trail heads northeast, then veers north up a gully to a low divide, from which it descends just beyond to a junction with a **spur trail (6310-1.0)** that heads south about a mile to Mazama Campground. Our trail now descends to meet

45
42
41
44

Road 30 (6130-0.5), which we'll follow all the way around the slopes of the Crater Lake rim. On this we start east, and eventually cross over a dozen tributaries of Castle and Bybee creeks before reaching a junction with Road 31 (5860-5.2). You can hike up this closed fire road that climbs 4.4 miles to the Rim Drive and then follow it north along our alternate route past spectacular lake views. Road 30 continues to descend, passing a spur road on the left before reaching a fork where Road 32 (5450-1.9) branches west. We keep right and follow our road as it quickly curves north and starts to climb, then descends slightly to the South Fork Copeland Creek. Just beyond it is the **Middle Fork (5470-0.7)**, which is likely to be your last fresh water until Red Cone Spring, 6.0 miles farther. We soon climb to a meadowy junction with Road 33 (5593-0.8), but continue on our northward ascent. Our road has taken us through a viewless forest of mountain hemlock, red fir, lodgepole pine and western white pine, but the scenery improves a little as our road climbs up to a spur, then heads east-northeast toward Red Cone. We get a glimpse of this unmistakable landmark a short way before a junction with Road 34 (6085-4.1), which descends northwest. Our road continues to climb, passing through meadows of lupine and phlox, then curves north and starts a gentle descent through yet another meadow. Almost immediately, we reach a short spur road that heads up 100 yards to

Red Cone Spring (6265-1.1) at the meadow's edge. This will be your last source of water—and your last good campsite—until the Thielsen Creek area, about 19 miles distant. If you're hiking through in August or September, be prepared for a long, dry day. Our route continues north gently down to a reunion with Road 34 (6128-0.6), where we turn east and follow Road 30 up to the lower north slope of Red Cone, a geologically recent cinder cone that formed just before the last eruptions of Mt. Mazama. Along the base of this cone you can find volcanic bombs, spindle-shaped rocks of ejected molten lava that solidified before hitting the ground. Our road becomes disrupted where it was crossed by an avalanche that cut a 50-yard swath down the slope and through the lodgepole forest. The height at which all the trees were decapitated probably represents the depth of hardpack snow on the ground when the avalanche swept down. We now curve southeast gently up to a junction with an

Abandoned road (6370-2.5), where Road 30 turns sharply south for 50 yards before heading east. This junction is amid a cluster of lodgepoles that have large burrs on their trunks. Beneath these trees flower some fleshy Newberry knotweeds, which seem to thrive in the dry pumice soil. We head down this abandoned road, which is being overgrown by lodgepoles, and find diversion by identifying a multitude of hues in the pumice and scoria beneath our feet. We reach the edge of the Pumice Desert (6000-2.2) and start on a trail toward Mt. Thielsen across this sea of pumice, sand and ash. To the east, cars skirt across this desert on the paved north rim access road. We curve northeast past isolated pussypaws and Newberry knotweeds, then, just before entering a lodgepole forest, we get our last view back at Crater Lake's north rim, dominated by Llao Rock. We also spy the light streak of green down the north slope of Red Cone that marks the path of the snow avalanche we crossed. Entering the advancing forest of lodgepoles, we follow a dirt road again and soon reach a junction with the

44
43
45

North rim access road (6029-1.7) and a reunion with the Rim Drive alternate route. The PCT crosses the access road and starts north-northeast along a dirt road. About 30 yards after passing a gravel pit on our right, we encounter two posts in the road, and this route improves to a trail. The trail makes a gentle descent to the **Crater Lake National Park north boundary (5956-1.5),** where it becomes a road again. Rather than continue north on it, our route turns right and follows a new trail east about half a mile along the park boundary before contouring north-

northeast to **State Highway 138 (5920-2.2),** which is crossed just
100 yards west of the drainage divide and county line. We continue up the trail through a predominantly mountain hemlock
forest to the **Summit Rock Road (#2710) (5930-0.7).**

The hiker who is low on supplies or who wants to avoid
some early-season snow or late-season drought can take
the following "business loop." Follow the Summit Rock
Road west, then north down to an intersection with the **Mt.
Thielsen Trail (#1456) (5310-4.6).** This trail climbs a steep
3.1 miles up to an intersection with the PCT. We follow the
trail west a quarter mile to its trailhead, then take a dirt
road 100 yards to the Diamond Lake Trailer Court road,
which we follow 0.2 mile to **State Highway 138 (5195-0.5).**
About 100 yards south lies the entrance to Broken Arrow
Campground; seventy yards north is the South Store and
Coffee Shop, where food and supplies are available. We
continue north on the highway alongside linear Diamond
Lake Campground to a **fork (5205-2.7),** where we veer left

45   down to the **Diamond Lake Resort (5195-0.2).** This resort
47   not only has one of the best supplied stores you'll find
         along or near the route, but its restaurant also serves
48A   first-class meals. Here too fishermen typically bring in
48B   foot-long trout daily. The resort also has the Diamond
46   Lake Lodge Post Office, to which you can mail your
         supplies. Well equipped to last until the smaller *Cascade
Summit resort at Odell Lake, 46 miles farther,* we now
hike north up the highway to the Diamond Lake Corrals,
where we find the **Tipsoo Trail (#1448) (5340-0.5).** We take
this trail east up to Tipsoo Creek (5915-2.5), parallel the
creek up to a junction with the **Thielsen Creek Trail
(#1449) (6060-0.7),** where in late summer we fill our canteens, then leave the creek and climb east up to a reunion
with the **Pacific Crest Trail (#2000) (7200-1.9-13.6).**

From the **Summit Rock Road,** two-thirds mile west of its
intersection with Road 2835 up from Highway 138, we continue
gently up the trail. After a mile our gradient steepens, and the
trail makes a few open switchbacks up the ridge before it chooses
to curve northwest around it. We now make a comfortable,
steady climb around a southwest ridge and up to an intersection
with the

Mt. Thielsen Trail (#1456) (7250-5.2), up which the old
Skyline route once ascended 3.6 miles from Highway 138

below. The summit of Mt. Thielsen (9182), sometimes called the "Lightning Rod" of the Cascades, is easily accessible and should not be bypassed. When you ascend it, however, leave your pack behind; it has probably one of the steepest trails in existence—more of a climb than a hike. The trail quickly exits above treeline and then climbs up increasingly loose pumice slopes toward a cleaver, where it seems to veer right (south) around it. This scree slope is the *descent* route. Rather than fight your way up this unstable slope, climb up solid rock along the left (north) side of the cleaver and continue up toward the 80-foot-high summit pinnacle, which can be climbed unroped only from its southeast ridge. The near-vertical north and east faces make this last few feet off limits to those with acrophobia. The view from the summit area is both spectacular and didactic. You can see north 108 miles to Mt. Jefferson (10,497), south 122 miles to Mt. Shasta (14,162), and down into Crater Lake. Amid the beetles, flies and butterflies carried here by the updrafts, gleeful violet-green swallows swoop and dive at their insect harvest while we contemplate the internal structure of a volcano. We can see from the dips, or inclinations, of the strata that Mt. Thielsen's summit once lay to the east, and about 1000 feet higher, above what is now a deeply glaciated canyon. Here is a vulcanologist's natural observatory, for the mountain's anatomy is stripped bare. Its original configuration was a broad "shield" cone of basaltic lava not unlike South Sister (10,358), 67 miles north. This broad cone was topped with a tuff cone, which in turn was intruded by swarms of narrow dikes and two large plugs, one of them remaining as the summit you're standing on. Howlock Mountain (8351), the prominent peak three miles north-northeast, is also a resistant plug, and its origin was similar to Thielsen's.

46

After downclimbing the summit pinnacle, we head south a short way along the ridge and pass some enormous pinnacles clinging to the east wall. Soon we come to an obvious spot, not too far from an isolated, scrubby whitebark pine, where nearly everyone begins to descend the scree slope to the trail.

Back on the PCT, we contour north to a northwest spur, cross the lower northwest face to another spur, then switchback down into the deep, glaciated canyon and reach hop-across Thielsen Creek. Over the last mile and a half of trail, snow lingers through late July. From our vantage point, we can see why Mt. Thielsen is often called the "Matterhorn" of the Cascades. Creekside avalanche boulders up to 20 feet in diameter attest to the constant forces of nature still dissecting the anatomy of this mountain. We cross the creek and follow it 70 yards to a trail spur left, then another 70 yards to a signed junction with the

Thielsen Creek Trail (#1449) (6910-2.2), which descends 2.2 miles along the creek to the Tipsoo Trail. We now parallel Sawtooth Ridge as we climb gradually north to open Pumice Flat, where tall posts mark our route across it to a junction with the obscure

Tipsoo Trail (#1448) (7200-2.7), which heads west and becomes more evident as it starts to descend along a southwest-oriented gully. This junction is the end of the described "business loop" alternate route. Under a cluster of hemlocks and lodgepoles you'll find a good campsite, if water can be obtained from nearby snow patches. We now proceed northeast, following posts across the grassy flat, then make a long switchback up to the northwest ridge of Howlock Mountain. On this trail segment we can see where the old trail climbed steeply up the slope in the days before this trail was stretched out to ease its gradient. The mileage markers you've been passing refer to the old trail; you have a greater distance to hike to Windigo Pass than they indicate. Snowfields may be a problem again as we head along the trail toward Tipsoo Peak (8031) and encounter posts that guide us up through meadows. Soon we reach a junction with the

46
48B
49

Cinnamon Butte Trail (#1472) (7550-2.1), which descends west to Road 2788 near Wits End, rather than all the way to Cinnamon Butte. Immediately beyond, you top a saddle (7560-0.1), where you can pat yourself on the back for having reached the high point—elevationwise—of the Oregon PCT. It comes as quite a surprise, for we would expect the high point to be on a slope of one of the more prominent Cascade peaks. From the saddle, snowfields obscure the trail through mid-July, and it is important that you follow the meadow posts and tree blazes rather than attempt a shortcut down the slope, which could take you unintentionally to Miller Lake. Our route starts northeast, crosses a long, 30-yard-wide meadow, and curves down along the base of cinnamon-colored Tipsoo Peak, which is a breached crater of late Pleistocene age. We almost unnoticeably cross a divide into the Umpqua River watershed and shortly reach a saddle (7100-0.8). Paralleling the ridge, we quickly pass an adequate campsite before we start another descent. We now follow a series of switchbacks that descend northeast below the realm of snow and into the realm of mosquitoes—through early July. The slope eases off and our trail winds down to a junction with the

Maidu Lake Trail (#3725A) (6060-3.8), which leads about 3.5 miles southeast over a low saddle and down to the Digit Point Campground at Miller Lake. The forest cover along our trail is mostly mountain hemlock and some lodgepole pine, but it also includes a fair percentage of noble fir, which we'll see more of as we progress north. It superficially resembles red fir, but its needles are grooved above and ridged below, whereas the red fir's are ridged both above and below. We now head north down our trail 200 yards and reach *another* **Maidu Lake Trail (#1446) (5985-0.1)** just 35 yards short of the lakeshore. Except for the questionably pure water of shallow Maidu Lake (5980), the south shore makes an excellent campsite, with its eight-man shelter

49

At Maidu Lake shelter, sitting out a storm

and a pit toilet. If you sit quietly in the shelter after an evening's meal, you may be visited by a variety of birds, including the Oregon junco, Audubon warbler, gray jay and—if you're lucky—northern three-toed woodpecker. Trail 1446 heads west past the shelter, then curves along the shore to a junction with the Lake Lucile Trail (#1459), which leads three-fourths mile west to that lake. About a hundred yards northeast, Trail 1446 leaves Maidu Lake and descends along the headwaters of the North Umpqua River. A lakeshore trail continues along the east side and back to the shelter. Before starting northeast up the Pacific Crest Trail, fill your water bottles, for by midsummer they'll have to last you until the Nip and Tuck Lakes, 13.5 miles farther. The PCT ascends the west slope of forested Miller Mountain (7513), contours north, then descends to a saddle (6430-2.7). We now climb up the east side of a ridge, top it, and soon reach a junction with the old, unmaintained Oregon Skyline Trail (6700-0.7), which climbs 0.3 mile up the ridge to a fair panorama east from Mule Peak View Point (6825). Our route descends around the west and north slopes of Mule Peak to a saddle, then traverses slightly down the ridge slopes to dry, shaded

49
50
51

Tolo Creek Campsite (6190-1.6) atop a saddle. We contour north from it to yet another saddle, then begin a moderate, sometimes steep, ascent around the slopes of Tolo Mountain (7046). Reaching the level section of its northwest spur, we meet the **Tenas Trail (#1445) (6610-2.1)**, ascending from the old Cascade Lakes Road (now Road 2507). Our trail turns east and descends to the ridge crest, then follows it for several miles before swinging west across a low saddle and up the lower slopes of a pyroclastic cone called Windigo Butte (6420). We now descend a half mile along its north spur and curve westward to a trailhead at **Road 2507 (5860-3.8),** 100 yards north of Windigo Pass. We follow this road north to a quick junction with

Cascade Lakes Road (5830-0.2), on which we descend to the **PCT trailhead (5710-0.7)** just 15 yards past a seasonal but obvious creek. We start northeast up the PCT, contour across gentle slopes of manzanita and sparse forest cover, then descend slightly to the **Nip and Tuck Lakes spur trail (5715-1.8).** This heads east-southeast for a level 200 yards to the two lakes, which are only one lake in early summer. The peninsula that juts between the two lobes makes an excellent campsite, and the warm, shallow lake water is very inviting. Our trail heads north-northwest and climbs gently at first, but then it makes a short, somewhat sunny, moderate-to-steep climb up to a ridge (5956-1.0), providing us with only one reward—a view south of Mt. Thielsen. The trail ahead is now downhill almost all the way

Shallow arm between Nip and Tuck Lakes

to Crescent Lake. We start moderately down and head north to
the west shore of Oldenberg Lake (5475-1.3), then north past two
of the Bingham Lakes to a junction (5450-1.1) with a west-
northwest trail to the third. This third Bingham Lake, at the end
of the hundred-yard spur trail, is the largest and perhaps the
clearest of all the shallow lakes near the PCT between Maidu
Lake and Crescent Lake. Continuing north along our route, we
pass through an "Oregon desert" of sparse lodgepoles, then
descend gradually and cross a seasonal creek whose luxuriant
green vegetation contrasts vividly with the surrounding sparsely
needled lodgepoles. We round a low ridge and then reach the
northeast end of murky, man-made

51

Pinewah Lake (5180-2.2), which has a habit of drying up in late
summer. Here, and for a short distance west, the Pacific Crest
Trail follows the immigrant road built and used by the Elliot
Wagon Train in October 1853. We go about a hundred yards
before our trail forks right (northwest) from the road and begins a
winding descent to a trailhead at the end of a 50-yard spur road
from the

Crescent Lake loop road (#244) (5000-1.0). We follow this road
one-third mile west to the Spring Campground spur road, which
descends half a mile to the campground at Crescent Lake (4853).
The lake is stocked with large, Kokanee salmon and rainbow and
Mackinaw trout. We continue past a junction with the Summit

Lake road (#211) (4860-1.2), then past the Tandy Bay Picnic Area and across Summit Creek, where once again we come to a

PCT trailhead (4860-0.6). We start in a flatland Douglas-fir forest, then reach gentle slopes on which grow lodgepoles that contrast strongly with the denser, shady forest below. Annuals such as lupine, phlox and bluebells adorn our trail's sides as we enter the Diamond Peak Wilderness and soon reach the rapids of Whitefish Creek. The trail usually remains within hearing distance of this refreshing creek as we climb northwest, then north up to a flat and a linear pond at an intersection with the

51
55   **Crater Butte Trail (#44) (5770-5.2),** four miles due east of Diamond Peak (8744). Should you wish to climb this peak, take this trail about 3.8 miles up to where it starts to descend south, then work cross-country northwest to the barren slopes of the south spur. Climb up this spur, following the path of least resistance, then head north up the narrow ridge to the peak's summit. When there is still a lot of snow on the mountain, we recommend a rope for the ridge section. From the trail junction, the PCT heads north past several shallow, somewhat stagnant ponds before arriving at large but shallow

Diamond Peak and Diamond View Lake

Diamond View Lake (5780-0.7). Photographs are best when the peak is snow-clad, which, unfortunately, is when the lake is mosquito-clad. We pass two good lakeshore campsites, then leave the lake behind as we make tracks north through swampy lodgepole flatlands to the headwaters of Trapper Creek. This creek remains unseen and unheard for a couple miles until the trail reaches slopes above the creek where it cascades north down toward a marsh. In a third mile, the trail reaches the creek and more or less follows it to the marsh, then goes east through a shady mountain-hemlock forest. In order to avoid the creekside's wet ground, the trail generally stays on the lower slopes just south of the creek. We follow the creek as it meanders east past tempting campsites, then cascades northeast down past a small breached dam. Almost immediately after sighting this concrete structure, we reach a

Trail junction (4880-4.9), where an access trail continues northeast, but the PCT turns north. The access trail descends 0.2 mile to the Southern Pacific railroad tracks and crosses them 20 yards west-northwest of a huge, steel overhead signal. Head east across the tracks and under the overhead signal for 17 yards to a dirt road that descends 100 yards to Road 2318 along the west shore of Odell Lake (4788). This lake was named for William Holden Odell who, with B.J. Pengra, surveyed the military wagon road up the Middle Fork of the Willamette in 1865. On July 26th Odell climbed a butte and discovered this lake; both butte and lake now bear his name. By heading 200 yards southeast along this road, you'll arrive at the Cascade Summit store and the Shelter Cove boat dock. Supplies are somewhat limited, but adequate if you plan your meals properly; they will have to last until *Olallie Lake Resort, a considerable 140 miles distant.* Backtracking to the PCT junction, we start north-northwest on the trail down to a bridge crossing of Trapper Creek 35 yards downstream from the breached dam. Leaving this creek behind, we contour the slopes and reach an intersection with the

55
56

Yoran Lake Trail (#49) (4880-0.5). This trail goes northeast moderately to steeply 180 yards down to the railroad tracks, from which you follow a dirt road 100 yards to Road 2318. You can follow this road a quarter mile east to the Trapper Creek Campground, then 0.4 mile farther to the Cascade Summit store. North of the trail intersection, the PCT parallels the railroad tracks below and passes a bubbling creek immediately before reaching a **spur road (4860-0.6),** which climbs northwest 0.4 mile to Pengra Pass. We start along this road from a point 50 yards west of the tracks and follow it up 80 yards around a bend to a resumption of the PCT, which branches right and ascends 130 yards northwest to a small creek under the shade of a Douglas-fir forest. Here we find shooting stars, bluebells, bunchberries and Oregon grapes, which are typically associated with this type of forest. Our trail now climbs gently northeast and reaches a junction with a new segment of the

Pacific Crest Trail (#2000) (5000-0.5), due to be completed in autumn 1975. As of September 1973 it dead-ended a few miles southwest of Pengra Pass, but it is slated to climb southwest toward Diamond Peak, skirt the peak's lower slope, descend south to the west shore of Summit Lake, and then traverse southeast past Cowhorn Mountain to Windigo Pass. The trail should be completed in a couple years. Both the new and the old trails continue climbing northeast, but the old Oregon Skyline path will eventually be abandoned, which is unfortunate, since it climbs out to a small bluff and provides you with the only good view of Odell Lake that you'll get along the route. Each trail eventually levels off, then they merge into one, which contours east to a pond on the right, from where the trail switchbacks down to

State Highway 58 (5080-1.2), a few yards northwest of Road 2318's branch southeast down toward Odell Lake. We diagonal east across the highway and locate the PCT trailhead about 15 yards north of a large highway-maintenance shed where pumice is stored. Our trail climbs steadily east through a forest of Douglas-fir, western white pine and mountain hemlock to a saddle, then it curves north and passes a hundred-foot-high rock jumble before reaching the ridge above **South Rosary Lake (5730-1.2).** This clear lake is deep in early summer, and in this it contrasts strongly with the other lakes its size we've seen so far along our entire route. By late summer, however, the lake level can fall more than twenty feet, due to seepage through the porous volcanic rocks, and leave its eastward drainage channel high and dry. We quickly encounter a very good ridgetop campsite with a table, then curve northward, cross the lake's outlet, and reach an equally good campsite. Now we climb northwest to a campsite near the southwest corner of deep, blue-green Middle Rosary Lake (5830-0.6), which is even more impressive than the south lake because it lies at the base of 400-foot-high Rosary rock. On a weekend, you're likely to see climbers scaling this rock. We walk alongside the lake, then pass by the low dividing ridge between the middle and north lakes, on which is an excellent campsite with a table. We reach shallower North Rosary Lake (5830-0.3), then follow the trail as it climbs west above the lake's north shore before switchbacking east-northeast up to a junction with the

Maiden Lake Trail (#41) (6060-0.6), which descends east-southeast before contouring east toward that lake. We continue east for 130 yards, then switchback west up to a saddle (6710-0.5), but not before getting one last glance back at Rosary rock and the Rosary lakes, and in the distance, Odell Lake, Odell Butte and Crescent Lake. We enter the Willamette National Forest and descend steeply to a cove, which we follow north along the east side of a gully. We step across trickling Skyline Creek and reach a meadow that is signed *T-M-R-Camp* (5920-0.4). Continuing down at a lesser gradient, we twice cross the now-bubbling creek, then pass by the unsigned Douglas Horse Pasture (5520-1.0) east of the creek. We soon reach the signed Bark Table Camp (5480-0.3), then meet Skyline Creek (5460-0.1) and cross it for the last time. After climbing a few yards to a divide, we start down a gully, then parallel unseen Skyline Creek a short way before curving north to Waithere Camp at an intersection with the

Maiden Peak Trail (#3681) (5300-0.5). This trail ascends from the southwest, crosses our trail, then climbs east toward the peak. We head northeast on the PCT, reach a sign that identifies Mt. Ray (7002) to the northwest, then contour northeast before curving north across wet meadows up to a junction with the **Bobby Lake Trail (#3663) (5440-2.5),** which strikes northwest. We turn right (northeast) and start up the trail as it curves quickly up to a triangular junction where two forks of the

Moore Creek Trail (#40) (5470-0.2) branch off from the PCT and merge just east of it. It's best for us now to head east a quarter mile down this trail to a nice campsite at the west end of large, clear Bobby Lake (5408), for our next reliable source of water will be Charlton Lake, about seven miles farther. It seems ironic that as we progress north into ever thicker, wetter forests, our water sources become spaced farther apart. We had expected drought over the miles of pumice-covered lands around Crater Lake and Mt. Thielsen, but we find it frustrating to be in a dense forest during a drizzling rain and yet have to hike miles to obtain running water to drink. In such areas, ground water percolating through the volcanic-rock structures certainly is the major form of water transport. Back on the PCT, we now head north past two large ponds, climb northwest to a saddle (5980-1.4), curve northeast gently down from it, and then climb to an intersection with the **Twin Peaks Trail (#3595) (6220-1.3).** A viewpoint is supposed to be 50 yards southwest down this trail. It isn't. Don't fret, for about a mile north from this junction you can follow red-orange plastic streamers 70 yards west across rock slabs and obtain an unobstructed view westward, from Diamond Peak north to Waldo Lake. After this side trip, the trail shortly starts a gentle descent and begins to cross gullies one after another. You eventually pass above a small pond, then quickly

57
58

reach a cluster of three ponds (6320-2.4) grouped around the small knob identified on the map as 6362. The route now descends northeast across gullies, reaches the watershed divide by a small pond, then descends west a short distance before curving north toward gentler slopes above Charlton Lake (5692). We head north through a forested flat area, reach the slopes above the lake, and descend to an intersection with the

Charlton Lake Trail (#3570) (5725-2.5), about a hundred yards north of a small pond. The lakeshore is 100 yards southeast; Road 204 is 150 yards northwest, just beyond a pond. Heading northeast for 0.1 mile, we reach a closed spur road heading southeast to the lake from Road 204. We diagonal north across the road to a broad trail that we follow north about 45 yards to where it bends northwest 40 yards to a roadside parking area. From this bend the PCT follows old blazes east-northeast and climbs gently up the divide to a diagonal crossing of

Road 204 (5480-0.6) at a 20° bearing. Our trail starts north, climbs northwest to the low watershed divide, and then contours north past small ponds and Charlton Butte to a junction on the right (east) with the **Lily Lake Trail (#19) (5965-1.4)**, which descends about three-fourths mile to that isolated lake. Continuing north on the ridge route through a forest of mountain hemlock, you might spot a red-breasted nuthatch inching down a tree trunk in search of bark insects. We keep following the divide down a north slope to a small flat, then climb over two low mounds before reaching the southwest arm of shallow Taylor Lake (5550-3.3). Our trail immediately angles away from the lake, heads north past a pond on the left (west), then reaches

Road 2049 at Irish Lake (5549-0.3). Popular Irish Lake Campground is a quarter mile east on the road. We can pick up the trail again by going west 25 yards on the road, then north 50 yards along a spur road that takes us to the trailhead. Our route heads north above the west shore of Irish Lake and passes west of shallow but clear Riffle Lake (5575-0.8), which has an adequate campsite on its west shore. We now climb a low ridge and descend slightly to a flat with two large lily-pad ponds before climbing up to a higher ridge, where we enter the

Three Sisters Wilderness (5730-1.2). The lakes and ponds of this area are shallow, and, like those in the Sky Lakes region, they support a superabundant mosquito population from late spring through mid-July. We pass a number of stagnant ponds and small lakes in rapid succession as we descend to a nice campsite on the east shore of Brahma Lake (5657-0.6). Some hikers undoubtedly wade out to its forested island and camp there. Our route continues north along its shore, contours west, and then climbs moderately up slopes and through a miniature

58
59
60

gorge before reaching the northeast corner of clear Jezebel Lake (5855-1.1). A campsite is perched on the low ridge north of this corner. Climbing northwest above the lake, we reach a shady glen, from which a trail once climbed a quarter mile west-southwest to Rock Rim Lake. Our trail rounds a linear ridge descending east, climbs west along its north slope, then angles north to a good campsite beside the outlet of

Stormy Lake (6045-1.1). The towering cliffs of Irish Mountain over a lakeside evening campfire leave us with a vivid memory of this choice spot. Leaving this lake behind, we descend to smaller, slightly cloudy Blaze Lake (5950-0.3), then contour northward past an abundance of ponds before the trail descends a ridge to a low divide just east of open Cougar Flat (5750-2.0). Our route winds down to Lake 5678, then passes smaller water bodies as it follows the ridge northeast down to Tadpole Lake (5340-2.1), perched on a forested saddle, where you may surprise some feeding ring-necked ducks. We traverse the lake's grassy north shore, then descend north to a grassy pond and a junction with the

Elk Creek (#3510) and Winopee Lake (#16) trails (5250-0.4). The Elk Creek Trail climbs northwest over a low saddle and descends into the Elk Creek drainage; the Winopee Lake Trail curves south around a knoll before descending to Winopee Lake. We continue northeast across the lower slopes of Packsaddle Mountain (6144), walk north past a polluted lake to the east, and arrive at a junction with the **Snowshoe Lake Trail (#33) (5250-1.3),** which descends east. We hike north past Desane Lake and enter the Willamette National Forest again as we cross a flat divide and descend into the Mink Lake Basin, where we meet a junction with the

Mink Lake Loop Trail (#3526) (5160-0.6). This 2.7 mile loop climbs northwest up a low, broad ridge before descending north to Mink Lake, stocked with eastern brook and rainbow trout. From there, the loop winds east, dropping to Porky Lake with more eastern brook, then climbs back to the PCT at the Cliff Lake outlet creek. Our route follows a string of sparkling lakes that make an appropriate necklace for South Sister. In rapid succession we encounter S Lake (5150), Mac Lake (5100) with rainbow, Merrill Lake (5080) and Horseshoe Lake (5039), a very shallow lake with both rainbow and eastern brook. The trail curves around to the north shore of this lake, then reaches a **spur trail (5040-1.4)** that bears 0.1 mile north to Moody Lake (5020). We cross the usually dry outlet of Horseshoe Lake, then continue north gently up and around a band of cliffs to a reunion with the

Mink Lake Loop Trail (#3526) (5130-0.8) beside the Cliff Lake

60
61

outlet creek. Just 130 yards southeast up a spur trail beside this creek is deep, green, rock-and-alder lined **Cliff Lake (5138).** The web of trails and the abundance of campsites attest to the popularity of this lake. The best campsites are atop the cliff along the lake's northwest shore, but should you be caught in foul weather, you can camp in comfort in the Cliff Lake shelter. Good eastern-brook-trout fishing justifies a stop at this lake, as do good diving rocks near large aspens along the northeast shore. Backtracking from these, we pass beargrass blooming between boulders, and, near the shelter, we avoid stepping on delicate bunchberries and shooting stars that grow on the moist, shady forest floor. Back at the loop-trail junction, we cross Cliff Lake's outlet creek, walk northwest, then round a pile of large boulders and climb gently to a seasonal creek (5225-0.9). We cross it, hike up a switchback, and then work up northeast to a junction with the

Goose Rock (#3542) and Senoj Lake (#3534) trails (5330-0.5). The Goose Rock Trail starts northwest down toward a meadow, then heads west and down to Goose Lake; the 5.6-mile Senoj Lake Trail starts southeast to an unnamed lake, heads east to the divide, then continues as Trail 14 east down to Cascade Lakes Highway 46. We start north, quickly descend to Reserve Meadow, and head northeast along its edge before curving northwest and climbing up to relatively deep Island Lake (5438-0.9), which has a patch of grass in its center. From this lake we climb up the trail to a rockpile, contour west past two stagnant ponds, and then hike north until we are just above a 50-yard-long peninsula that juts southwest into **Dumbbell Lake (5502-0.7).** Excellent campsites exist on this rocky spur, from which you can fish or dive in the lake's warm, clear waters. Our trail now gradually climbs north past many ponds to a low divide (5660-2.2), then descends to a junction with the **Oregon Skyline Trail (5460-0.5).** Here the PCT route branches east and approximately follows the old **Island Meadow Trail (#3517).** Since the OST route is still more popular, it will be described first.

61
62

This segment of the Oregon Skyline Trail passes numerous ponds and lakes, including the popular Horse Lake, and it is therefore the route we recommend you take after mid-July, when the mosquitoes have abated and the PCT segment has become virtually dry. The OST descends gently 50 yards to a continuation of the Island Meadow Trail, which starts west-northwest gently up toward the McBee Trail, about a mile away. We continue north down gentle slopes and reach a junction with the

McBee Trail (#3523) (5100-1.7), which starts west-southwest on the level from our trail. Descending north a bit more, in 130 yards we reach an intersection with the **Sunset Lake Trail (#3517A) (5075-0.1)**, which descends west one-half mile to the Horse Creek Trail and northeast 70 yards to Horse Creek. We now angle northwest down a ridge to a junction with the

Park Trail (#3530) (4960-0.2), which descends southwest before climbing west to Mile and Park lakes. In 50 yards we arrive at a campsite on the west side of willow-and-gooseberry lined Horse Creek. There is nothing particularly outstanding about the site except for an abundant array of wildflowers that include Sitka valerian, paintbrush, groundsel, corn lily, ligusticum, pussy paws and subalpine spiraea. You might identify others. We now jump across ten-foot-wide Horse Creek and curve northeast along the trail to a junction with a spur trail that bears 300° for 270 yards to adequate campsites along the southeast shore of Horse Lake (4930). Twenty feet past this trail junction, we meet the

Horse Creek Trail (#3514) (4940-0.2), which leads northwest half a mile to the north shore of Horse Lake, from where you can head southwest to very good campsites atop a bluff along the lake's northwest shore. From the trail junction, we curve east and make a gentle climb to a junction with the **Horse Lake Trail (#3516) (5040-0.4)**, which climbs gently eastward 1.7 miles to the ridge crest PCT, then continues east down to Cascade Lakes Highway as Trail 2. Our route starts east-northeast up the **Red Hill Trail** and curves gradually northward as it ascends increasingly steep slopes to a saddle east of forested Red Hill (5800-2.0), then finishes the climb just before reaching a cluster of shallow lakes and ponds. We descend an often soggy trail past these and finally reach a meadow that contains Camelot and Sisters Mirror lakes. Hiking northwest to the south shore of Camelot Lake (5995), we reach the **Pacific Crest Trail (#2000) (5997-1.7-6.3)**, which descends north from Koosah (Indian for ''sky'') Mountain to this lakeside junction with the Red Hill Trail before turning northeast.

62

From the junction with Oregon Skyline Trail a mile and a half south of Horse Lake, the **Pacific Crest Trail** branches east. After a few minutes' hiking, we reach an obvious spring seeping from the ground only ten yards downslope from the trail. This is a good place to obtain water, for the route beyond may be dry until Camelot Lake, 8.8 miles farther. Continuing east, we descend toward Island Meadow, but stay within the forest's edge as we hike southeast along its southern border. We soon reach a bridge across a small, seasonal creek and find a fair trailside campsite above its east bank, 70 yards south of the meadow. Our trail strikes southeast again, but shortly turns and makes a wandering route northeast before descending north to a mile-high meadow, across which we traverse north-northeast to a junction with the

Sunset Lake Trail (#3517A) (5280-1.9), which passes that lake midway in its descent to the OST. We now go east-southeast on our trail, enter forest and pass a large pond 50 yards south, then snake east over an undetected drainage divide before descending to a junction where the PCT leaves the

62

Island Meadow Trail (#3517) (5260-1.3) and angles north. The 1.1-mile Island Meadow Trail makes a southeast descent before turning east and dropping to Cascade Lakes Highway 46, on which you can head south 100 yards to the Elk Lake Lodge entrance. Down at the lakeside lodge, you can obtain dinners plus limited supplies. If you visit the lodge by early July, you'll likely see barn swallows nesting in the rafters above its entrance. Large, 57-foot-deep Elk Lake (4884) offers very good trout fishing and is a nice place for a layover day. Although the lake has no outlet and no permanent inlets, its water stays quite clear because fresh groundwater continues to seep into the lake at about the same rate that groundwater leaves it. Rather than

Lunch stop

backtrack up the Island Meadow Trail, you can head north on the road 0.2 mile past its trailhead and start up the Horse Lake Trail (#2), which takes you 1.6 miles northwest up to the PCT.

Back where the PCT leaves the Island Meadow Trail, the PCT climbs north toward a cinder cone (5676), rounds its eastern half, then heads north to a lesser summit before reaching an intersection on a saddle with the **Horse Lake Trail (#2/3516) (5300-1.3).** Following the divide, our trail climbs gently north at first, but steepens as it curves over to the western slope of Koosah Mountain (6520). Here we make a long switchback up to the ridge, then contour to its east slope, where, by stepping a few yards east, we can absorb an eastern panorama from Elk and Hosmer lakes north past conical Bachelor Butte (9065) and deeply glaciated Broken Top (9175) to South Sister (10,358). Although we can't see Cascade Lakes Highway below, we can hear the rumble of the logging trucks on it. Hiking northwest, we encounter switchbacks down the north slope, then reach a flat and continue north to a junction at the south shore of placid, shallow

Camelot Lake (5995-4.4). Here the OST route heads southwest along the Red Hill Trail. The PCT starts northeast, and we follow it to **Sisters Mirror Lake (5995-0.2),** which in the tranquil morning and evening air is a photographer's delight. The reflected view of South Sister won't last forever, for lodgepoles are invading the open flat, and this lake, stocked with eastern brook trout, is gradually being choked with vegetation. In the meantime, you and the nesting spotted sandpipers can enjoy the lake's serenity. Here, your best "nest" is on top of the rocky bluff along the northwest shore. Our trail soon leaves the lake and heads due east to a junction with the

Mirror Lake Trail (#20) (5990-0.3), which descends southeast 3.5 miles to the Cascade Lakes Highway. We start a level hike east-northeast, but quickly begin a short, moderate climb up this Trail 12A segment to a junction with the **Nash Lake Trail (#3527) (6010-0.1),** which ascends gently from the west. We hike east up through a forest of lodgepole, with its trailside red heather, then descend to a meadow containing cinquefoil flowers, where our trail, which was once a road, turns northeast toward a gully that has a 50-foot-high lava flow above its east slope. We start up this gully and reach a point where the

Wickiup Plain Trail (#12A) (6080-0.7), which we've been on, forks east across the gully and then turns south. We continue north on the jeep tracks, pass The House Rock (6745) on our left (west), and reach the partly forested Wickiup Plain. As we approach Le Conte Crater—a low cinder cone to the

62
63

northeast—we begin to picture a sequence of events that molded
this volcanic landscape. The thick stand of mountain hemlock on
the northern half of Le Conte Crater indicates that this cone is at
least several thousand years old. An educated guess, based upon
comparisons with cones of known ages, is that an eruption took
place 6000 to 8000 years ago and built up the cinder cone. Immediately following this eruption came outpourings of fluid,
basaltic lava that breached the cone's south rim and flowed south
down the gently sloping Wickiup Plain. We see this flow today as
the forested, undulating surface south of the cone and off to our
right (east). The section of Wickiup Plain over which the trail
passes is probably no more than 20,000 years old, for it shows
little sign of erosion. We can be quite sure its age is greater than
10,000 years, since it was in existence when the last great Pleistocene glaciers marched down from South Sister and deposited
their debris on its eastern side; a conspicuous moraine ends on
top of the plain roughly a mile and a half due east of the cone.

North of Le Conte Crater we see a vast, desolate, steep-sided,
chaotic jumble appropriately called Rock Mesa. The high point
near its east side marks the location of the vent from which dacite
lava was extruded 2000 years ago. Because the dacite lava was so
viscous, the flow not only solidified before reaching Le Conte
63 Crater but it also solidified halfway down the relatively steep
slopes of the Mesa Creek drainage just north of us. It did suc-
ceed, however, in covering up any trace of a conduit that might
have given rise to the older flows of Wickiup Plain.

By now you've probably noticed The Wife (7054)—a conspicuous summit off to the west—and you've probably observed
that South Sister (10,358) is a redhead. Should you wish to climb
to its summit, strike east from a point just south of Le Conte
Crater, then head northeast along the east margin of Rock Mesa.
When you reach the peak's lower slope, climb north directly up it
and pass between the Clark and Lewis glaciers as you near the
summit cone. When you top its rim, you'll find it crowned with a
snow-clad lake (10,200) that occupies a crater which may have
been active in the last few thousand years. South Sister, with at
least three major periods of eruptions, is a geologically complex
volcano; its slopes contain over two dozen types of volcanic
rocks. This sister is the youngest of the three, and it still retains
much of its symmetry because it has been exposed only to
late-Pleistocene and Recent glaciation.

By the time you finish reading the above digressions, you
could have been well on your way to the north end of Wickiup
Plain. The posts along the route seem unnecessary since the
route is so obvious. Newberry knotweed and scattered grass

attest to the dryness of the pumice soil, but plentiful gopher mounds indicate that at least one mammal thrives here. At the northern edge of the plain, the trail curves northwest over a low saddle, then descends to a creek (6010-2.3) which passes through a large meadow. In early July this meadow is a continuous field of yellow cinquefoil that contrasts sharply with the wintry chill of deep snow patches on the surrounding forested slopes. We regretfully leave this island of sunshine behind and press onward northwest into the forest and down alongside a small gully. Our trail makes a switchback east and leads us down to South Mesa Creek. We step across it, hike north into a large, grassy meadow, reach another tributary, then 100 yards later arrive at North Mesa Creek (5710-0.9). You *could* camp anywhere in the meadow, but if you discreetly select a campsite near its edge and away from the trail, you'll help preserve its pristine appearance. Leaving this meadow and its sparkling creeks behind, we turn our backs on the frozen "tidal wave" of Rock Mesa and climb northwest up to a junction with the

James Creek Trail (5920-0.5), which makes a gentle ascent west before curving north along the old OST route. We ascend east, curve north, and then round a murky lakelet just east of us. Continuing to climb north, our route tends to follow the break in slope between the foot of South Sister, to the east, and the Separation Creek headwaters, to the west. Along our course we pass through numerous small meadows and beside a fine, six-foot-diameter mountain hemlock before we descend slightly to a crossing of Hinton Creek (6320-2.1). After hiking to the other side of a low divide, we descend past a cliff of a high-density, parallel-fractured, shalelike flow. Here we cross Separation Creek (6400-0.5), whose flow, like that of Hinton Creek, has usually sunk beneath the pumice by mid-July. We now come face-to-face with Middle Sister (10,047), which can be easily climbed up its south or west slope. Continuing north, we follow posts and rock piles across a pumice flat and reach a shallow, clear lakelet (6460-0.4), beside which good campsites can be found. The fragile timberline ecosystem here is very sensitive to human impact, so treat it gently. Beyond, we tread across level bedrock that has a previous glacier's signature etched upon it in the form of striations. The glacier also left souvenirs of its visit: erratic boulders. Our route north now crosses half a dozen seasonal, step-across creeks as it descends toward Linton Creek and finally bends west down to a meadow at whose north end we meet the

Foley Ridge Trail (#3511) (6270-1.3), which heads south-southwest down a slope. About 25 yards west, at a forested flat,

63

is a justifiably popular campsite. The Husband (7524), off in the west, is the resistant plug of an ancient volcano that once reigned over this area before the Three Sisters matured. Just after we start north again, we reach a tributary of Linton Creek, then 70 yards farther reach a second tributary. From these seasonal creeks, our trail climbs gradually north through a hemlock forest to where it meets the **Linton Meadows Trail (6440-1.7)**, descending steeply southwest. The PCT ascends moderately northeast to a spring, then angles north to a gentle slope from which we can look south and identify, from east to west: the Mt. Thielsen pinnacle (9182), the Mt. McLoughlin pyramid (9495) and the Diamond Peak massif (8744). We now follow an open, post-lined, undulating pathway north over loose slopes with trailside rose paintbrushes, yellow cinquefoils, pink heathers and white pasqueflowers. Then we cross a rocky meadow, perhaps while being watched by a marmot, and descend to a junction with the

Obsidian Trail (#3528) (6380-2.1), just above Obsidian Creek. This five-mile trail takes you down to Frog Campground by the McKenzie Highway. We start hiking east moderately up to a slope, then go northeast up to the trickling, 50-foot-high Obsidian Falls, from which we top a small shelf and cross Obsidian Creek. We now tread north on a trail that sounds and feels like glass. It is. The black obsidian is nature's own glass. Our trail soon leaves the shelf, descends a ridge, and then turns east and intersects the

Glacier Way Trail (#3528A) (6370-1.6), which descends moderately 0.7 mile to the Obsidian Trail, which can be followed 3.4 miles to Frog Campground. An efficient mountaineering party can follow this route up from the campground, climb North and Middle Sisters via the Collier Glacier col, and return to camp late the same day. From the col, Middle Sister (10,047) can be climbed via its north ridge without any special equipment. Likewise, North Sister (10,085) can be climbed via its southwest ridge to the south arête, but the climb north along this sharp crest requires a safety rope. The view from Middle Sister is particularly instructional, for from it you can compare the degree of glaciation on all Three Sisters. North Sister, the oldest of the three, has suffered repeated ravages from quite a number of glacial advances. South Sister (10,358), the youngest, retains her symmetry, for she hasn't lived long enough to feel the icy tongues cut deep into her body.

Twenty yards east of the Glacier Way intersection, we bridge Glacier Creek, then reach a pleasant, hemlock-shaded campsite where Sunshine Shelter once stood. We make a minor climb

63

64

north over the western spur of Little Brother (7810), then descend slightly to the edge of the steep south slope above White Branch creek (6210-0.9). After climbing east along this stream, we eventually descend slightly and cross the trickling creek. Here you can camp above its north bank at a flat called Sawyer Bar. Our trail bears north 200 yards part way across a basalt flow, then angles east up a ridge of solidified lava to the breached Collier Cone—the obvious source of this flow. Here, mountaineers' paths take off south up to Collier Glacier. We turn north and work our way across several lava ridges before descending north to Minnie Scott Spring (6650-2.2), which is likely to be snowbound through mid-July. You can camp on the level ground west of the spring. Our trail now makes a curving, counterclockwise descent almost to the Minnie Scott Spring creek, crosses a ridge, descends north to a large, grassy meadow and shortly meets the

Scott Trail (#3551) (6300-0.9). Descending west to the McKenzie Highway in about five miles, this trail follows the narrow strip of land between the Four in One Cone (6258) basalt flow on its north side and the Collier Cone (7534) basalt flow on its south side. The age of these flows, and of the Yapoah Crater (6737) basalt flow immediately north of us, is about 2600 years. Our route follows the Scott Trail north, which curves northeast and switchbacks up a northwest spur of the Ahalapam Cinder Field. It then curves around the slopes of Yapoah Crater and enters Deschutes National Forest. Looking north, we can see a row of peaks: Mt. Washington (7794), Three Fingered Jack (7841) and the snowy Mts. Jefferson (10,497) and Hood (11,235). We now wind along and around ridges of the Yapoah lava flow and are thankful that the rocky trail exists, even when it is covered with snow patches. A cross-country hike across this material would be very exhausting. We reach the edge of the flow and parallel it north on a blocky cinder trail to

South Matthieu Lake (6040-2.5) at Scott Pass, from where the Scott Trail (now numbered 95) descends east-southeast toward Trout Creek. If your backpack is a bright red-orange color, you might find that here, as in other places, hummingbirds buzz up to it and try to extract nectar from your alluring "flower." At this pass, you get one of your best views eastward of central Oregon, which is drier than the west countryside because of the rain shadow cast by the Cascade Range. In beauty, 70-yard-wide South Matthieu Lake is a far cry from North Matthieu Lake, which has long been a favorite camping area. The north lake, however, got too much use, so the section of trail descending to it was closed after a new high route was completed in 1972. Now,

64
65

unfortunately, the smaller south lake, with windy campsites, must bear the brunt of the backpackers. We follow the old trail above the north shore of the south lake, then take the new trail around the west slope of Summit 6302 and are rewarded with excellent views below of the Yapoah lava flow, which was deflected northeast around the lower slopes of Belknap Crater. Our trail soon begins a moderate descent and eventually arcs west in its descent to the north end of the blocked-off OST route (5400-2.3). On almost level terrain now, we proceed northwest alongside the flow's edge to where a

Spur trail (5300-0.4) continues straight ahead but the PCT turns left (west) and climbs up the flow. Since your next permanent source of trailside water is at Coldwater Spring, 11.1 miles distant, you had better head over to Lava Camp Lake first. Follow the spur trail 0.2 mile northwest to the trailhead, parking area and Road 1550, which are reached just after a crossing of the seasonal Lava Camp Lake outlet creek. Road 1550 goes north 0.1 mile to the McKenzie Highway. We follow Road 1550 east 0.4 mile to Lava Camp Lake, where the people and the jays outnumber the six-inch trout, yet water, campsites and good summer swimming are always available. Backtracking to the PCT, we follow its zigzag course west over the blocky lava field and leave the Three Sisters Wilderness as we cross the narrow

McKenzie Highway (State 242) (5280-1.1) 500 yards west of the Dee Wright Observatory—a lookout tower well worth visiting for its views. Just 0.2 mile west down this highway is a parking area with a trailhead for those starting their hike north from McKenzie Pass. This pass was named for the river that was explored in 1811 by Donald McKenzie, a member of John Jacob Astor's Pacific Fur Company. It was opened to travel in 1862 when Felix Scott, with a party of 250 men, chopped their way through the forest, building the road for their 106 ox-hauled wagons as they traveled. They crossed the divide by what is known as the Old Scott Trail, two or three miles south of the

North and Middle Sisters, from McKenzie Pass

Mt. Washington towering over the Belknap lava field

present road. Our route, which now enters the Mt. Washington Wilderness, starts north from the highway, then makes a curve and a switchback down to this trailhead (5210-0.3). We now make an ascent northwest up the Belknap Crater basalt flows and pass between two forested islands of older, glaciated basalt that stand in a sea of younger basalt. The desolate young basalt flows look as if they had cooled only a few years ago, yet those emanating from Little Belknap (6305) are 2900 years old. The flows seen today on Belknap Crater (6872) and its flanks are mostly 1500-4000 years old. All the flows between North Sister and Mt. Washington compose a 65-square-mile field that represents the Cascade's greatest post-Pleistocene outpouring of lava. Belknap Crater is an excellent example of a shield volcano, and is quite similar to the shields that the Three Sisters and Mt. Thielsen grew upon. Our route now takes us up to a junction with a

Spur trail (6120-2.3) that leads east-northeast up to the summit of Little Belknap. This area we're in looks quite lifeless, yet up here among the rocks you might spot a whistling marmot scurrying for its hole, or even more astounding, you might discover a western toad perhaps searching for those white-abdomen spiders you've seen crawling over these flows. Mountain chickadees sing out their name as we enter a strip of forest near Belknap Crater and descend through it to the eastern edge of a fresh-looking flow (5320-2.5). We first head north, then west up along its edge, which borders the south slope of Mt. Washington. After ascending a switchback up this slope, we climb steadily west-northwest to the Cascade divide, where our trail levels off. We follow the same bearing for a way, then angle northward for 0.3 mile to a gully where the

Washington Ponds spur trail (5710-2.5) curves 200 yards northeast to the shallow, 25-yard-wide lower Washington Pond, beside which people have camped. Beyond this unmarked junction we climb slightly higher through a meadow that affords us an excellent view of the basalt plug that makes up the steep-walled summit block of Mt. Washington (7794). An ascent of its 500-foot-high south arête or its 700-foot-high west arête requires a complete set of technical rock-climbing equipment. This extremely glaciated peak probably once stood as high as North Sister at a time when that peak was still undergoing its growing pains. Our route arcs west and descends moderately alongside the west spur, then descends northward around it to an overused meadow that contains an obvious well (16-inch-diameter pipe) known as

Coldwater Spring (5200-2.4). Since this meadow is the only good PCT campsite in the Mt. Washington Wilderness that has fresh water, it has been overused. On weekends, as many as two dozen mountaineers will make this their base camp and then climb up the north spur to the 300-foot-high north arête of the summit block—the easiest summit route, but still requiring ropes and other equipment. The organic evidence lying profusely around the grassy meadow lets us know that horses use this site too. There may be some question about the water quality of the shallow well. It is, however, our last fresh water on route until Rockpile Lake, about 21.5 miles farther. Less desirable ponds and lakes exist near the trail, and snow patches linger through mid-August on the northwest slope of Three Fingered Jack. Our route continues its northward descent through a hemlock forest occupied by clicking Oregon juncos and drilling red-shafted flickers. We pass by an unmarked trail (5050-0.5) that ascends east-southeast toward the peak's north spur, then we descend northwest to a fork where a log blocks the old

66
67

Oregon Skyline Trail (4760-1.0), descending straight ahead. This trail still approaches the noisy ski-boat-infested Big Lake (4644). Our route veers right (northeast), soon leaves the Mt. Washington Wilderness, and then crosses dry gullies on the way north to a crossing of west-trending

Road 130 (4680-2.1), which was part of the old Santiam Wagon Road. This crossing is 200 yards east of a spur road south to the Big Lake Youth Camp. We hike northeast through a ghost forest of burned lodgepole snags and past abandoned logging roads on a route that gradually turns north and reaches a hundred-yard-long lily-pad pond (4790-2.0) just west of the trail. This unsightly stretch we have just passed through is easy to follow, despite the junctions, because it has an adequate posting of both gray and

PCTS diamonds. Southbound along it, the hiker at least has open, if not scenic, views of Mt. Washington. Just north of the pond, we climb over a low saddle and into a green forest once again. After traversing north over a gentle, open-forested stretch, we hear the drone of automobiles, then our trail turns northeast and heads for a crossing of the

Santiam Highway (State 20) (4810-2.0) about 200 yards west of the national forest boundary at Santiam Pass. This pass was first crossed in 1859 by Andrew Wiley. He explored an old Indian trail up the Santiam River and worked his way farther east each year on his hunting expeditions from the Willamette Valley. Just 240 yards west of our crossing is a PCT access road that curves 0.2 mile northeast to a parking area at a popular trailhead. We cross the highway and after 200 yards spy the parking area, immediately west. Our trail bears north, curves northwest and enters the Mt. Jefferson Wilderness, then climbs increasingly steep slopes and passes a few stagnant ponds just before a junction with the

Santiam Lake Trail (#3491) (5200-1.4), which curves northwest around a prominent boulder pile. We climb northeast up to a forested ridge, then follow it north-northwest toward Three Fingered Jack. The trail eventually leaves the ridge and curves northeast across a prominent cliff above Martin Lake, then heads up a small gully and quickly curves north-northwest **(6000-2.5)**. If you are in desperate need of water, you can now head east cross-country, starting from an obvious flat atop the cliff, then follow markers 0.4 mile north down to sparkling Summit Lake (5800), a favorite among mountaineers. Back on route, we follow the PCT as it switchbacks up to the ridge again, crosses it, and traverses the lower west slope of Three Fingered Jack (7841), which up close has a totally different appearance than when we saw it from a distance: he seems to have considerably more than three fingers. The easiest route to the highest summit is a Class 3 ascent that starts on a faint trail up its southwest talus slope, then climbs its south ridge. Most of the routes up to the serrated crest require climbing equipment. Our trail rounds the peak's northwest spur **(6390-2.6)**, turns east toward a snow patch that lasts through mid-August, then curves northeast up to a

Saddle (6500-0.5) along the Cascade divide. From this vantage point we can observe the remaining structure of an ancient volcano that stands today as a crest called Three Fingered Jack. In two ways it differs from most of the other glacially eroded volcanic peaks we've seen. First, the plug that filled the throat of the volcano does not compose the summit but lies on the east arm

67

68

of the glacial cirque *below* the summit; this plug, unlike others, must not be very resistant to erosion. Second, this peak is composed of remarkably uniform, thin, alternating beds of cinders and flows that dip west about 20°; their *regularity* over such a great thickness indicates a long period of minor eruptions. The reddish-brown, unsorted cinders consist of ash, lapilli, blocks and bombs that contrast strongly with the brownish-gray andesite flows. We now descend several switchbacks, soon recross the divide, and then descend northeast several miles along forested slopes to a smattering of stagnant ponds just southwest of an intersection with the

Minto Pass Trail (#3437) (5350-3.2) at Minto Pass. This trail descends south one-quarter mile to large, green, ten-foot-deep Wasco Lake, whose shores see a lot of campers in August once the mosquitoes have left. The PCT quickly turns north, climbs to a saddle and reaches the **Wasco Lake trail (#65) (5430-0.5),** which descends southeast half a mile to an unnamed lake before curving west to Wasco Lake. We continue north up the divide, switchback as it steepens, and then traverse across to the southeast spur (6210-2.2) of Peak 6488, from where we can look south and see how Three Fingered Jack got its name. Continuing north, we contour to a saddle, then contour across the east slope of Rockpile Mountain (6559) and pass the Two Springs Trail (#70), descending southeast, just before we reach a pond and beautiful

68
69

Rockpile Lake (6250-1.0). This shallow but clear lake has an excellent campsite above its southeast shore and a very good one at its north end. Our trail heads north on the rocky slope along the lake's west shore and then descends the divide to a saddle where the **Summit Trail (#65) (6140-0.5)** forks right, down the east slope. Our route stays west of the divide and climbs up to a level, open area just east of a breached cinder cone. Although there are no lakes or ponds near us, we nevertheless find that in midsummer this flat is crawling with one-inch toads. Continuing north, we pass a second cone, South Cinder Peak (6746), which is of post-Pleistocene age, as is the other one. We soon reach a saddle and an intersection with the unmaintained

Swallow Lake Trail (#3488) (6300-1.0), which descends two miles southwest to Swallow Lake and two miles northeast to Carl Lake. The PCT continues north along the west slope of the divide and reaches a saddle (6400-1.2) on a northwest ridge, from where a spur trail climbs west-northwest to a small knoll with a good view of Mt. Jefferson, six miles north of us. Our trail now crosses a snow patch that lingers through late July, then arcs eastward to the divide and descends it to a level section that contains an adequate campsite beside a small, fresh-water pond

Left: Three Fingered Jack

50 yards east of the crest. Hiking a few minutes longer, we encounter an unsigned trail (6240-0.9) that descends southeast about a mile to large, emerald Carl Lake (5500). From the junction we hike once again up the ridge route, then contour across the forested west slopes of North Cinder Peak (6722) to a small,

Grassy meadow (6240-1.7) that has obviously been camped at, and for a good reason. A hidden, rock-lined pond lies on the other side of a low pile of rocks that borders the meadow. This is a good water hole to stop at if you are passing through late in the summer. After a brief ascent north, we arrive at an escarpment (6340-0.4) where Mt. Jefferson (10,497) towers above us in all its presidential glory. On March 30, 1806, Lewis and Clark saw this snowy peak from the lower Willamette River, and they named it after their president. At the base of its south slope below us lies a bizarre glacio-volcanic landscape. During the last major glacial advance, glaciers cut a deep canyon on each side of the resistant Sugar Pine Ridge, seen in the east. After these disappeared, volcanic eruptions burst forth and constructed Forked Butte (6483), east of North Cinder Peak. This butte was subsequently breached by outpourings of fluid basaltic andesite that flowed east down the glaciated Jefferson Creek and Cabot Creek canyons. A smaller cone with a crater lake, north of us, also erupted about this time, but it was aborted by nature before any flows poured forth. To its north stands the flat Table, and between it and the ridge of Cathedral Rocks is a large, deep, enigmatic depression that may represent a collapsed flow. Time, which allowed nature to sculpt this surrealistic art work, now forces us to press onward. We descend northwest, still marveling at the configurations below, then leave the ridge and switchback down to a junction where a faint, unsigned trail (6130-0.7) climbs 100 yards back to the divide before descending into the marvelous basin. After more switchbacking down, we reach a **saddle (5910-0.5),** from where three variations of the **Pacific Crest Trail** continue northward.

69
70

The **oldest route** starts north steeply down the glaciated valley and curves west to shimmering, pure Hanks Lake (5144-1.2). Along its north shore, the Hunts Cove spur trail climbs north up to another gem, Hunts Lake (5236-0.4). It also descends west to a junction with a newer PCT route (5020-0.5-1.7).

The **newer route,** which was the standard one through 1972, starts on a contour northwest from the saddle, crosses over a low ridge, then makes a descent to the Trail

3493 junction (5640-1.8), near a saddle, before it switch-backs down to the **Hunts Cove spur trail (5020-1.4).** The older route joins the newer one here, continues a descent into the glaciated valley and finally arrives at the southeast shore of shallow Pamelia Lake (3884). Paralleling the shore, the route curves west to a junction with the **Pamelia Lake Trail (#3439) (3970-3.1),** which takes us down to many campsites near the lake's deeper end. Early in the season, the lake is high and attractive, but by August, Pamelia is reduced to a putrid puddle populated with people. Leaving this potential eyesore behind, you can ascend north, then northeast up toward Milk Creek and reach a junction (4320-0.8-7.1) with the newest PCT route.

The **1973 PCT** route starts on a gentle descent north-northeast from the saddle and heads along the lower slopes of the inspiring Cathedral Rocks, which, judging by their color, must have been constructed in the Dark Ages. Our route curves northwest to the crest of a lateral moraine well above sparkling Hunts Lake, then leaves this escarpment and winds north to the west shore of placid **Shale Lake (5910-1.8),** which is a logical spot to stop for the night. Very good campsites beneath mountain hemlocks can be found near the north and west shores of this warm swimming hole. The shale implied by the lake's name is actually basaltic andesite that has become highly fractured along many parallel planes. Just north of this popular lake, we reach a shallow, seasonally larger lake that in late summer dwindles to a mudhole. Beyond it, our trail drops west to the glaciated escarpment, then oh-so-gently descends it before entering a Douglas-fir forest and reaching a junction with the

69
70

Oregon Skyline Trail (Old PCT) (4320-5.0), just south of Milk Creek. We start up the gravelly, bouldery outwash deposits of Milk Creek canyon and pass a lavish display of wildflowers and shrubs before hiking north to a crossing of aptly named **Milk Creek (4320-0.1).** Its silty color is caused by glacially ground "rock flour" that is transported down Jefferson's slope by this minor torrent. We shall see many more creeks like it as we encounter glacier-clad volcanoes along our journey north. We now make tracks northwest across many small, deceptive ridges before we reach the real Woodpecker Ridge and a junction with the

Woodpecker Trail (#3442) (5040-1.8), which descends west. We head east gently down from the ridge and soon pass a stag-nant pond with a fair campsite at its west end. The open forest here is quite choked with an understory of spiraea, corn lily, gooseberry, rhododendron and the ubiquitous huckleberry. Not much farther along, we pass a small spring, then enter a shady forest. Trickling Jeff Creek and its tributary are crossed, then we veer north and start a climb up around a slope to milky **Russell Creek (5520-2.7)**. The early-morning hiker might wonder about a sign which states that it is dangerous to ford this creek after 11 a.m. If he stays through the afternoon, he will see that the warmer temperatures greatly increase the snowmelt from the Russell and Jefferson Park glaciers, and that the flow just might sweep him down the cascading creek. This diurnal fluctuation is a second characteristic of glacier-fed creeks that we will encounter. Our trail now curves around a minor, westward-descending ridge, crosses two frolicking tributaries of Whitewater Creek, and arrives at a very good campsite just east of the second crossing. Our trail now turns west and in 100 yards reaches a junction with the heavily traveled

70
71

Jefferson Park Trail (#3429) (5540-0.5), which descends 4.0 miles west to Road 1044. This is the shortest trail into popular Jefferson Park, where you'll probably find more backpackers and mountaineers than in any other backcountry area along the Oregon PCT. We climb east-northeast across a slope, ford two more tributaries of Whitewater Creek, make a short switchback up above a third and head east-northeast up its swale, then angle north up to Jefferson Park, with its emerald lakes. We quickly reach a junction with a **spur trail (5930-0.6)**, which descends northwest to cool, deep, green Scout Lake (5910). Other paths lead down to it and across low ridges to Bays and Rock lakes just beyond it. Good-to-excellent campsites are everywhere; the best at Scout Lake are under mountain hemlocks above its northwest shore. These trees beautifully frame views across reflective Scout Lake of stately Mt. Jefferson (10,497) with its ermine robe of glaciers. At this lake and the adjacent lakes of Jefferson Park, you might make a strange catch while fishing for trout: Pacific giant salamanders that inhabit these lakes' shady waters.

The PCT turns right (northeast) at the first spur-trail junction, follows blazes past radiating, narrow spur trails, then curves north past a seasonal pond and reaches a signed **spur trail (5930-0.3)** that heads west to Scout and Bays lakes. We now hike north-northeast across the open flat of Jefferson Park and obtain impressive views back at the peak all the way to a junction with the

South Breitenbush Trail (#3376) (5870-0.5), which starts west-southwest before descending northwest. Just 30 yards

Right: Mt. Jefferson, from Scout Lake

farther, a prominent spur trail branches northeast 250 yards to good campsites around shallow Russell Lake (5856). The PCT turns abruptly northwest at this junction, then quickly descends northeast to a step-across ford of South Fork Breitenbush River (5840-0.1). As you begin your ascent northeast, you can spot an excellent campsite 40 yards southeast just above the other side of the "river." The trail now climbs steeply up a slope and into a glacial cirque, where we again step across the river. Here, a steep shortcut northeast looks more like the trail than the trail itself does. It developed, as so many shortcuts do, when early-season hikers chose to descend straight down the slope rather than follow the buried trail across snow patches. The real trail parallels the trickling river a short way north, then curves and climbs moderately southeast to a spur on the Cascade divide. This is climbed in an arc up to Park Ridge, which is then traversed 70 yards west to a

Signed viewpoint (6920-2.0), where you obtain your last look down at justifiably popular Jefferson Park. A short trail climbs 200 yards west up to Peak 7018 for an even better view. In the distance, just east of north, towers magnificent Mt. Hood (11,235), and just to the west of north stands southern Washington's conical Mt. St. Helens (9677). We now descend the trail—or rather, the semipermanent snowfield—toward small, shallow lakes and ponds. As the gradient eases, the trail becomes very obvious as it selects a pond-dotted route north out of the alpine realm and into the hemlock forest. Our path momentarily takes us over a low saddle (6150-2.1), then leads us down a winding, verdant forest path to a grassy meadow with a seasonal pond by which the **Pyramid Butte Trail (#740) (5770-0.7)** starts a zigzag path to the summit of Pyramid Butte (6095). The PCT strikes east-northeast and gradually descends toward Breitenbush Lake, leaving the Mt. Jefferson Wilderness behind shortly before we enter under the portals of the littered

Breitenbush Lake Campground (5505-1.3). Rather than fight the camp's motorized crowds, it is better for you to camp near a shelter at the south end of the lake or to continue hiking north to Gibson Lake. In an effort to get the populace to pack out its trash, the Forest Service removed all its trash cans. Some irritated car campers have turned outhouses into garbage cans, and not one of these remains in decent shape. Other car campers have just littered the ground. Evidently, those who make the least effort to get into the wilderness are the same ones who make the least effort to preserve it. At least you can obtain fresh tap water in this campground. Walk north through it to its entrance at **Skyline Road (#S42) (5530-0.3),** where the PCT takes off east-

ward and follows the lake's shore northeast to a crossing of
Skyline Road (#S42) (5530-0.5) at the north-shore parking
area. We make a short, brisk climb northward, then angle northwest up to the shallow, rockbound Gibson Lake (5675-0.3).
Considering its closeness to hectic Breitenbush Campground, it
is surprising that this lake isn't used all that much. Our now-
rocky trail passes possible lakeshore campsites, arcs westward
to a fine vantage point of the lake-dotted basin below, and then
descends to a saddle and more comfortable underfooting. Here
we meet the
Horseshoe Saddle Trail (#712) (5510-1.3), which descends
three-fourths mile northeast to the Horseshoe Lake
Campground, between the lake and Skyline Road. A short distance northwest along our ridge route, we encounter the Ruddy
Ridge Lookout trail (5600-0.3), which climbs west. We now
contour northward through a thick forest, then climb up to a low
knoll before descending slightly to Many Lakes Viewpoint
(5600-1.2), which lives up to its description. Mile-long Olallie
Lake is the focal point of the basin, and andesitic Olallie Butte
(7215) rules above it. ("Olallie" is what the native Indians called
the huckleberries.) After hiking counterclockwise down the
knoll's northern slopes, we reach a dry flat, from which the   **71**
southbound traveler sees the lofty crown of Mt. Jefferson beck-   **72**
oning him onward. Here our trail crosses a seasonal creek, then
descends north steeply alongside it, and veers northwest to a
very good campsite at reposeful
Upper Lake (5380-0.9). Continuing north, we pass several
seasonal ponds and shallow, linear Cigar Lake (5350), then
switchback northeast down to Top Lake (5170), which has a very
good campsite on its west shore. At the lake's northwest corner
we meet the **Top Lake Trail (#725) (5180-0.8)** ascending west
from Skyline Road and Olallie Lake. Climbing north, we leave
the pleasant lake behind and soon cross a grassy meadow with a
tiny pond that may last only a few tens of years longer before it is
completely engulfed by the meadow—the fate of all ponds. The
forest, in turn, is engulfing the meadow. We soon reach a mile-
high fork on a ridge where the **Oregon Skyline Trail (5280-0.3)**
branches left. This route offers you more lakes than does the
PCT, but the PCT offers you another view of Mt. Jefferson plus
supplies at Olallie Lake Resort. We'll describe both.

The older **Oregon Skyline Trail,** like other old trails, has
the annoying tendency to climb over hills rather than to
contour around them, but the route is mostly downhill if
you're traveling north. This trail climbs up the ridge, then

contours and descends northwest to a junction with the
Red Lake Trail (#719) (4920-1.2), which descends west.
We make a sharp turn right and follow the OST east up
past a shallow lake (4930-0.1) and a lily-pond (4910-0.5),
then arrive at minute Middle Lake (5050-0.2), which
nevertheless is perhaps the most scenic gem along this
alternate route. We now descend a trail segment that is just
as steep as the one we've ascended, to an intersection with
the

Fish Lake Trail (#717) (4760-0.6) at the outlet of
much-fished-at Lower Lake. A fine campsite is just above
the northwest edge of this relatively deep lake. Lower
Lake Campground, which lacks water, is reached by hiking east 0.7 mile up the Fish Lake Trail. From Lower Lake
the OST surmounts two low ridges, contours north-
northeast under three sets of power-lines (4560-2.1), then
eventually makes a short, curving climb east to rocky-
bottomed, water-strider-inhabited Triangle Lake
(4550-0.8), which in late summer you can boulder-hop
across. Beyond it, we start hiking northeast but soon reach
Skyline Road (#S42) (4570-0.3). Our route continues
northeast as we start down a gully, quickly reach a junction
with a **connecting trail** that weaves 230 yards southeast to
the PCT, then head north to a junction with the

Russ Lake Trail (#716) (4500-0.3). You *could* walk north
0.2 mile up Road S822 to Olallie Meadow Campground,
but you would be disappointed—nothing there but an outhouse and a few parking spaces. From the campground,
the old, unsigned, unmaintained and unaesthetic OST continues north. It is far better to hike east up the Russ Lake
Trail, camp or pass by Brook Lake (4600-0.2), and then
rejoin the **PCT (4640-0.2-6.5)**.

Back at the trail fork just north of Top Lake, a 1972 segment of
the **Pacific Crest Trail** contours north along the divide, curves
northeast and crosses it, then follows it east down past a small,
triangular, semiclear lake (5180-0.9) and arrives at the shore of
deep, clear Head Lake (4950-0.7). Here a short spur trail curves
eastward about 100 yards to the Olallie Lake Forest Service
Station beside Skyline Road. As our trail climbs above the
southeast shore of Head Lake, we spot a very good trailside
campsite, then in 50 yards reach
Skyline Road (#S42) (4990-0.1) at a point 20 yards north of its
signed 4991-foot divide. If you're hiking the entire PCT, you'll

Mt. Jefferson and Olallie Lake at sunset

definitely need supplies, so head 100 yards south to a "Y" junction, from where you follow a spur road 200 yards east to Olallie Lake Resort. It has a limited food selection, as did the Cascade Summit store, 140 miles south at Odell Lake. Northward, you can look forward to good, but expensive, meals at Timberline Lodge, 56 miles distant. You will have to go to the settlement of Government Camp, out of your way, if you need more supplies by that time. Now you can head back toward the "Y" junction and, seven yards before it, turn north for 270 yards, first along a spur road, then along a short trail to the PCT. From Skyline Road, the PCT starts northeast, quickly reaches this short-trail junction, then makes a long, gentle descent north along the lower slopes of Olallie Butte (7215) to an intersection with the

Olallie Butte Trail (#720) (4680-2.2), which descends 220 yards **72** west alongside the southern power-line to Skyline Road. We cross under the three sets of power-lines and parallel the unseen road, going north-northeast until we observe a flat, bushy, open depression on the right (east). Then our trail veers northeast, but a blocked trail continues north. This trail (4570-1.0) is a 230-yard link between the PCT and the OST. We continue northeast on a low ridge, angle north and intersect the

Russ Lake Trail (#716) (4550-0.3), ascending southeast from the Oregon Skyline Trail and Olallie Meadow Campground. This trail continues 0.3 mile southeast past an adequate campsite at Jude Lake to a better one at deeper Russ Lake (4600). We start north, then ramble northeast to shallow Jude Lake (4600-0.2), which has a good campsite on its northwest shore. Get a good drink of water, for you now hike a gently graded trail north around the lower ends of two ridges before descending to trickling

Lemiti Creek (4360-6.0) at the lower end of Lemiti Meadow. The trail arcs clockwise through the forest around the meadow's northeast fringe to a signed **spur trail (4400-0.5)** that gently descends 70 yards southwest past a spacious campsite to a five-yard-wide fresh-water hole known as Trooper Springs. On a weekend, you may have to compete with the Scouts as well as with the frogs—your next water will be at a spring 8.3 miles farther. Our trail continues southeast for 0.1 mile, then turns north and climbs over the low Cascade divide. It more or less follows the divide north through a viewless forest, until South Pinhead Butte (5337), where we reach the trailside

Chinquapin Viewpoint (5000-2.8), rather disappointing, but at least it permits us to see over the forest. Better views are just ahead. We contour the butte's slopes northward, cross a saddle (4980-0.8) with an abandoned spur road going west, then reach the southeast slope of North Pinhead Butte (5447), which is the youngest of the three andesitic buttes. Looking south, we see Mt. Jefferson once again and are reminded of the beauties of Jefferson Park. We now descend north to a lava flow, where a signed spur trail (4640-1.4) heads north-northeast 60 yards across it to an open view north of Mt. Hood (11,235) and east of the Warm Springs River basin. We then make a switchback, descend back into the depths of the forest and generally follow a gentle ridge route down to a junction with a **spur trail (3860-3.3)** that descends moderately west-southwest 70 yards to a seeping spring. The slopes steepen, and so does our route, which switchbacks down to a dry creek, contours northward almost to the Warm Springs Indian Reservation boundary, then turns west and makes a bridged crossing of

73
74
75

Warm Springs River (3330-2.3). A very good, spacious campsite is just 20 yards north of this crossing. We now climb north above a tributary gully and reach a flat, where we meet another signed spur trail (3450-0.4), which heads 70 yards east-southeast to a spring. Camp can be made almost anywhere in this open-forest area. Beyond it we cross a northwest-trending, linear meadow that is being invaded by lodgepoles, then we climb gradually increasing slopes up to a junction with

Road S649 (3720-1.0), which is closed 0.3 miles east, at the Warm Springs Indian Reservation boundary. Traveling southwest along this road, you would reach Skyline Road in 3.4 miles. We walk 17 yards northeast up Road S649 to a resumption of the trail and follow it north up to the east slope (4240-1.7) of andesitic Summit Butte (4790). Without getting a view anywhere, we make a gentle descent north, pass under a six-cable power-line, cross northwest over Red Wolf Pass (4120-1.4) without noticing it, then reach a jeep road (3990-0.8) that diagonals northeast across our route. Our trail continues its northward descent and parallels a seasonal creek on our right (east), shortly before intersecting the closed **Road S549 (3580-1.3)**, which, like our trail, heads toward the Clackamas Lake area. We cross this road and roughly parallel it northwest to a junction with the

Miller Trail (#534) (3400-1.9). The permanent, trailside creek depicted on the topo map does not exist, nor does any trace of a creek bed exist. The Miller Trail makes a moderate descent northwest before contouring west to fairly large, well-maintained Clackamas Lake Campground, 0.3 mile distant. Why it is so popular is a mystery, for nearby Clackamas Lake is little more than a polluted cattle pond, and campground vistas are virtually nonexistent. Could it be the campground's two old-fashioned, muscle-powered water pumps? Judge for yourself. The PCT turns north and proceeds through the forest bordering the meadow's edge to a usually dry crossing of Oak Grove Fork Clackamas River (3350-0.7) shortly before a junction with now paved

Skyline Road (#S42) (3370-0.2). The PCT crosses this road about 240 yards northeast of where Road S57 forks west from it over to the Timothy Lake campgrounds. We start west on the trail and soon see Oak Grove Fork Clackamas River below us on our left (southwest). We momentarily descend to this creek, then climb a little just before reaching the

Timothy Trail (#528) (3320-1.3), which makes an eight-mile traverse around the west shore of Timothy Lake (3217), passing campgrounds, picnic areas and creeks before rejoining the PCT near the lake's northeast end. You can see the lake from this junction, from which the PCT winds gradually down to its unappealing east shore. The shoreline improves as you head north, where you are perhaps tempted to swim across the lake's narrow arm or make an adequate campsite beside it. Farther north, the arm enlarges to a shallow bay that in late summer becomes a swamp, and the trail contours northeast around it, passing several trailside springs a few minutes before you reach a bridge over wide, clear

Crater Creek (3220-4.3). About a hundred yards north of this crossing, the Timothy Trail (528) rejoins our route from the west. Just 250 yards beyond this junction, we reach another, where the **Little Crater Lake Trail (#500) (3230-0.2)** strikes east 220 yards to 45-foot deep, extremely clear Little Crater Lake, which is an oversized artesian spring. Its purity is maintained by a fence that keeps out the cattle and a sign that bans camping. You can camp either back near the trail junction or at pleasant Little Crater Campground, which is just 200 yards east of the lake. Little Crater looks like the ideal swimming hole, but stick your arm down into it—brrrr!—as with most springs, its water stays an almost constant year-round 40°F. We re-enter forest and get back on the PCT. Our path north to Mt. Hood is now deficient in views, lakes, creeks and hikers, but it is great if you like the solitude of a shady forest, such as this one, that has Douglas-fir, western and mountain hemlocks, western red and Alaska cedars, silver, noble, grand and subalpine firs, and western white and lodgepole pines. Our trail starts northwest, then gradually curves north up to

Road S481 (3360-1.6), which gently descends northeast to a crossing of Crater Creek. We bear north for 30 yards on a diagonal across the road, then continue north up an increasingly steep trail to the gentle summit area (4040-1.5) of Basin Point. Descending north-northwest, we soon reach a junction with the **Jackpot Meadow Trail (#492) (3960-0.3),** which descends northwest along the old OST route. We veer north-northeast and quickly arrive at paved, new

76

77

78

79

Abbot Road (#S457) (3920-0.1), which would lead you back to Little Crater Campground and Skyline Road. Traversing through a forest of mountain hemlock and lodgepole, we pass a faint, unsigned-but-marked trail (3900-0.4) striking east, then reach the **Linney Creek Road (#S407) (3910-0.4).** Now our trail angles northeast and soon encounters a signed spur trail (3910-0.2) that descends southeast to a small campsite and a seeping spring about 50 yards from the PCT. This is likely to be your last water until Lower Twin Lake, 5.9 miles farther. The PCT now climbs north to a saddle (4010-0.5), then makes a long northeast traverse through a beautiful forest with rhododendrons to a junction with the Blue Box Trail (#483), which strikes south to Clear Lake (3500). In 50 yards you reach **U.S. Highway 26 (3910-3.5)** at Wapinitia Pass.

If you have inadequate supplies to last until *Cascade Locks, 61 miles farther,* then you will have to take an alternate route on paved roads that lead you to the small settlement of Government Camp. This route follows U.S. Highway 26 north past a junction with State Highway 35 at the **Salmon River Campground (3596-4.5),** then northwest to a junction with the **Timberline Lodge road (3980-2.4).** Obtain supplies at **Government Camp,** which is just off the main highway and one-quarter mile west of this junction, then return to it (3980-0.5). Now you can backtrack all the way to Wapinitia Pass, backtrack to State Highway 35 and ascend it 2.5 miles to Barlow Pass (4161), or better yet, start northeast up the Timberline Lodge road. This climbs up past the entrance to **Alpine Campground (5450-4.5),** then finally tops out at giant **Timberline Lodge (5940-2.2),** which in 1973 was undergoing further expansion with the addition of an east wing. The Pacific Crest Trail (5960-0.1-13.2) traverses the slope above the lodge and can be reached by a hundred-yard spur trail that climbs up to it from the east wing.

Thirty yards northwest of the PCT trailhead at **Wapinitia Pass** is a small parking lot for those hiking south. Southeast 0.1 mile from this trailhead is a spur road that goes northeast 100 yards to a huge parking lot and trailhead north, then bends southeast for three-fourths mile to Frog Lake Campground. From the pass, we hike east 250 yards to a spur trail. This goes 50 yards southwest to a junction with the Frog Lake Trail (#530), then continues 70 yards to a trailhead at the aforementioned parking lot. We veer northeast through a solemn forest of western hemlock, curve southeast upward, then make a switchback north and climb to Twin Lake Summit (4325-1.3). Now we descend northeast to a gully, where a spur trail descends south to Lower Twin Lakes (4200), but we hike southeast a bit farther to a junction with a shorter **spur trail (4230-0.6),** which descends 70 yards to a good campsite at the lake's northeast shore. At the campsite, the Lower Twin Lake Trail (#532) departs south along the east shore toward Frog Lake Buttes. A fishermen's trail circles the lake and exposes you to other campsites. The PCT now makes a gentle, protracted ascent up a ridge north to a good campsite on the south shore of cool, shallow **79** **78**

Upper Twin Lake (4380-0.7), where the Upper Twin Lake Trail (#533) starts its semicircular path around this lake's west shore. Proceeding around its east shore, we encounter, after a hundred yards, a junction with the Palmateer View Trail (#482), which climbs north-northeast up toward a low summit. As we near the northeast lakeshore, we reach a very good campsite with a toilet. Just beyond it at this clear lake's north end, the Upper Twin Lake Trail reunites with ours (4380-0.3). Since the next water we'll reach won't be until the headwaters of the Salmon River, 8.4 miles farther, we fill our canteens here before making a short climb up to a saddle on the Cascade divide

(4500-0.2). After making an equally short descent, we get a glimpse of Mt. Hood, then head northwest and quickly reach a second junction with Trail 482 (4395-0.3), which descends east-northeast. Our trail now rounds a northeast slope, contours west, and then climbs gently north to an open slope of huckleberry, yarrow, fireweed and pearly everlasting. Soon we reach our *third* and last junction with Trail 482 (4550-1.4), which this time descends southeast. We contour over to the divide (4570-0.3), with its unrestricted views east, and descend it to within a few yards of paved

Old State Highway 35 (4157-1.2) at Barlow Pass. Over this pass was built the first wagon road across the Cascades into the Willamette Valley. Developed by Samuel K. Barlow in 1845, it enabled immigrants to avoid the dangerous and expensive raft trip down the Columbia River from The Dalles. A very short **spur trail** takes us a few steps northwest to a trailhead and a parking lot for those hiking south. The old highway is blocked off immediately west of this lot. Our trail continues northeast, immediately crosses **Road 30** beside its junction with the old highway, then heads east and curves north to

New State Highway 35 (4155-0.3). This junction is 40 yards **78** northeast of the new Barlow Pass elevation sign (4161), which in turn is 40 yards northeast of the old highway junction. We **79** diagonal north across Highway 35 and start up the PCT, which regains the divide and follows it north to an elevation of 4700 feet, then climbs its west slope to a gully (4870-2.7) that has water only in the early season, even though this spot is designated on the Mt. Hood Wilderness map as a campsite. From this cool forest retreat, our trail methodically climbs over to the slopes of the Salmon River canyon, where we can look west toward Alpine Campground and see a cliff below it of loose hornblende andesite debris. Our trail then climbs northeast up to a junction with the

Timberline Trail (#600) (5340-0.8), which starts a descent east to the White River. This trail, which stays near timberline as it circles Mt. Hood (11,235) counterclockwise, is an alternative 22.7-mile route that takes you to a reunion with the Pacific Crest Trail near Bald Mountain. From the junction our trail starts northwest up a ridge of loose, gravelly debris, and soon it ramifies into a number of sandy paths that parallel one another up the ridge.

If you look east at the cliff composed of unsorted volcanic debris that is above the White River, you'll get an idea of the type of sediments you're walking on. These deposits, which are on the south and southwest slopes of Hood, are remnants of a huge debris fan of hornblende andesite that was formed 1700-2000

Right: Mt. Hood and White River Glacier

years ago when a crater was blasted out near the mountain's summit and a plug dome of viscous lava welled up, melting the surrounding ice field. The sudden release of frozen water created devastating mudflows that carried the volcanic debris down to these slopes that the PCT crosses today. Due north of us, we can identify Crater Rock (10,560), which is a remnant of that plug dome. Just north of it, numerous fissures still emit steam and hydrogen-sulfide gas. On clear, windless days the gas emissions from these fumaroles are visible from as far away as Portland. Mt. Hood had minor eruptions during the last century, and we can be sure that it is still alive today.

Our pathways eventually merge and curve westward as a single trail, which first crosses a dry creek bed, then crosses the upper **Salmon River (5960-1.2)**, which derives its flow from an arm of the Palmer Glacier. The trail now contours southwest past an ascending dirt road, then reaches a **spur trail (5960-0.3)**—one of many—which at a sign starts a south-southeast descent 100 yards to the eastern end of towering

Timberline Lodge (5940), where our alternate supply route from Government Camp ends. No hiker should pass up the opportunity to inspect this grand structure built by the Works Progress Administration in the late 1930s. This is also the place to register if you intend to climb the snow-capped peak. Just east of the ski lift is a trail that ascends north to the Silox Warming Hut (6930). From it, you climb up the Palmer Glacier and head for a bowl containing the fumaroles of Devils Kitchen (10,400). From here you can climb northwest to a ridge, then northeast to the summit. Plan your one-day ascent so that you reach the hut by sunrise. That way you'll be well on your way down by early afternoon and will avoid the minor avalanches, caused by the melting snow, that tend to occur later in the day. A rope is definitely recommended, even though this popular climb has been done in tennis shoes.

After ascending the spur trail from the lodge back to the PCT, we hike west under the ski lift and past a microwave tower (5980-0.2) below us, then gradually descend westward with views south across a rolling topography to lofty Mt. Jefferson (10,497). Several seasonal creeks are crossed before we make a three-yard boulder-hop across silty Little Zigzag creek (5760-0.9), then continue our descent to a junction with the

Hidden Lake Trail (#779) (5680-0.4), which goes southwest down a moraical ridge to Hidden Lake. Our trail continues its rambling descent, then climbs to a narrow ridge from where we get a great view of Mt. Hood and glaciated Zigzag Canyon. We switchback down the steep slope, jump across the silty Zigzag

79

River (4890-1.3), and climb moderately into a tributary canyon, then out of it up to a slope where the **PCT (#2000) (5140-0.5)** splits into two routes.

The recently constructed **horse trail** starts west-southwest and switchbacks up to a broad ridge where we intersect the **Paradise Park Trail (#778) (5390-0.4)**, a footpath that climbs northeast. The horse trail ascends north across the ridge and passes a camping area below us just before it turns northeast and descends to splashing Lost Creek (5390-0.6), which cascades down a cliff just east of us. We cross it and its more reserved tributary, then pass another camping area below us as we make a climb west up to a ridge, top the ridge, and descend once again—this time to a crossing of Rushing Water Creek (5440-0.6) just below its narrow waterfall. After climbing steeply north out of this cliff-bound canyon, we follow a rather direct trail down to a reunion with the **foot trail (5400-0.5-2.1)**.

The older **foot trail,** which is by far the more scenic route, starts northeast, enters the Mt. Hood Wilderness, and zigzags up the tributary canyon of Zigzag Canyon. If you're wondering about the composition of the loose cliffs—yes, they are part of the debris-fan deposits that originated from the Crater Rock area. Our ascent finally eases off just after gaining access to a ridge and meeting the **Paradise Park Trail (#778) (5740-1.0)**, a footpath descending west-southwest through an alpine meadow. We now hike over to Lost Creek (5720-0.2), whose banks are ablaze with common and Lewis monkey flowers, lupine, bistort, corn lily, Mariposa lily, yarrow, paintbrush, pasqueflower, aster and eriogonum. Remembering that campsites must be at least 100 feet from any creek or body of water, we push onward and quickly reach the **Paradise Park Shelter (5730-0.1)** in an open forest of dwarf hemlock. This ten-foot-square shelter, constructed with andesite blocks from the surrounding lava flow, even has a built-in fireplace. Beyond it, our trail makes a slight climb, then contours across more alpine meadows, and perhaps gives us a chance to spot a pair of sparrow hawks before it switchbacks down to a reunion with the

80

PCT horse trail (5400-2.2). We now make a switchbacking descent and leave the Mt. Hood Wilderness, but not before obtaining two fantastic views: up toward the glacier-mantled summit above and down upon the mountain's anatomy below, exposed by the incising Sandy River. We get one more view—

from a vertical-sided ridge at the end of a 50-yard spur trail—and it is the most revealing of all: the cliffs of the Sandy River canyon and its tributary canyon are composed of andesite flows and interbedded pyroclastic deposits. As if this flood of magnificent scenery were not enough to satisfy, our trail takes us down to the west side of the ridge where, from a viewpoint, we are saturated with the impressive, naked cliffs of Slide Mountain (4872) and of the Rushing Water Creek canyon all around us. After such a day as this, one is bound to reminisce about his alpine adventure, and a good place to stop and talk it over is at large, flat

Scout Camp (3400-3.0), which is beside Rushing Water Creek at the bottom of the switchbacks from the viewpoint. Leaving this forested campsite, we descend the trail northwest 100 yards and arrive at the bouldery, bushy bottom of the Sandy River canyon. We immediately make a log crossing of the three-yard-wide river, which in high runoff expands to fill its 30-yard-wide channel. Continuing northwest downstream on a sandy trail, we wind 270 yards between bushes and over bars to a low cliff of unsorted, poorly bedded sediments of a glacial moraine. Our trail makes a short climb up it and reaches the

Sandy River Trail (#770) (3280-0.2), which is signed here as the *Ramona Falls Loop Trail 797.* Just because we've left the mountain behind doesn't mean that we have run out of good scenery, for we find that, after hiking eastward through a dry, open forest, we reach beautiful **Ramona Falls (3520-0.5),** 70 yards past a large, leaky-roofed shelter that nevertheless makes an excellent campsite. The location of this shelter is not fortuitous; it is close enough to the falls' creek to make water easily accessible, yet far enough away—in the open forest—that few mosquitoes bother us. Descending northeast from the shelter to the cascading, "bridal veil" falls, our trail crosses the creek and, after a few yards, reaches a fork where the

80

Yocum Ridge Trail (#771) starts a three-fourths-mile climb up to that ridge. During the summer of 1973, a new section of the Pacific Crest Trail was being blasted out of the rock north of Yocum Ridge; it should be ready to hike on by the 1974 season. Hikers were barred from this trail in 1973, but we did see parts of it and have drawn on our map a "best guess" route, based on our observations, on the 1973 Federal Register, on the "lay of the land," and on our knowledge of modern trail-design principles. Over about a 4.7-mile stretch, it should go up the Yocum Ridge Trail to Yocum Ridge, contour the slope eastward to the Muddy Fork of the Sandy River, and then climb gently northwest up to the open slopes beneath Bald Mountain (4591), along which you'll get truly scenic views of the mountain above and the canyon below. The trail should then re-enter the forest and gently descend northward to a junction with the Timberline Trail and the pre-1974 PCT.

Leaving the hidden grotto of Ramona Falls behind, we cross its creek again, then walk alongside the stream on a soft, verdant forest path that is unquestionably the best creekside mile of trail along the Oregon PCT. Farther down, we cross the creek a third time and soon leave this cliff-lined green strip of mountain hemlock, Douglas-fir, alder, vine maple, rhododendron, coral root, fern and moss. Then we descend a drier slope with lodgepoles and soon meet the southwest-bearing

Ramona Falls Loop Trail (#797) (2820-1.6), which is shown on topographic and planimetric maps as the "Portage Trail." We pass a very good, roomy campsite and in 30 yards reach a bridge that crosses the aptly named Muddy Fork, which is larger than the stretch of the Sandy River we recently crossed. Our trail starts west beside the rushing fork, then climbs north before reaching steeper slopes and switchbacking up them. You would expect to get a superb view of Mt. Hood, but the thick forest sees to it that you get nary a glimpse. We top the ridge of this glaciated canyon, start to curve northeast, and reach a junction with a spur trail (3910-1.7) that descends 100 yards to a bend in Road S238J. Our trail now climbs steadily east-northeast to a junction with the

80
81

Timberline Trail (#600) (4270-0.7), ascending gently east-southeast, and the **1974 Pacific Crest Trail (#2000),** ascending gently south-southwest, then veering east to some spectacular views of the Mt. Hood country. From this junction, our route is mostly downhill to the Columbia River. Descending northwest 50 yards, we reach a junction with the 0.4-mile-long **Top Spur Trail (#785),** which curves west down to a trailhead at Road S238J. A trickling creek can be found halfway down this trail. We continue our forested route northwest to the crest's end (4200-1.4), then start down a series of switchbacks northward. The thorny gooseberries, thimbleberries and giant Devil's clubs attest to the cool, moist slope of this forest, which we leave behind as we descend a drier north ridge to a flat clearing immediately south of the

Lolo Pass Road (#N12 west/#N18 east) (3420-1.4) at Lolo Pass. A quarter mile west of here, you can find water running down to the road. The north trailhead is about 20 yards southwest along paved Road N12 and 30 yards before this road's junction with paved Road 238. We start northwest, quickly cross north under four sets of buzzing power lines, and then glance back northeast at Mt. Hood's deeply glaciated north face. Before the glaciers performed their cosmetic surgery, the peak's summit towered to about 12,000 feet. You soon reach a gully with a trickling creek (3520-0.4), then climb gradually north to the divide, and circle around the east slope of Sentinel Peak (4565). Rejoining the divide, we contour northwest past two low summits before arriving at a junction with the

Huckleberry Mountain Trail (#617) (4020-3.9), which descends slightly for 0.3 mile to a trickling creek in the gully below the Preachers/Devils saddle. If you descend this trail farther, you reach Lost Lake (3143-1.7), follow its east shore north to Lost Lake Campground (3160-0.8), then finally reach a small store (3160-0.3-2.8) by the lake's north end. The Oregon Skyline Trail once followed this shoreline route, but the trail segment has since been abandoned. From the junction we contour 270 yards to a sharp bend in the trail, where a spur trail descends 50 yards to a trickling creek and a small flat called Salvation Spring Camp. Back on route, we continue north to an obvious gully and then switchback up to the

Preachers/Devils saddle (4340-0.9). Avoiding sermons from its two summits, we follow a huckleberry-lined path in a forest of hemlock and fir, descend to a saddle, climb north up the ridge above Lost Lake, and then descend west to a notch (4250-1.9). Now, a short, stiff climb north takes us to a saddle and a junction with the

81
82
83

Buck Peak Trail (#615) (4500-0.5), which continues along the ridge up to Buck Peak (4751). We descend north across the west slope of this peak and discover a small spring (4340-0.4) a couple feet below the west edge of the trail. A little farther down the trail, we reach the ridge (4230-0.3) again, then switchback down to a long saddle, from which we can get a glimpse below of Blue Lake (3780) to the southwest. As we arc northeast, we leave the Multnomah County's Bull Run Watershed behind for good, and with it the posted *no camping* signs that have bothered us while within that section of the county since Lolo Pass. They don't want fires. Our route follows a fairly level crest northeast, contours across the southeast slope of a low, triangular summit, then, just below a saddle, reaches the abandoned

Oregon Skyline Trail (4190-2.2), which climbs from the southwest to merge with the PCT. Climbing gently northeast, we quickly reach the Larch Mountain Road (#N20) (4240-0.1), which is momentarily atop the ridge. We locate the trail on the northwest side of the road, parallel it north-northeast and then round the narrow north spur (4400-1.6) of Indian Mountain (4890), from which we see Mts. St. Helens (9677), Rainier

(14,410) and Adams (12,276). Then we descend eastward to logged-over

Indian Springs Campground (4300-0.3), which has few car campers because of the rough, rocky nature of Road N20, which is used to reach it. The spring is just beyond the west end of the camp's road loop, and just beyond it, the brushy, unmaintained Indian Springs Trail (#435) starts northwest toward the north spur, follows it, then steeply descends it to the Eagle Creek Trail (#440) (2800-2.0). The PCT recommences at the east end of the loop and parallels the road, first below it, then above it to a saddle, where it leaves the roadside and winds gently down a forested slope, then northeast down to a junction with the

Eagle Creek Trail (#440) (3750-2.6) just above the south shore of Wahtum Lake (3732). This trail, which is especially popular on sunny summer weekends, continues east past shoreline campsites, then climbs as a wide, manicured path up to Wahtum Campground (3960-0.6) and the Larch Mountain Road (#N20), both on a saddle. We turn sharply left and follow Trail 440 west to the lake's outlet, where the **PCT (3740-0.1)** branches 30 yards down to it and then climbs north.

The hike from Wahtum Lake down to the Columbia **83** River is far more scenic along the **Eagle Creek Trail** then along the PCT. From the Wahtum Lake outlet, which is the East Fork of Eagle Creek, Trail 440 begins as a typical trail, for it descends through a Douglas-fir forest with an understory that includes inconspicuous annuals such as coolwort, false Solomon's seal, queen's cup, bunchberry and vanilla-leaf. In a north-draining canyon, we reach an adequate campsite beside a trickling creek (3300-1.2), then arc westward gently down to a ford of the **Indian Springs fork (3040-0.8)** of Eagle Creek, which could be tricky to cross in early summer. Along its bank is a very good campsite. We now begin a descent northwest that takes us past rhododendron, gooseberry, red elderberry, thimbleberry, huckleberry, Devil's club and Oregon grape. Along this cool descent, you'll probably not notice the camouflaged, unmaintained

Indian Springs Trail (#435) (2800-0.4), which you can climb perspiringly for two miles up to Indian Springs Campground. After reaching a viewpoint (2350-1.2) at the tip of a north spur, our trail turns south and descends past a campsite (1920-1.0) by a shallow gully, crosses seasonal creeklets, and then makes a switchback (1600-0.7) north.

The slope is now much gentler, and in the near distance we can hear Eagle Creek splashing merrily down its course. In a short distance we reach a rockbound creek (1440-0.5) and pause for a drink. Don't be too surprised if a red-spotted garter snake is climbing up a rock behind you; he needs water too. It is not uncommon to encounter half a dozen of these beneficial snakes in a day's hike along this verdant route. Just beyond this refreshing creek we meet several trails that descend about 50 yards west to

7½ **Mile Camp (1380-0.1),** complete with a primitive shelter. If you intend to camp before reaching the trailhead, this certainly is a good place to stop at. Before us lies the string of impressive waterfalls that make this last half of the trail so popular. Our trail gradually descends to the bank of Eagle Creek, and we see a 50-foot cascade (1180-0.7)—not too impressive—but a sample of what's to come. The creek enters a safe, very deep, crystal-clear pool (1120-0.3) that is extremely tempting for an afternoon swim, but the cool water will ensure that you won't stay in for long. Immediately beyond it is a two-stage, 100-foot-high waterfall, sliced into a narrow gorge, which we don't see until we round a vertical cliff, where our precariously exposed trail, blasted from the cliff, heads toward 150-foot-high

83
84

Tunnel Falls (1120-0.2). This trail is definitely not for the faint-hearted, nor is its ceiling sufficient for those on horseback. The fall, in its grotto of vertical-walled basalt, is spectacular enough to make it the climax of this route, but our sensations of it are heightened even more as we head through a wet tunnel blasted behind the fall about midway up it. Exuberant from the wall of water around us, we leave this grotto of the East Fork in expectation of more high adventure. Below us, Eagle Creek cascades 30 feet down to another layer of this Miocene Columbia River basalt. We walk enthusiastically northwest and unexpectedly reach a junction with the unmapped

Eagle Benson Trail (#434) (1000-0.8), which climbs steeply up to the PCT. This narrow footpath is not recommended by the authors, who believe it is too narrow to be safely climbed or descended with a heavy pack. In places it is quite easy for you to slip on loose gravel and then fall over a hundred-foot cliff. Just around the corner from this junction, our trail enters another side canyon and bridges a murmuring tributary a hundred yards downstream from its slender, 80-foot-high fall. Unseen above it is the Eagle Benson Trail, which descends near the mossy brink of this graceful fall. Continuing northwest, we soon enter another side canyon, and this one provides us with the very good

Wy East Camp (960-0.5), which is just above the trail and is equipped with a 15-foot-square shelter. Progressing farther downstream on this trail, we reach a bridge (710-0.7) across Eagle Creek, 20 feet below. A daredevil instinct may urge some to jump from the bridge into the tempting 8-foot-deep pool below, but better judgment takes hold and we pass up the opportunity for another time. Now above the creek's west bank, we follow the singing creek down to the popular, excellent

4 Mile Camp (680-0.6), also known as the "Tenas Camp." How many campsites do you know of that have a beautiful waterfall near them? We've seen just a few. This one has a two-step, 40-foot fall, and near it, you'll find the dipper, or water ouzel, which is a gray, chunky, water-loving bird that tenaciously clings to the bottoms of swift streams in search of aquatic animal life. The name "dipper" refers to the bird's bobbing motions while standing on land, and, taking that word as a suggestion, we decide to take a dip in the 57°F creek ourselves. After a quick, invigorating frolic in the pools below the lower fall, we stretch out in the afternoon sunlight to thaw out before hiking once again. Back on the trail, we walk spiritedly north to a

84

Bridge (690-0.3) across a 90-foot-deep gorge that is only 30 feet wide. A hundred yards downstream from this crossing, the swirling creek has cut, with the aid of churning boulders, deep potholes that would make superb swimming holes were it not for the cool temperature. The six-inch trout don't seem to mind it though. Above the potholes, wispy Loowit Falls emerges from the vegetation to flow silently down the polished rock and into one of the pools. Continuing downstream, we soon enter another side canyon, bridge a creek 50 feet above it, then pass by massive, vertical-walled flows of this Columbia River basalt. The contact between two flows tends to be a weak point, and both the creek and its tributaries tend to flow along such contacts. The height of a waterfall often represents the thickness of a single flow. The minutes pass by quickly, and before we know it, we cross Tish Creek and arrive at an overlook (500-1.4) above

Punch Bowl Falls, which drops 40 feet into a churning

cauldron below us. It's hard to judge just how deep this huge pool is, but right beneath the falls a depth of 20 feet wouldn't be much of an exaggeration. Here our trail starts to climb high above the now-impassable gorge, and we soon see more reasons why horses aren't allowed on the trail. At times, the overhanging walls seem to press us terribly close to the brink of the dead-vertical cliff below us, and we're thankful that the trail crew installed cables along these stretches. We now reach another overlook (520-0.7), where we can look 200 yards upstream to

Metlaka Falls, whose silvery course plummets another step down into the inaccessible gorge. Our route gradually begins to descend toward the trailhead, and we leave the threatening, moss-covered cliffs behind as we descend into the realm of a cedar-and-Douglas-fir forest. Alder, maple, dogwood, ocean spray, blackberries, thimble-berries, moss, three species of ferns and dozens of wildflowers harmonize with the conifers on these canyon slopes to create a symphony of nature at her best. All too soon, our verdant route reaches the

Trailhead (160-1.1-13.2), and we follow the creekside dirt road past a parking lot and picnic area, then reach a paved spur road (100-0.6) that climbs 0.5 mile east to Eagle Creek Campground. Continuing northwest, we pass the Cascade Salmon Fish Hatchery and reach **Interstate Highway 80N (90-0.1).** If you intend to continue north into Washington, you'll now have to hitchhike or walk east along it for 1.4 miles to the next exit (Cascade Locks), then follow the offramp north to the east end of **Bridge of the Gods (100-2.2).** Here you walk up the steps to its toll booth (170-0.1-16.2) and brace yourself for an exciting journey through Washington. (For those traveling south up the Eagle Creek Trail, you must drive *east* on Interstate 80N just past huge Bonneville Dam, then take the offramp immediately beyond a tunnel.)

84
86
83

From the outlet creek of Wahtum Lake—which could be your last trailside water until Herman Creek, 11.6 miles farther—the **Pacific Crest Trail** switchbacks north, then curves northwest up to a junction with the eastward-contouring **Chinidere Mountain Trail (4250-0.7).** A few steps later, this trail leaves our route and climbs northwest to the summit of Chinidere Mountain (4673) while our trail contours northwest around it. Our route descends to a saddle (4130-0.6), then contours across the southwest slope

Left: along the Eagle Creek Trail

of Summit 4380 before descending along a disheartening, burned-over crest route to a good rest stop known as

Camp Smokey (3810-2.4). Perhaps someone smoked too much. From here, the Eagle Benson Trail (#434) descends three miles to the Eagle Creek Trail, but it is not recommended because the last few hundred feet are quite exposed and could be treacherous if you're descending with a heavy pack. You might, nevertheless, start west on it, for a nice campsite lies 150 yards down it, and a pipe spring 50 yards beyond that. We now start a climb up to Benson Plateau, which is a layer of Pleistocene or Pliocene volcanic flows that cap the underlying Pliocene olivine basalt flows. These flows, in turn, overlie the thick, mid-Miocene Columbia River basalt flows, which tend to have well-developed columnar jointing on the lower part of each flow, and lesser jointing on the upper part. Just before we top the east edge of the plateau, we reach the west-climbing **Benson Way (4080-0.4),** then continue north up to the summit area and soon descend slightly northeast to the

Ruckle Creek Way (4120-0.7). This departs west-northwest toward the creek and goes down to Interstate 80N. Our descent north stays close to the plateau's east edge, which eventually becomes a ridge, then we encounter our first switchback (3600-2.5). After a few switchbacks down, we reach an open spot on the ridge from where we can see Mts. Hood (11,235), Adams (12,276) and St. Helens (9677) as well as the dammed Columbia River below us. Our route re-enters forest, switchbacks down the east slope of the ridge, and then crosses to its drier, northwest slope. By 1975, when a new trail segment is completed, you'll be able to continue westward down this slope to the Bridge of the Gods toll booth. If you're expecting to see any rattlesnakes in northern Oregon, this is the stretch to look for them. Our trail now takes a rambling course down to a bridge above spirited

83
85

Herman Creek (560-4.3). We cross it or, like others, stop to fish at it, then take a short switchback up to a bench, where we reach a jeep road. This we parallel for 35 yards west to where our trail merges with it. Seventy yards later, the road dwindles to a trail and we come to a large, heavily used campsite, which is a popular spot for weekend hikers and fishermen. Our route progresses west to the crest of a low ridge, where we meet a junction with the

Herman Creek Trail (570-0.5). This trail climbs steeply up the ridge to the jeep road that curves back down to our trail beside Herman Creek. We continue on and descend to a **power-line road,** which we follow northeast for 85 yards, then cross north under the power line, and continue for 35 yards to a **resumption (420-0.2)** of the PCT. Here we switchback down into a beautiful Douglas-fir forest and arrive at the

Pacific Crest trailhead (120-0.3), which is located at the west end of the Mt. Hood National Forest Columbia Gorge Work Center and, appropriately, beside a bench and a drinking fountain. Below us is a grassy, roadside parking lot with all the amenities of civilization: a drinking fountain, a table and an outhouse. (Those who intend to take the PCT south from here can reach this trailhead via Interstate 80N by taking the Cascade Locks offramp if coming from the west or the Forest Lane offramp if coming from the east.) The hiker who intends to cross into Washington should follow **Herman Creek Road,** in front of us, southwest to a junction with

Forest Lane Road (140-0.5). On this you walk west immediately over Interstate 80N, then past houses until you reach the entrance to the **Cascade Locks KOA (130-1.2).** At this campground, you'll be able to resupply, shower, and try to get a good night's rest beside the sometimes-busy Union Pacific Railroad tracks, which run almost through it. Continuing toward town, we reach a junction with old **U.S. Highway 30 (135-0.5),** and follow it past Cascade Locks Marine Park, with a campground, to the **Cascade Locks Post Office (120-0.4),** across from 5th Street. We pass a few cafes as we walk to the **Bridge of the Gods (100-0.4),** then climb the steps to its toll booth (170-0.1), start west across the bridge and midway reach the **Oregon-Washington State Line (180-0.2).** The steel grating beneath our feet allows us to look down at the Columbia River as we cross it to a junction with

85
86
87

Washington State Highway 14 (160-0.2). A proposed Pacific Crest Trail route is supposed to descend southeast from Table Mountain (3400) to this junction, but it will be years before the trail is actually built, if it ever is. We start north on Highway 14 and walk along it to the town of Stevenson, which has stores and cafes, plus the **Stevenson Post Office (110-2.7)** at the corner of First and Russell, one block south of the highway. *Your next supply point will be at White Pass, 132 miles distant.* East of Stevenson, our highway climbs the rocky bluffs and provides us with scenic views up and down the river. Douglas-fir and maple provide plenty of shade even if you're doing this stretch in the afternoon. Our road now descends slightly to a junction with the **Wind River Road (#30) (280-3.4),** which is an "all weather" route you can take north.

The authors do not recommend the first 27 miles of the old Cascade Crest Trail (Washington's PCT) because 1) the trail, where it exists, is largely unmaintained and heavily vegetated (hence concealing rattlesnakes and creating a "fog drip" problem); 2) part of the route has been subject to clear-cut logging, and the trail through that eyesore is a rough one; 3) the trail often climbs and descends steeply; and 4) the route follows roads for several miles.

The alternate route, which is just a fast-access route, also follows roads, but it lacks most of the hazards and frustrations found along the first two-day hike on the Cascade Crest Trail. This route starts northwest up the paved **Wind River Road,** reaches the sleepy settlement of Carson (450-1.0), heads north past houses, then curves northwest to a bridge (570-2.5) across the 200-foot-deep Wind River gorge. Continuing northwest up the gently dipping tableland, we reach a **junction (802-2.3),** on the right, with a paved road that is signed *Panther Creek*. We follow it east to the

87
88A
88B
91
92
89A
89B

Panther Creek road (#N605) (802-0.1), up which we walk north to a junction with **Road N406 (832-0.9).** It is possible to take this road northeast 0.6 mile to the Big Huckleberry Trail (#186), but you would find that this trail up to the PCT is excessively steep and is, in part, overgrown with vegetation. After starting north again up our paved road, we soon angle northwest, then follow the mildly winding route up to a junction with **Road N405 (938-1.9),** which climbs west over low Warren Gap. The proposed new PCT, if it is ever built, will descend the (hopefully improved) Big Huckleberry Trail and cross our road near this point. We now curve northeast along this creekside forest route, cross Panther Creek (995-1.3) and climb above it, then recross it (1810-3.8) just beyond Big Huckleberry Creek. After climbing steeply up a ridge above the creek, our Road N605 becomes a dirt road and climbs moderately to a junction with the **Carson-Guler Road (#N60) (2798-3.5).** This we tread east up to **Crest Campground** (not on the real crest), where we meet the **Pacific Crest Trail (#2000) (3490-2.3-19.6).**

Those wishing to do the complete, unabridged Pacific Crest Trail, regardless of cost, should continue east along Highway 14, bridge the lagoon of Wind River (90-1.9), curve around the base of monumental Wind Mountain (1903), pass by Grant Lake (72-3.8), and finally arrive at the Crest Trail Inn (120-0.6), which is a cafe at the west end of a long parking lot. Backpackers who leave their cars in the lot should leave them at this end and walk to the

Cascade Crest trailhead (#2000) (130-0.1) at the east end of the parking lot. From it, you walk east 100 yards up a dirt road and reach the **Cascade Crest Trail,** on which you start north, then switchback steeply up a rocky route on Columbia River basalt which is lined with poison oak. The river views are pleasant diversions as you climb west up the sunny slope to a grassy flat where an old road used to end. Here we angle north and pass a grassy campsite just before the trail begins its steep climb again. After starting up it, we reach in 200 yards a signed, 15-yard spur trail that climbs east to a trickling

Pipe spring (960-0.9). Other animals besides humans use this spring too, including some pretty sizable black bears. You now climb in earnest—particularly if you've met a bear—and begin to wonder if a mountain goat blazed this trail, which has such incredibly *steep* switchbacks that they would allow you almost to pick up, without bending forward, a rattlesnake slithering across the trail in front of you. After much toil, particularly with your heavy pack, you climb "dog tired" to the upper slopes of Dog Mountain (2980) and reach your only reward:

89B

Observation Point (2480-1.6). If the Columbia River gorge is filled with clouds—as it often is—then all your efforts have been in vain. Furthermore, it means that you will soon experience the frustrations of "fog drip." The view on a clear day is far-reaching

Columbia River, view west from Dog Mountain

and particularly spectacular to the west when, in the late afternoon, the Columbia River becomes a sinuous band of reflected sunlight that beams toward us in stark contrast with the dark outline of Wind Mountain below. Our trail now climbs moderately to the southeast ridge, descends it slightly, then commences a winding, sometimes-steep descent along a very overgrown trail down to the usually dry west tributary of Dog Creek (1680-2.2). It's a likely bushwack for accidentally stepping on garter snakes, and we wouldn't rule out the possibility of stepping on a rattler, so be careful. If the day has been overcast, you'll probably be soaking wet—from the thighs down—by the time you reach the *dry* tributary. The clouds that impinge upon these slopes leave part of their moisture behind in the dense crown of this Douglas-fir forest. Gradually, this crown starts "raining" drops onto the luxuriant growth below, which gets so thick at times that you almost have to crawl through it. If the weather is cloudy, you can expect to stay continuously wet, except on the roads and logged-over trail sections, until you reach the saddle north of Big Huckleberry Mountain, about 18 miserable miles more. Our wet, overvegetated trail follows the dry creek bed for a short distance, then climbs northwest to an overgrown,

89B
90

Abandoned road (1930-0.4). We follow this road 20 yards east up to a resumption of the trail, then hike west up trail before contouring a southwest slope and dropping to a trickling creek (1880-0.6). We now climb to a minor saddle and descend steeply to a large trail sign beside an unused

Jeep road (1720-0.7). Now we struggle north up this steep road for 30 yards, to where it turns abruptly west and temporarily eases its gradient before curving north. Then we trudge up to a junction with a level

Power line road (2200-0.7). Grateful for this next easy stretch, we hike briskly west along this road to where it **forks (2160-0.5)** while between two sets of power lines. We take the right fork, which curves north as it descends, and follow it past a merger with a level road from the south. Our route, now quite verdant, contours northeast to a junction with the

Larson Lakes road (1970-0.2), which is the first maintained road we've seen since the CCT trailhead. We start southeast up this road, then follow it northeast up to a bend where a spur road (2050-0.7) descends 0.2 mile west to lower Larson Lake (1920). Just past this junction we reach 100-yard-long, milky blue-green upper Larson Lake, beside which it is possible to camp. You might as well stop here, for it is quite a way to the first good campsite, now that the Little Wind River Camp no longer exists.

Our road now climbs, for no apparent reason, up to the lower slope of imposing Augspurger Mountain (3667) before winding down and heading north-northwest to a junction with a

Power line road (2160-1.1) that descends southwest alongside two power lines. The Cascade Crest Trail starts at this junction, winds through thorny brush under the power lines, then reaches a shady, fairly steep northwest slope—all in 100 yards. You now head northeast across the slope on the severely overgrown trail, curve east to a gully, then reach the border (2240-0.5) of a desolate, clear-cut area. Here your trail contours over to a **logging road (2250-0.1)**, which you follow 200 yards east to where it curves and starts to climb moderately southwest. The trail resumes its eastward contouring course, but makes short, steep detours to avoid downed logs. You finally arc southeast, spot a road across a ravine, then follow the trail to it. This road you descend northeast 130 yards to where it dead-ends (2250-0.7). Locating the trail once more, you follow it southeast to a nearby gully, contour out of this gully, then break, slide, roll or tumble northeast very steeply down the "trail" to the

Little Wind River (1970-0.6). This creeklet looks clear enough to drink from, but if you followed the new trail east up alongside it, you'd reach man-made, stagnant ponds and would have second thoughts. Nevertheless, it is our only permanent water source for the next 7.2 miles, so we purify it and tank up before climbing steeply northwest to the western edge of Section 5, where we finally enter the Gifford Pinchot National Forest (2350-0.6) for good. Leaving the desolation behind us, we enter the "rain" forest again and slog our way along a rambling crest route to a saddle and a crossing of

Road N408 (2300-1.7) just north of its junction with Road N428, which descends to Carson. Now on a better trail, we climb west up a ridge, then north to a crossing of Road N408D (2700-0.9) that is only 20 yards east of Road N408. Our trail starts up an open slope, then quickly enters forest and climbs moderately-to-steeply up a ridge to the cliff tops of Summit 3603 (1.2), where we get a view north of the lodgepole-forested Big Lava Bed, about 5000 years old, which is a lava flow that descended from its source at an obvious cinder cone (4100) six miles north of us. Hiking along the northwest-trending crest, we reach a saddle (3420-0.8), then switchback steeply up to the concrete foundation blocks that remain to mark the site of the **Grassy Knoll Lookout (3649-0.3),** now under the watchful eye of a lurking coyote. (For the southbound traveler trying to find the trail down, start at these blocks and head 35 yards northeast to the south side of an obvious row of trees, by which you'll find the

Fern and thimbleberry

trail.) Bearing west-northwest, we resume our traumatic adventure along a windswept ridge before entering forest again and climbing to a small but good trailside campsite just above the trickling

Cold Spring (3870-1.7). Fill your canteens here, for your next *good* water will be at Blue Lake, 15.4 miles farther. Leaving the campsite, we make a short initial climb, then descend steadily along a wet, forested southwest slope before making another short climb to an adequate campsite (3760-0.9) immediately east of a trickling creek. Here, rather than logically climbing around the south ridge of Big Huckleberry Mountain (4202), our trail climbs northwest steeply up to the ridge, contours west, and then climbs 20 feet directly up the slope to a junction with the

Big Huckleberry Trail (#186) (4000-0.6). The proposed new Pacific Crest Trail is slated to come up this trail, but if it is ever built, we hope that it will join our Cascade Crest Trail at a saddle one mile north of the summit, thereby sparing us a steep ascent or descent. We turn right (northeast) and climb steeply for 130 yards up to a junction with the

Big Huckleberry Mountain summit trail (4070-0.1), which climbs steeply east 200 yards to the summit. Our path eases off, curves northward and descends a "fog drip" ridge route, which is steep at times, to a saddle (3730-1.3), where we leave the wet wildflowers—but not our wet pants—behind and descend a peaceful forest slope to a trickling creek (3550-0.3). From it we contour northward through a shady forest of Douglas-fir, western hemlock and western white pine, reach a saddle (3580-0.9), and then descend steeply north toward Road N500, coming within 100 yards of it (3280-0.4) before turning northeast. Contouring counterclockwise around Summit 4170, we follow the edge of the Big Lava Bed, cross one of its western overflow channels—which reveals the detailed intricacies of the flow—and then contour around another summit and cross another channel to the back of the

Crest Campground (3490-3.5), which is on the south side of the Carson-Guler Road (#N60). Ascending this road from the southwest is our "all-weather" route. The campground has a horse corral but no water, so we pick our packs off the tables, put them on our backs and trudge north up the signed Pacific Crest Trail. This moderate ascent up a fern-decked path is really quite nice if you aren't running short of water. We climb to a flat and reach a duck pond (4020-1.9), which is no more than an oversized mud puddle after your arrival frightens the ducks away. Nevertheless, it boasts the name *Sheep Lake*. After climbing northwest through a more open forest, we reach another 35-yard-wide puddle signed

91
92

Green Lake (4250-1.1), which gets as deep as a foot in early summer and serves as a vital water supply. When one of the authors (Schaffer) visited this "lake" in late August 1973, it had just been converted into an oversized latrine by an unscrupulous packer and his family who let their eight horses defecate and stomp around in it. Having followed in his tracks for several days, I observed that he always let his horses do this, presumably after the family first got its share of water. I wish I could say that he was the only packer I encountered who had such disgusting trail manners, but in fact, *every* packer that I saw camped near water disregarded the 200-foot Forest Service shoreline limit and allowed his animals to graze and defecate right up to the water. Since you'll probably find Green Lake too polluted to suit your standards, prepare for a dry march and start northwest past a meadow, then reach a junction with the

Shortcut Trail (#171A) (4240-0.4), which strikes west-northwest half a mile to a large, stagnant pond and to the Racetrack, which supposedly was used by Indian horsemen. We hike north-northwest through a forest, then climb several long switchbacks up the sunny south slope of Berry Mountain before reaching its crest. The abandoned Cascade Crest Trail, on the shady slopes way below us, led thirsty hikers past a spring. Our trail provides us with excellent views of Mt. St. Helens (9677) to the northwest, Mt. Adams (12,276) to the northeast and Mt. Hood (11,235) to the south. Upon reaching the north end of linear Berry Mountain, we descend short switchbacks to a saddle (4730-2.9), follow a rambling path down past the seasonal outlet creek of Lake Sebago (4640-0.9), and come to an overlook of a 100-yard-wide stagnant pond beyond which we finally reach the welcome, clear waters of

Blue Lake (4630-0.2), nestled at the foot of Gifford Peak (5368). Here, at the lake's southeast end, we find a junction with the Tombstone Lake trail (the old CCT), which winds 0.2 mile south to that lake. At Blue Lake there is a very good campsite on its south peninsula as well as one on its northeast shore. As our trail climbs northwest above the lake's north shore, we can easily see how this deep lake got its name. A few minutes later, we pass a good campsite at shallow, circular Lake Sahalee Tyee (4680-0.3), then climb a creekside trail up to a junction with the

Thomas Lake Trail (#111) (4800-0.3), which curves northwest through lake-bound Indian Heaven. We hike north through a pond-dotted flat that is mosquito heaven before midsummer, then cross a meadow and pass more ponds before curving north-east around East Crater (5250), beyond which we reach the **East**

East Crater, view south

Crater Trail (#48) (4730-1.4) at the west end of Junction Lake (4730). This trail goes east to a good lakeshore campsite, then veers southeast. We cross the lake's outlet and arrive at a junction with the

Lemei Lake Trail (#33A) (4730-0.1), which climbs east. After walking north past a seasonal pond, we make a descent to an open field in Indian Heaven, where a faint trail (4630-0.5) departs southwest from our post-lined route and bends north to another field. In times past, Indians picked huckleberries and hunted deer here. Nowadays the berries and deer thrive but the Indians have largely disappeared, and you can consider yourself lucky if a solitary bear, coyote or mountain lion crosses your tracks. The avian population, however, seems not to notice the change, and you can hear or see the hairy woodpecker, the red-shafted flicker, the gray jay, and of course the omnipresent Oregon junco. After crossing the three-yard-wide Lemei Lake creek bed, which has banks of vesicular basalt, we leave heaven behind as we progress north past shallow Acker Lake and immediately come to a fork where the

Indian Heaven Trail (#33) (4630-0.6) veers right (northeast) steeply up to the southeast shore of Bear Lake (4730). Our trail veers left and switchbacks north up to a good trailside campsite at the northwest corner of the lake. The best campsite, however, is out of your way on the southeast peninsula. A few yards farther, we reach the **Elk Lake spur trail (4740-0.3)**, which descends west-northwest 250 yards to more secluded but less inviting Elk Lake (4685). After filling our water bottles at beautiful Bear Lake, we quickly pass two stagnant ponds, then spy an unmarked spur trail (4850-0.5) that climbs a few yards before descending southeast 90 yards to a nice campsite by unseen Deer Lake (4830). Now we start north, get a southeastward glimpse of this lake, and climb north, passing small ponds before we reach a fork where the

93

Lone Butte Trail (#29) (4980-1.2) splits northwest down toward Placid Lake while our trail continues north. After climbing and then descending a northwest spur of Bird Mountain (5706), the PCT is met by a 0.3-mile spur trail (5010-0.4) that ascends northeast from the Lone Butte Trail. Nearby roaring of lumber trucks and crashing of falling trees on the west slopes below remind us that we are hiking through a wilderness *corridor* rather than through a wilderness area. After climbing eastward, we reach an adequate campsite at the west end of a semiclear pond, from where the **Wood Lake trail (5075-0.3)** descends half a mile toward that lake and the noise of progress. Not much farther toward Canada, we reach a junction with the

Cultus Creek Trail (#108) (5140-0.2), which climbs northeast to Saddle 5237 before descending to large Cultus Creek Campground along Road 123. We now contour around a low summit, descend a ridge to a forested saddle, then switchback up the south ridge of Sawtooth Mountain, where we curve around to its west slope and stop at a small spur (5160-2.0) that projects a few yards west of the trail. Here we get an excellent view of Mt. St. Helens, to the west-northwest, and if we climb third class up past dwarf junipers to the knife-edge crest of Sawtooth Mountain (5353), we get an exhilarating view down its east cliff as well as an unobstructed view of Mt. Adams. If you are not a climbing freak, you can still see that volcano, for it is plainly visible as our trail switchbacks north down the ridge before curving northeast to a fork where an unsigned spur trail (4440-1.5) angles right and descends toward Surprise Lakes. We keep left and weave down the ridge to the Sawtooth Huckleberry Field, where we parallel a spur road 60 yards northeast to a large, brown *Pacific Crest Trail No. 2000* sign at a crossing of

Road 123 (4260-0.7). We'll see more of these readily visible signs as we progress north. The large berry field at this flat was being harvested by Indians when George B. McClellan's exploration party came through in 1854. Needless to say, it had probably been harvested for countless generations. Roads were built up to it around the turn of the century, and today the Indians have exclusive rights only to the berries *east* of the road. Frankly, we were hard-pressed to find many bushes on that side, and wondered whether some midnight raiding party of pioneers had transplanted some of the bushes to the west side.

Our trail now descends gently east-northeast, enters forest, and passes above two outhouses of the little developed Surprise Lakes Campground. Continuing northeast on the 1972 Surprise-Steamboat lakes section of the PCT, we descend to a saddle (4070-1.4), then climb northwest up this well-graded trail and round the west slopes of East Twin Butte (4690). We reach a platform between the two Twin Buttes, which are obvious cinder cones, descend northwest below unseen, dumpy Saddle Campground, switchback northeast, and descend to a crossing of a trickling creek immediately before reaching

Road N819 (3915-2.5) at a junction 35 yards southeast of the west-trending Little Mosquito Lake road. Our trail bears northeast from Road N819 and quickly reaches the wide, refreshing outlet creek from Big Mosquito Lake (3892). The PCT leaves the creek and climbs gently east along the upper margin of a sheep-inhabited clearing, then rounds a spur and shortly crosses a dirt road (4090-2.5) that snakes northwest 130 yards up to Road 123. We continue northeast and descend to a small gully where the

Steamboat Lake spur trail (3980-0.4) climbs north moderately 0.2 mile up to that lake (4022), from which you can then follow an east shoreline road northward. By the time you've reached the lake's northeast corner, this road deteriorates to a log-strewn trail. Then you can take a steep trail northeast up to Road 123 and small, waterless Steamboat Lake campground (4100-0.7). At the northeast edge of the camp, the old CCT descends to a shallow, unnamed lake and then rejoins the PCT (3970-0.5-1.2) at a bend. From the Steamboat Lake spur-trail junction, the PCT curves counterclockwise from the gully and makes a gentle descent to an outlet creek 70 yards downstream from an unseen, unnamed lake, then climbs gently northward to a saddle, where it meets the blocked-off, old **CCT (3970-0.8)**, which climbs west to Steamboat Lake campground. Here our trail turns east and starts on the old, undulating, weaving path through quiet forest down to a junction with

Road N88 (3470-1.2). The swath this road cuts through this forest is so oriented that we have an open view directly at Mt. Adams. Our trail recommences at a large sign 50 yards northeast up this road, and on it we top a minor ridge before descending to a bridge over three-yard-wide Trout Lake Creek (3310-0.4). North of the trail at a point 25 yards east of this creek, we see a very good campsite, and 100 yards later we cross the smaller Grand Meadows Creek. Our trail now ascends eastward, steeply at times, but momentarily descends to a tributary before making a final, stiff climb up to **Road N85 (4110-1.4).** Continuing east up the slope, we reach the crest (4570-0.6), then begin a generally descending route north-northeast along the ridge down to a trailhead at

95
96
97

Road N85 (3854-2.8). We walk east 50 yards to this road's junction with north-trending **Road N84** and a trailhead for the Mt. Adams Wilderness. Our trail drops to a two-yard-wide creek just east of Road N84, then climbs north around the slopes of a low summit to a crossing of east-trending **Road 84M (4020-0.9).** After hiking for a few minutes north, we reach a small, good campsite near a bridge (4110-0.3) over a permanent creek. Continuing up an increasingly steep trail that turns east and enters the Mt. Adams Wilderness, we climb the slopes earnestly to a junction with the **Stagman Ridge Trail (#12) (5700-3.6),** which starts a gentle descent southward. Pressing onward, we climb north, then east up to a timberline meadow and meet the

Round the Mountain Trail (#9) (5900-0.7), which starts on a southeast traverse and continues for 6.5 miles to Timberline Camp at the end of Road 81. The easiest and most popular route to the summit of Mt. Adams (12,276) starts there and climbs up the south ridge. You should have no trouble attaining the summit in good weather, for this is the route that mule trains used in the 1930s. Back then, a sulfur claim had been staked out on the summit, but it didn't pay off. This massive andesitic stratovolcano, like the others we've seen, should still be considered active. It probably erupted at least once in the last century, and in May 1921 its near-surface magma generated enough heat to initiate a large snow slide that eradicated the forest on the slope below it.

On the high slopes east of our junction with Trail 9, we can see the White Salmon Glacier. The Pacific Crest Trail climbs northwest around a ridge that separates this glacier from the Pinnacle Glacier, immediately north of it. Our northward, round-the-mountain route is quite a contrast with that of Mt. Hood: it stays at a relatively constant elevation, and where it climbs or descends, it usually does so on a gentle gradient. To the north and northwest, we can often see Goat Rocks and Mt. Rainier. After traversing to a saddle (5950-3.2) just east of Burnt Rock, our trail descends toward 70-yard-wide, 5-foot-deep Sheep Lake (5768-0.3), which is 40 yards northwest of the trail, then reaches milky, jump-across Riley Creek (5770-0.2). Next on our menu, Mutton Creek (5900-1.3) is approached, and we follow it up beside a geologically recent, rather barren lava flow over which we eventually diagonal quite a distance up. Our route then bounds from one wash to the next, and crosses milky Lewis River (6060-1.3) and then the silty tributaries of West Fork Adams Creek before it curves north-northwest to a junction with the

Divide Camp Trail (#112) (6020-0.3), which descends northwest toward Road 101. Directly upslope from us is the overpowering, steeply descending Adams Glacier, which appears to be a gigantic frozen waterfall rather than an advancing snowfield. Along our journey north, our glances back toward this massive peak will always single out this prominent feature. We head northeast across a 330-yard swath of bouldery glacier outwash sediments, then jump across silty Middle Fork Adams Creek. After climbing its bank, our route contours northeast past a 70-yard-wide pond (6110), and in a few minutes we arrive at a junction with the

Killen Creek Trail (#113) (6084-1.4), which starts beside a seasonal creek as it descends northwest toward Road 101. We contour onward, descend to a large flat through which flows clear Killen Creek, then cross this creek as it reaches a brink and cascades merrily down 30 feet to a small meadow and a beautiful campsite (5880-1.0) nestled under a cluster of subalpine firs. As we are about to head north away from the mountain, we reflect

97
98

Right: Mt. Adams and Adams Glacier

upon another characteristic of this crescentic trail which distinguishes it from its counterpart on Mt. Hood: this trail stays on the mountain's lower slopes, and we never feel like we've set foot on the mountain itself—the upper slopes don't begin until a "distant" 2000 feet above us. In this respect, the trail resembles those around Mt. Jefferson and the Three Sisters. A short distance from the campsite, our trail intersects the

Highline Trail (#114) (5900-0.1), upon which you may find *footprints* leading east toward the Yakima Indian Reservation. Just north beyond this intersection we spy a 70-yard pond a hundred yards northwest of us. It is better to descend 80 feet down the slope to this pond than to continue onward to a second, readily accessible one (5772-0.4) that receives too much impact from packers. The PCT now becomes a rambling, evenly graded pathway that descends north-northeast into a mountain-hemlock forest whose monotony is broken by an intersection with an

Unsigned trail (5231-2.1), which starts east-northeast toward a junction two miles later with the Highline Trail. Meeting no traffic other than perhaps chickadees or juncos, we continue northward and reach a sturdy bridge across the 5-yard-wide Muddy Fork (4770-1.7), by which we find a small campsite. Curving northwest, our path soon reaches and then parallels an alder-and-willow-lined silty creek westward to a very good campsite (4600-0.6) immediately before a log crossing of the creek. A short distance farther we round the nose of a recent lava flow and head north to the vibrant, crystal-clear waters gushing from a trailside spring (4520-0.3) at the foot of the flow. Since its water is among the best you'll find along the *entire* PCT, you might as well rest and enjoy it. A water ouzel may be camped here; you can camp at a spot 25 yards up a short trail south-southeast from the spring. Leaving it and the tranquil, little-used Mt. Adams Wilderness behind, we follow the 40-foot-high edge of the flow a short way, then climb gently through a predominantly lodgepole forest to a trailhead parking lot a few yards north of paved

Road 1011 (4750-1.6). From the lot we walk northeast 50 yards along an old jeep road, then veer north-northeast along a trail that ascends gently toward Potato Hill (5387). Although motorized vehicles are specifically barred from the PCT, they or their tracks are likely to be encountered along this rather unscenic stretch through second-growth forest. We quickly reach the jeep road again and follow its northwest-curving path around Potato Hill, then take this dusty road north-northwest past huckleberries and mountain ash to a junction with

Road 101D (4490-2.0). By walking 0.3 mile west on it, you'll

98

99

reach Midway Guard Station beside Road 101 and Midway Creek. As our trail curves northwest above Road 101D, we reach closed **Road 101E (4520-0.1)**, which descends west-southwest 0.1 mile to Road 101D. We'll walk across no more roads until near U.S. Highway 12 at White Pass, 42 miles distant. Our trail starts west-northwest up toward Midway Creek, crosses it (4690-1.5), then climbs up through alternating forested and cleared land toward the crest. As the gradient eases off, we enter forest for good and follow a winding path that takes us past eight stagnant ponds. You could have an adequate campsite at any of them if you're willing to purify the water. After leaving the last pond (5070-2.8), on our left (west), we hike around the west slope of a knoll, descend gently to the west side of a broad saddle, then climb moderately to a switchback (5220-1.6) beneath Summit 5632. Now we climb east to a saddle (5450-0.7), curve northeast and enter the Goat Rocks Wilderness. Two small ponds on the left are passed as we ascend toward a prominent, open

Ridge crest (5600-0.8) that stands directly south of Walupt Lake (3926). North of us we see the glistening summit of Old Snowy Mountain (7930), in the heart of the Goat Rocks country, over whose slopes we must soon climb. Our route now winds southeastward down auxiliary ridges and enters a forest of mountain hemlock, western white and lodgepole pines, and Alaska yellow cedar. As the trail begins to level off, it crosses a trickling creek that you shouldn't overlook, for it contains the best water you'll taste for miles. After descending gently eastward, we pass a 50-yard pond, then immediately arrive at a shallow lake (5058-1.8) on a forested, flat saddle just southeast of Coleman Weedpatch. Leaving a campsite at this lake, we tread an easy path northeast through a dense mountain-hemlock forest across the lower slopes of Lakeview Mountain (6660). As we veer east, our forest transforms into an open stand of lodgepoles, and we finally curve southeast to a junction with the

Walupt Lake Trail (#101) (4960-2.9), which descends gently north. After hiking southeast for a few minutes, we arc east to a large, shallow pond (4960-0.2) where one could make a fair campsite. The countryside now is quite open, and the topography stretches out below us as we hike the trail up the west slope of a long, north-trending ridge. Fireweed, yarrow, lupine and pearly everlasting proliferate along the trailside before we reach the shady confines of a coniferous forest. We now contour for several miles before reaching the diminutive headwaters of Walupt Creek (5520-4.0). If there were enough level ground here, a primitive campsite by the stream would be fine. Instead, it is better to continue southwest up toward a saddle where you'll

99
100A
100B
101A

see shallow, clear 130-yard-long Sheep Lake (5710), which has good but open campsites. Just north of it, we meet a junction with the

Nannie Ridge Trail (#98) (5770-0.6), which descends about six miles to mile-long Walupt Lake. Our route north through the Goat Rocks country will take us on ridges high above glaciated canyons. Walupt Creek canyon was the first major one we've seen in this wilderness, and the ones north of it are even more spectacular. If you look northwest toward the saddle on the next ridge, you can spot the PCT. From our junction we traverse north on a new trail segment and come to a campsite among mountain hemlock and heather at the headwaters of Nannie Creek (5840-1.5). This creek is located below a small but formidable-looking volcanic knob. We now make a descent westward before climbing a stiff trail up to a saddle (6080-1.0). Rather than contour over toward Cispus Pass, our trail descends steeply north for a 300-foot drop, climbs moderately northwest, then makes another steep descent and a steep ascent before arriving at a junction with the abandoned

Cispus Pass Trail (6340-1.6). This trail climbs 0.2 mile to Cispus Pass (6460) then continues south around the previously mentioned volcanic knob and arrives at a saddle above Nannie Creek. The head-on view down the deep, glaciated Klickitat River canyon as seen from Cispus Pass is certainly worth the 0.2-mile effort up to it, but the authors feel that you should not take the remainder of this obvious trail through the Yakima Indian Reservation. We certainly didn't, for we felt that Indian lands have already been too overrun by ''Americans.'' Our timberline trail passes by dwarfed specimens of mountain hemlock and subalpine fir as it descends toward the headwaters of the Cispus River. The basin is much smaller than it first appears, and we quickly reach an open campsite beside the easternmost tributary (6140-0.5). The scale of the canyon is put in true perspective when backpackers hike past miniature conifers that are now seen as only 30 feet high instead of as 80, as we originally presupposed. After contouring west, we jump across the base of a splashing, 20-foot-high waterfall, then continue a winding contour over toward a southwest spur, which we climb up and arrive at a junction with unsigned

Trail 86 (6120-2.0). This trail switchbacks about one mile down to Trail 96 and closed Snowgrass Flat, which is being trodden to death because of its accessibility to both hikers and packers. To alleviate the pressure, the Gifford Pinchot National Forest Service has built Bypass Camp (5560) a half mile south of this flat, and Alpine Camp (5940) a quarter mile northwest of it. We didn't

101A
101B

see any *No Camping* signs along the actual PCT route when we surveyed it in 1973, but it is possible that such postings may appear in the future. Upper Snowgrass Flat certainly has the right proportions of rock, snow, trees, wildflowers and scenery to make it one of the most beautiful spots along the entire PCT. In 300 yards we reach a spur trail that cuts across to Trail 86, then pass several very good campsites above the trail and gushing springs below it shortly before coming to a junction with the

Snowgrass Trail (#96) (6640-0.8), the shortest route into the Goat Rocks area, which descends about a mile from Alpine Camp. Forty yards from this junction is 40-foot-high "Split Rock," which broke apart eons ago, since full-sized conifers now grow in the gap between the two halves. This rock is excellent for bouldering—as volcanic rocks go—and it has dozens of routes ranging from moderate to extemely difficult. A top-rope belay is desirable for the strenuous overhanging routes. Our route, considerably easier, goes north up a ducked alpine trail that passes a few specimens of pasqueflowers and Rainier gentians. A half mile beyond our junction, we tread across rocks with deep striations, convincing fingerprints of past glaciers. Climbing up to the low west ridge of Old Snowy Mountain, we encounter the stone-walled

101B
102

Dana May Yelverton Shelter (7040-0.9), 12 feet square, which provides plenty of protection from the frequent summer storms. The six-inch-high junipers here attest to the severity of this environment. Above us lies the realm of rock and ice—the habitat of the alpine mountaineer. After a gentle 100-yard climb north, we reach a trailside, two-foot-high windbreak assembled from loose stones at the edge of a permanent snowfield. Upslope 35 yards from this windbreak is a larger, three-foot-high one. Neither gives you much protection if you are caught in a storm, but both shield you from the misty, howling winds that you might encounter at night. Crossing the snowfield takes us to the brink of the severely glaciated, 3000-foot-deep Upper Lake Creek canyon, which will become even more impressive as our northbound trail provides us with even better views down and across it. To the northwest we see perpetually frozen Goat Lake (6450) nestled in a classic glacial cirque at the southeast end of the Johnson Peak ridge. At the brink, most hikers contour northeast across the gentle upper slopes of the Packwood Glacier. Who could blame them, for the bypassed trail segment is partly snowbound for most of the summer. If, however, you do decide to follow the dozen or so short switchbacks east up to the

North shoulder (7620-0.8) of Old Snowy Mountain (7930), your efforts will be amply rewarded. Not only have you reached the highest Pacific Crest Trail point in all of Washington and Oregon, but you have an almost full-circle panorama of the Goat Rocks country. Looking above the canyons to the northwest, you see the monarch of the Cascade Range—the mighty Mt. Rainier (14,410)—ruling above all the other stratovolcanoes. To the south rises Mt. Adams (12,276), the crown prince and second highest peak in the range. Off to its west lies the youthful princess, Mt. St. Helens (9677). The Multnomah Indians had a different interpretation. They said a feud developed between Klickitat (Mt. Adams) and Wyeast (Mt. Hood) over the beautiful Squaw Mountain (Mt. St. Helens), who had just moved into the neighborhood. She loved Wyeast, but Klickitat triumphed in a fight, so she had to reside in Klickitat's domain. She refused to bed down with him, however, and after a while, as would be expected, his flames of love for her died, and both volcanoes became dormant.

A steep descent north along a narrow ridge takes us to a saddle (6850-0.6) where those who contoured the glacier join us. This Egg Butte section of the PCT, constructed with heroic efforts in 1953-54, now continues along the jagged ridge, contours around its "teeth" and provides us with alpine views across the sparkling McCall Glacier toward Tieton Peak (7768), due east of Old Snowy. We reach a small saddle, from which the trail makes a precarious descent across a steep slope as it bypasses Summit 7210. You can expect this narrow footpath to be snowbound and hazardous through most of July. Crampons may be required,

Old Snowy Mountain and McCall Glacier

Mt. Rainier, Packwood Saddle and Elk Pass

particularly in early-summer descents. Reaching the ridge again, we follow it down to

Elk Pass (6680-1.1). Here the windswept whitebark pines stand chest-high at most, and the junipers creep but inches above the frost-wedged rocks. Despite its foreboding appearance, the pass does have animal life. Excluding invertebrates, the most common wild animals seen are chipmunks and ground squirrels. A sparrow hawk may dive swiftly past you, and if you're lucky, you might even have a weasel dart across your path. As for the mountain goats—well, there's not much chance that you'll see any as long as you adhere to this popular trail. The goats have good reason to fear man. From this pass, the faint

Coyote Trail (#79) starts steeply downslope before relaxing its gradient northwest toward Packwood Saddle. The tremendous erosional power of glaciers is attested to by the spectacular Upper Lake Creek canyon below us. The retreating ice has left bare the steep, massive cliffs of Johnson Peak (7487), in which we can identify numerous, level layers of Eocene-Oligocene andesitic lava flows. In places these are offset by what appear to be postflow intrusions by vertical dikes. Leaving the rockbound pass, we contour the east slope of Peak 6768, then descend its northeast ridge to

102

Alpine campsites (6320-0.5) just north of the Elk Pass snowfield. If you're heading south, these are the last good campsites you'll see until south of Old Snowy. Our trail descends east-southeast along the foot of the Elk Pass snowfield, crosses its runoff creek and several others, passes by glacially striated bedrock, and then makes short switchbacks down to a small pond at the foot of another snowfield. By late afternoon the snowfields in this basin are melting at a good rate, as evidenced by the roar of the cascade to the west. From the pond we now climb steeply 200 yards to a saddle (5820-0.8). Descending east-southeast from the saddle on a trail that is just as steep as the one we've climbed, we get our last good views south of the McCall Glacier below Goat Rocks, and then enter a forest on our way down to wet, meadowy

McCall Basin (5190-0.8). Very good campsites can be found here, but often this bench is as thick with campers as it is with mosquitoes. By going a few hundred yards southeast across the bench, you can at least find peace from the other campers. Leaving the basin, our trail curves north and winds over an east slope of Peak 5755 to a saddle on which lies Lutz Lake (5100-0.9), an oversized, stagnant puddle. Beyond it we descend north around the west slope of Peak 5493 to

Tieton Pass (4750-0.8). Here, by a dry campsite with springs downslope, the **Clear Fork Trail (#61)** starts a moderate descent west-northwest on its route north toward U.S. Highway 12. The **North Fork Tieton Trail (#1118),** which at 4.6 miles is the shortest trail approach to this pass, descends east before curving northeast down to the North Fork Tieton Road (#134) at a trailhead near Scatter Creek. Our trail starts a gentle descent northwest, then gradually makes a winding route north past two stagnant ponds just before crossing east over the divide (4930-1.4) and rounding Peak 5472. We now continue our viewless path east until we climb the southeast spur of Peak 6427 and then reach a junction with the

Shoe Lake Trail (#1117) (5750-2.1), which ascends from the southeast. From this merger we climb north to an open ridge, from where we can look down on clear, cool, shimmering Shoe Lake (6130). Tucked under the mountain hemlocks on its south peninsula is an excellent campsite. The only drawback to this site is that it is too beautiful—it attracted the wrong sort of packers, and the lake's shallow waters got littered with trash. Consequently, the Snoqualmie National Forest Service has closed this lake to overnight camping. We pass by a number of trails leading down to this lake, then switchback steeply north up to a

Saddle (6620-1.3). Mt. Rainier pokes its head above Hogback Ridge and Mt. Adams just manages to lift its crown above Goat Rocks. The volcanic flows around us here superficially resemble sedimentary rocks, for they have broken along close, evenly spaced horizontal joints to give the illusion of alternating, stepped beds of sandstone and shale. We make one switchback, descend a well-graded trail past a thumb above us and Miriam Lake below, then reach the stepped slope of Hogback Mountain (6789). As we descend its northeast ridge, we obtain views of Mt. Rainier, whose slopes we should set foot upon in a few days' time. Entering forest once again, we cross a vaguely defined saddle, then climb gently to a junction with the

White Pass Chair Lift spur trail (5830-2.6). Many hikers truck 0.4 mile north up it, then take the lift down to the White Pass ski lodge (4480), which houses the Continental Cafe, open year-round. From it they can walk east 170 yards past the White Pass Village, with its Nor'wester Restaurant, then in 70 yards reach the Cracker Barrel Grocery and Post Office at an Exxon Station. Minimal supplies are available here, but you can wash your clothes and make a phone call home. *Your next supplies will be at Snoqualmie Pass, a distant 98 miles away.* A half-mile walk northeast on U.S. Highway 12 takes you to a spur road that heads northwest to the trailhead.

From the spur-trail junction, the PCT makes a winding descent northeastward to a junction with the little-used **Hogback Trail (#1144) (5400-1.1),** which starts on a gentle descent east before curving north. Our trail curves northwest, passes a small, stagnant pond, then reaches green, 100-yard-long Ginnette Lake (5400-0.2), by which there is a small, poor campsite. We now start north, get a glimpse of the chair-lift jeep road northwest of us, and then switchback down to a trailhead 50 yards south of

U.S. Highway 12 (old State Highway 14) (4400-2.1). A posted sign warns the southbound hiker that he cannot camp closer than 100 feet from most lakeshores, and if he has horses, they must be kept at least 200 feet away—a wise policy for this overused area. We walk north 50 yards on a dirt road that takes us past Douglas-fir, western hemlock, Alaska yellow cedar, western white pine and grand fir before we reach the highway. After walking 30 yards southwest on it, we turn right on a spur road and follow it northwest to Leech Lake (4412) and an obvious

Trailhead (4420-0.3) and parking lot above the road where it curves west to White Pass Campground, which is immediately west between the road and the lake. Our well-graded, comfortably humus-padded trail switchbacks easily up a gently slope forested with mature western hemlock, Engelmann spruce and giant western redcedar. PCT emblems and blazes adequately mark the route when snow is shallow. Leveling, the trail leaves the highway sounds behind, and approaches an unsigned junction (4720-0.7) with a trail that descends east-southeast. The

103
104

well-rounded hills traversed here are built of easily weathered Pliocene-Pleistocene volcanic material. Traversing northwest, we reach a junction with the **Dark Meadows Trail (#1107) (4780-0.5)** and then climb west to Deer Lake's outflow creek (4920-0.4), which is easily crossed even during spring runoff. In late summer all our water for the next 9.6 miles will come from lakes, tarns and mudholes, so it is worthwhile to fill canteens here. White glacier lilies and vanilla leaf decorate the forest floor in early summer as we approach the large, marshy meadow near Deer Lake. The trail skirts the east fringe of the triangular clearing, heading roughly south toward the apex at **Deer Lake (5206-0.5)**. A hitching rack and a toilet mark this established and pleasant, though well-used, campsite. Deer Lake is a favorite with fishermen, and deer haunt the meadow near dawn and dusk. Doubling back very sharply, we follow the west edge of the meadow north toward Sand Lake. The next 200 yards are especially unpleasant in early season, as backpackers have been known to almost completely disappear in the seemingly bottomless muck (at least up to their ankles). Such hazards inevitably plague early-summer hikers, while those passing through a few weeks later suffer from unquenched thirst . . . *chacun à son goût!* When our trail arrives at

104   **Sand Lake (5295-0.6),** it follows the west shore. During the season of snowmelt and spring rains, the submerged path goes through the west edge of the lake. At this time we may either follow the trail "come hell or high water," or stay just far enough west of the trail to avoid the water. A short distance along the PCT, we meet the Sand Lake Trail (#60) (5295-0.1), which heads west 100 yards to the Sand Lake Shelter (functional but abused) and beyond to Clear Fork Cowlitz River. Skirting the lake for another 250 yards, we pass a few inviting tent sites, then re-enter typical forest at the north tip of the lake. Strolling among unmapped lakes and tarns through a picturesque preview-in-miniature of the Cowlitz Pass flatlands, we appreciate deer, finches and chipmunks, and depreciate the prevalent mosquitoes. Soon the

Cortright Trail (#57) (5610-1.4) forks north 35 yards beyond an infant gully with an incipient trail. Turning east, we glimpse Goat Rocks in the south, then contour north across a clear area with impressive views of Cramer Mountain (5992) and Spiral Butte (5920). These wooded hummocks demonstrate the easy weatherability of the Pliocene-Pleistocene andesitic bedrock. Uphill from our trail is a small outcrop if it, readily accessible to interested hikers. Soon another signed **Cortright Trail junction (5520-0.6)** appears. This trail is a cutoff for southbound PCT hikers who wish to exit via the Cortright Trail. Northward we immediately cross the divide near two serene alpine tarns bordered by corn lily, glacier lily, lupine and bistort. Snow may linger in the moderately steep north-facing couloir that our trail descends, but it presents no safety hazards—just a short glissade. However, care may be needed to stay on the snow-covered trail. As the grade lessens, we reach an unmarked junction with a mapped trail (5300-0.4) which heads southwest to a campsite near the headwaters of a tributary of Summit Creek. We view Mt. Rainier (14,410), fragmented by the thick forest, as our trail completes its descent to

Buesch Lake (5081-0.5), where there is a deviation from the older PCT. The newer route, part of the Cascade Crest Trail (#2034), parallels the west and north shores of Buesch Lake, crossing its outflow creek before entering the flat Cowlitz Pass region of lakes, tarns, mud puddles and swamps. Campsites are numerous in this 4.6-mile stretch of trail, but water is stagnant except in June and early July. Purification is strongly advised. Canadian elk, unperturbed by the plentiful mosquitoes, can be spotted, and paintbrush, lupine and huckleberries add color to the grassy meadows. Following Trail 2034, we soon reach a fork that starts south to **Dumbbell Lake (5130-0.7).** This lake, a half mile off the PCT, is one of the largest lakes in this area, and a favorite for camping and fishing. Passing a popular campsite at small but pretty Benchmark Lake, we approach two liberally signed trail junctions. The **Shell Rock Trail (#1142) (5200-1.0)** descends southeast to the White Pass Highway. Just beyond this junction, the

Cowlitz Trail (#44) (5191-0.1) frames Mt. Rainier in its trail cut. A bench mark implanted in a boulder at this junction gives Benchmark Lake, immediately south of the first junction, its name. We follow the sometimes rocky, sometimes muddy trail as it meanders over and around minor hummocks and among (or through) uncountable ponds. Eventually we reach the **Twin Sisters Lakes Trail (#980) (4880-2.5),** which forks east-northeast to Twin Sisters Lakes, on the edge of a Tertiary granitic instrusive body. Prospectors have left evidence here of their hopes of finding ore in this contact region. Soon we pass a meadow campsite by an early-season creek that has an impressively eroded vesicular volcanic bed, and take leave of this land of stagnant waters. Reaching a junction with the **Jug Lake Trail (#43) (4670-1.1),** which ascends southwest to Fryingpan Lake (4814), our rutted trail continues to an established campsite, a reliable creek (4650-0.1). The PCT fords this creek, which you may prefer to cross via logs upstream. Heading north through a forest of mature hemlock interrupted by bright but marshy meadows, we make a leisurely descent toward Fish Lake. We cross the infant Bumping River on convenient logs 20 yards before reaching the

Bumping Lake Trail (#971) (4080-1.5). Just west of here is the Fish Lake area, which is popular with fishermen and hunters as well as hikers, and boasts many campsites. Yellow monkey flower, red columbine, Devil's club, bistort, and dwarf bramble are among the botanical wonders of this moist locale. Our trail continues levelly along the north shore of Fish Lake to a poorly signed junction with the

Cannon Creek Trail (Carlton Creek Trail) (#22) (4120-0.4). Here we leave the lake and start the 1200-foot climb to a bench on a shoulder of Crag Mountain (6208). Thirteen switchbacks bring us to a welcome creek—when it has water. With half the elevation gain behind us we deserve the reward of a cool draught. In late season there is no guarantee of trailside water until Anderson Lake, about 8 miles distant, so we check that our canteens are full and gear down for the remaining 11 switchbacks. Until midseason there should be water in the small creek we follow for the last couple hundred yards to the signed Crag Lake turnoff (5320-2.0). Pleasant camp spots on this sheltered bench are inviting and have fairly convenient water most of the hiking season. If, in August or September, the stream runs dry, Crag Lake (5000), 0.5 mile east beyond a low ridge, and a closer, smaller lake offer congenial tent sites. Turning west, the PCT climbs yet a little more along a bench on Crag Mountain. Some trails heading north up the ridge peter out before reaching their probable goal: the PCT on the other side of the crest. It seems that not everyone appreciates the apparent detour to the Laughingwater Trail. However, in an effort to minimize human impact on the wilderness, we observe proper trail etiquette and follow the beaten track. Columbine, lupine, paintbrush and phlox brighten our route as we finally cross the ridge into Mt. Rainier National Park and descend to meet the

Laughingwater Trail (#22) (5360-0.7). A forest of trail signs marks this junction. Between this junction and Chinook Pass, steep-sloped traverses above 5500 feet remain generally snowbound and potentially hazardous until mid-July. Ohanapecosh Campground and Ranger Station are less than 8 miles down the Laughingwater Trail. From here to Sheep Lake, just north of Chinook Pass, the PCT roughly follows the eastern boundary of Mt. Rainier National Park, the Cascade crest. The park was created on March 2, 1899, by an act of Congress. The outstanding features that earned it a national-park designation early in the

105
106

Right: Mt. Rainier   *Fred Hartline*

national-park program are its wonderful subalpine flower fields and Mt. Rainier's spectacular glacier system. These same features impress park visitors today, over 70 years later.

The National Park Service is the sole authority regarding activities within the park's boundaries. In July 1973 Mt. Rainier National Park instituted a new backcountry management plan, which will be revised as more feedback becomes available and is evaluated. This plan is designed to protect the overused backcountry in the park. The best current source of user information is the Backcountry Desk, Mt. Rainier National Park, Longmire, Washington 98397, or (telephone) (206) 569-2233. Hikers who do not wish to get backcountry permits may camp legitimately anywhere on the east side of the crest. Examples of possible campsites are American Lake, Two Lakes and Dewey Lake. However, even outside the park fires may be prohibited in dry periods, or may require permits at the discretion of the Snoqualmie National Forest officials.

From the Laughingwater Trail junction our route meanders briefly through subalpine meadows as it climbs slightly to begin a long traverse. Obvious trails south up to the ridge are attempts to bypass the Laughingwater junction. In the national park such straying from the trail is firmly discouraged, since attempted **106** shortcuts become heavily eroded and result in the trampling of numerous flowers. Shortly before we leave the park via a minor pass (5680-1.0), views of Mt. St. Helens and Mt. Adams in the south join the excellent vista of Mt. Rainier in the west. From the pass, One Lake (5050) appears below us in the northeast, and we contour along the east slope. Occasional shady oases are welcome places to rest on a hot day. The traverse ends as the

Two Lakes Trail (5660-1.7) heads due south on its 0.3-mile descent to those lakes, which have a nice campsite and a reliable water supply. We engage a pair of switchbacks to help us over the crest into the park, and then embark on a long, scenic traverse. Along a bouldery, flowery meadow we revel in the overwhelming, quiet beauty of Mt. Rainier's Cascade wonderland. Proceeding onto a steeper slope, the PCT reveals a five-star view of Mt. Rainier. To the south is an impressive though not so dominating panorama, including Mt. Adams, Goat Rocks and Mt. St. Helens. As the local terrain encroaches on the distant scenery, we approach a small, sheltered lunch spot in a level col. The headwaters of a crystal brook provide the early-summer water supply. Unless park headquarters declares this a campsite, no overnighting will be permitted in this choice site. Common flowers here are red columbine, pasqueflower and phlox. Resuming the traverse, we descend gradually, then make a switchback steeply down through a mature forest of fir and western redcedar, to drop out of the national park near a junction with the

American Ridge Trail (#958) (5300-3.0). Heather, paintbrush, glacier lily and lupine entice the flower photographer slowly on as, like a bee, he flits from blossom to blossom, every new plant more worthy than the last. A congenial camp and late-season water are available at American Lake, one-half mile and only 80 vertical feet down Trail 958. Cougar Lakes, the name source for a possible wilderness area that would include the PCT between White Pass and Chinook Pass, are reached via a side trail off the American Ridge Trail. Moving steadily, we climb a short, moderately steep stretch to re-enter the park at a heathery pass. Ascending a bit more, we are afforded a view of Goat Rocks and several glimpses of Mt. Rainier as the trail levels, then descends to Anderson Lake (5350-1.2). Camping here is subject to approval by the Mt. Rainier National Park headquarters, though anyone is welcome to picnic near the rich but delicate meadowlands around the shallow pond. Leaving Anderson Lake and the park through a marshy notch, we soon cross the seasonal headwaters of a fork of American Creek. After traversing volcanic scree slopes, the PCT descends through flowery meadows and a mature mixed-conifer forest to Dewey Lake (5112). Along the southwest lakeshore, the adjacent steep slope abates, revealing

Dewey Lake *Bev Hartline*

several campsites along the trail and worn paths to more-obscure tent spots. The
Dewey Lake Trail (#968) (5150-2.7) heads east past inviting campsites to follow the American River out to "civilization." On the persistent climb to the **Tipsoo Lake Trail (5840-1.2)**, mosquitoes plague us while hermit thrushes soothe us. Two options are available for the last short stint to State Highway 410.

One choice, favored when snow is a problem or when one wants to visit Tipsoo Lake, follows the Tipsoo Lake Trail west. This trail leads past a tarn to a minor crest with a view of Dewey Lake. Descending a traverse of a steep, open slope, we pass weathered outcrops of vesicular Eocene-Oligocene andesite. Fields of glacier lily, pasqueflower, heather, lupine, huckleberry and mountain ash explain why this route is popular with day hikers and park visitors. Turning north, we amble down to Mather Memorial Parkway (5330-1.5), meeting it just south of Tipsoo Lake. North along the highway 200 yards is the Tipsoo Lake parking lot, picnic area and facilities. To rejoin the PCT after this brief excursion to civilization, hike one-quarter mile up the highway to Chinook Pass (5450-0.4-1.9).

107

The other choice follows the true Pacific Crest Trail around the east side of Naches Peak (6457). From the divide, we look back at Dewey Lake, and farther still to Mt. Adams' peak. Leaving these vistas, you wander down flowered alpine meadows and around a charming little lake, and finally traverse on an even downgrade to
Chinook Pass (5450-1.5). A log-bridge overpass spares us direct interaction with the perpetual traffic below. Chinook Pass is the northernmost pass on the Cascade crest from which water flows east and west to the Columbia River. The Mather Memorial Parkway over Chinook Pass, named in honor of Stephen Tyng Mather, first director of the National Park System, is a favorite and spectacularly scenic recreation highway through the Cascades.

Reshouldering our packs, we hike parallel to the Mather Parkway for the long traverse to Sheep Lake. Initially the PCT follows an old roadbed. This peters out within a quarter mile and we leave the lush subalpine gardens of Chinook Pass to traverse a steep, huckleberried slope with scattered timber. Views of State Highway 410, Naches Peak, and the valley of Rainier Fork American River dominate the scenery. The final short climb to the lake passes through a mature forest of cedar, spruce and hemlock, and then we skirt popular, signed **Sheep Lake** **(5740-2.2)** along its south shore. Several unofficial trails, "maintained" by the many day hikers and weekend backpackers who come here, cross Sheep Lake's subalpine basin. Jumping the lake's outflow creek, we bid Mt. Rainier National Park farewell and fill our canteens for the next 8.2 dry miles. Southbound travelers have no water worries for a while. A gently graded path guides us effortlessly through the grassy bowl where, soon after the snows leave, a spring crop of diverse, many-colored wild flowers encourage one to pass leisurely. A final climb brings us to

Sourdough Gap (6410-1.1), the gateway to an old mining district. Though not much of value was extracted there, the major features have kept the names given them during the mining era. Tunnels and prospects dot the area; they and jeep roads remain to remind us of efforts to make a fortune from the low-grade, short, fractured gold and silver veins. Leaving the views of Mts. Adams and St. Helens, we descend north across a large scree slope. At a pair of switchbacks, an unsigned side trail (6380-0.1) contours north through the next notch. Just beyond the next and last hairpin turn, another unsigned trail forks downhill east to Placer Lake. Our descent abates here to a dusty, sandy, rocky, **107** sloping traverse and arcs northeastward. An inviting trailside **108** campsite (6140-0.9) offers a fabulous view to those who are carrying sufficient water or are willing to hike downhill to get some. Since there are not many trees, firewood should be used sparsely if at all. Roughly 300 yards farther, an unsigned path worn in the heather forks north through a gap. After crossing an outcrop of the common Eocene-Oligocene andesite, we reach

Bear Gap (5882-1.3), with its three major signed trail junctions. The Bear Gap Trail (#967) heads east to Highway 410. The Hen Skin Lake Trail (#1193) contours initially due west to begin its descent to Hen Skin Lake. The Silver Creek Trail (#1192) drops northwest to the Crystal Mountain Ski Area. The PCT crosses the divide to contour northward to signed Pickhandle Point (6000-0.3). Doubling back to traverse the upper slopes of signed, glacially carved Pickhandle Basin, we reach Pickhandle Gap (6000-0.6). Almost immediately a trail (6000-0.1) signed for Fog City and Gold Hill forks southwest down the east side of the ridge. The PCT heads almost due east to diagonal up the south slope of Crown Point, then, from the saddle just east of it, goes west to a junction with the

Union Creek Trail (#956) (6160-0.3). Views of Mt. Rainier and Mt. Adams are revealed to the delight of photographers, as we continue west up Crown Point. A fresh outcrop of blue dacite with quartz and plagioclase phenocrysts here stimulates an inquisitive pause by amateur geologists. Pressing on, we balance along signed, knife-edged Blue Bell Pass (6400-0.5), and descend slightly to a trail junction (6320-0.2) near a small grove of Alaska yellow cedar. This trail descends northwest to a jeep trail in Bullion Basin. Circling above Bullion Basin, we pass a few paths that drop precipitously toward the basin. These are either deer trails or routes for hikers with very strong knees. At narrow, signed Bullion Pass (6100-0.5), another, even steeper, trail crosses the crest. Soon we approach the reasonably graded **Bullion Basin Trail (6160-0.1),** which drops southwest down to the small, meadowy glacier bowl. A climbing traverse leads us out of the mining district to **Scout Pass (6560-1.4),** and then we cross the divide above Lake Basin to traverse high above Basin Lake. Use-defined trails into the basin were made by previous hikers lured to some pleasant camp. An official **Lake Basin Trail (6400-0.4)** departs from ours at a grassy knoll at the north end of the traverse, and we descend northwest toward Big Crow Basin. Signs mark the junction with

Crow Lake Way (#953) and Norse Peak (#1191) trails (6320-0.5) at the south edge of upper Big Crow Basin. A spring 20 feet downhill from the PCT, less than 50 yards south of this junction, is the most convenient water source before Arch Rock, 7.7 miles distant. One-half mile down Crow Lake Way Trail, a large trail shelter with more-abundant water provides an ideal camp spot. If snow still lingers on this well-worn trail, one can cross the upper basin guided by three-foot-tall cylindrical posts. Along the PCT, which also has posts, the first part of the next traverse looks down on the Big Crow Shelter, and worn paths downhill are evidence that quite a few passersby have accepted the open invitation. **Barnard Saddle (6090-1.0)** greets us with a cheery

Walter Barnard 1889-1964
There are no strangers in the mountains—
Only friends one hasn't met.
Walt was a friend to all.

A short stroll through a friendly glen brings us to **Hayden Pass (6080-0.3)** and a view of Little Crow Basin. Descending into the basin we meet the **Castle Mountain Trail (#1188) (5930-0.4).** Just beyond this junction is

Little Crow Basin (5900-0.1), a charming camp and a favorite with elk as well as backpackers and horse packers. There is a creek with reliable flow about 200 yards downhill from the Castle Mountain Trail sign. Firewood is available, but fires are an unjustifiable risk in late August and September. Resuming the traverse, we cross a steep slope that quite clearly is scoured frequently by avalanches. Droopy Alaska cedar and sickly white pine join the more common hemlock and fir on this southeast-facing hillside. On one dying pine an aged sign points downhill to water. In the Cascades there is always water downhill; time of year determines how far one must go to find it. After passing a layer of a mudflow breccia, we climb into grassy **Stool Camp Gap** **(5700-1.4)** and are guided across it by the now-familiar cylindrical posts. An old trail forks northeast in the meadow, but we turn northwest to regain some needed elevation. Pearly everlasting, paintbrush and lupine decorate the bouldery slopes of Peak 6373, which we climb around. Cresting at a notch, we cross to the west side in a forest of dead trees, possibly remnants of an old burn. A vegetation discontinuity on the hillsides below may mark the downhill edge of the fire. For the next stretch the PCT follows the Cascade crest faithfully, and in the north panoramas of the Cascades beyond Snoqualmie Pass supplement still-good views of Mt. Rainier in the southwest. After passing junctions with two minor trails, we reach the

Arch Rock Trail **(#1187) (5930-2.4),** which descends gradually down the west flank of the broad, rolling divide. Saddle Springs campsite is about two-thirds mile down Trail 1187. In this region, elk hoofprints are more common than the waffle pattern of hiking soles, suggesting that not very many people pack this far "in." The easy trail, the lack of significant elevation gain, and the pleasantly distracting scenery make these miles among the most enjoyable along the PCT in Washington. During a storm, though, things could be quite miserable, because the terrain provides no protection. With snow on the ground, the broad-crest trail would be very difficult to follow exactly. By the time we meet the **Cougar Valley Trail** **(#951) (5800-0.6)** the country is really open. In our approach to Arch Rock Shelter, we seem on top of the world—a very beautiful world from this vantage point. The flowers along the crest here are fantastic in the "spring-time." Descending easily to the **Arch Rock Shelter access trail** **(5750-1.5),** we notice erratic chips of white chert in the brown dust of the trail. Only 250 yards down the access trail is Arch Rock Shelter, a large, clean, rustic cabin. The park below the trail offers excellent campsites for those who prefer not to use the shelter. Leaving the open high country, we descend across the headwaters of South Fork Little Naches River. The next trail-side water is a Government Meadow, 5.3 miles north. Gradually losing elevation, the PCT is efficiently routed to follow the crest closely, but views to the east toward Raven Roost Lookout are

108
109

more frequent than those to the west. We soon meet a junction with the

Middle Fork Trail (#951) (5220-1.6) at Louisiana Saddle, from which a long, descending, forested traverse brings us to **Rods Gap (4820-1.2).** At the one switchback required to climb out of the gap, a wooden sign, introducing us to Mike Urich, a Forest Service trail-maintenance worker during the late 1940s and early 1950s, warns us that:

> The trails you travel through these lands
> Were made by Big Mike's mortal hands,
> And still his spirit rides the breeze
> To punish those who mar his trees.

Very soon the PCT crests to follow the broad divide, and the swinging rhythm of the perceptible descent is broken only by a signed junction with the **Maggie Way Trail (#1186) (4850-1.7)**. It is hard to believe that less than one-third mile west, Maggie Creek's canyon wall drops 1000 feet to the canyon floor. Hemlocks and small mountain meadows randomly cover the terrain, over which our grade remains easy as we descend into Government Meadow and

109
110

Meadow Creek (4720-0.8). Born in Naches Pass (4940), this creek, which intersects the trail at the west edge of the meadow, probably does not run dry during the hiking season. **Camp Urich,** a rustic camp with four bunks, two stoves and a table, is but 50 yards ahead on the meadow's fringe.

Government Meadow is a heavily used site, since a jeep road, the first "highway" across the Cascades, provides access for motorbikes and four-wheel-drive vehicles. Despite this, and possibly because of two Forest Service poems, the campsites and shelter are clean and in good shape. On the cabin is displayed this verse:

> Camp Mike Urich. Dedicated to the memory of Mike Urich
> (1888-1957)
> The mountain Gods from seats on high
> Rejoiced to see Mike Urich die.
> And at his death gave this decree
> "To all who pass here know that we
> Entrust to Big Mike Urich's hands
> These camps, these trails, these forest lands
> To rule, protect, to love and scan
> Well as he did while mortal man;
> And deal out sentence stern and just
> To those who violate his trust"

Stranger, beware, leave not a fire—
Foul not Mike's camp, rouse not his ire.

The dirt-road track in front of the cabin and the PCT behind it
merge in 200 yards. Leaving the meadow, we pass a bent-
wagon-wheel monument to the Longmire party of pioneers,
which in 1853 was the first wagon train to cross the Cascade
Mountains into Puget Sound.

In early 1853 residents of Olympia wished to increase the
Puget Sound population. At that time, pioneers from the east
followed the Columbia Gorge to Portland, and many were captured by the fertility and beauty of the Willamette Valley before
they ever got to Puget Sound. The Olympians wanted a wagon
road across the Cascades from Fort Walla Walla, to bring some
of the immigrants to the Puget Sound basin. After Congress
granted $10,000 to build a wagon road through Naches Pass,
Territorial Governor Isaac Stevens commissioned George B.
McClellan to survey the route and begin construction. McClellan, pessimistic from the start, left with some men and returned
much later to report that the venture was impossible. In June,
with no activity started, the settlers themselves began working
on a trail, as they expected the Longmire party to come through
in the early fall. By September the summit had not been reached, **110**
and no word was available about the immigrants, so the effort
was abandoned for the winter.

About this time the Longmire party arrived at Fort Walla
Walla and prepared to leave the beaten pioneer path to strike off
across the Cascades. To cross the Columbia, they had to build
rafts, but in comparison with the trails ahead this task was nearly
trivial. Guided by Indians, they worked up the Yakima River,
crossing it several times. Then they turned up the Naches, and
had to ford it 68 times before they reached Naches Pass. The
beautiful meadows and sheltering forests were unexpected bles-
sings to the tired and hungry immigrants. Unfortunately it was
already early October, and prudence would not allow them a
long enough stay to recoup their strength and that of their animals.

Leaving Government Meadow, they got only about 2.5 miles
before they were stopped by the 1000-foot-high steep slopes of
the canyon of the Greenwater River. Splicing together every-
thing they could use for rope, they were still several hundred feet
short of the length required to enable them to lower their wagons.
One dedicated expedition member volunteered the hides of as
many of his steers as would be necessary. In all, three precious
steers were sacrificed to produce enough rawhide to sufficiently

lengthen the rope. Anchoring to a sturdy tree, they lowered the wagons, which were dragging smaller trees for added braking power, one by one. This resourceful technique was so successful that only one wagon was smashed. Continuing toward Puget Sound, they faced more hazards, but the final leg for their pathbreaking journey was relatively easy. Longmire, Washington, the headquarters of Mt. Rainier National Park, is named for David Longmire, a nine-year-old member of this party. David settled at Longmire Springs, which he deeded to the national park when it was established. Following the road-sized trail cut 50 yards north-northeast from the memorial, we cross the

Naches Trail (#942) (4800-0.2), a dirt jeep trail. After passing a sign prohibiting motor vehicles, we follow our trail as it winds through the forest. A small marshy area (4870-0.7) offers water of questionable purity throughout the hiking season. Soon the Naches West Trail (#1175A) (4870-0.4) forks south and then turns west to meet the Naches Jeep Trail. We continue to climb slowly along the divide past the **Pyramid Peak Trail (#941) (4960-0.5),** which heads east. In 15 yards, energetic hikers may choose the direct route, true to the crest, and follow the Pyramid Peak Trail over the crown of Pyramid Peak. The vantage point afforded by the 5715-foot elevation of the summit was exploited **110** by a lookout tower, which has since been abandoned and removed. Backpackers whose loyalty lies with the Pacific Crest Trail (and who want to avoid unnecessary elevation gain) may prefer to contour around the west slopes of the peak. The views from the official PCT are not as spectacular and broad as those from the summit route, but they are respectable, including some glimpses of Mt. Rainier. Dwarfbeard masks the identity of the sickly conifers that have a tenuous roothold on the steeply canted hillside. Pearly everlasting, lupine, brambles and huckleberries thrive in open areas around the volcanic outcrops. The two trails merge (5200-0.9) where a sign just south of **Windy Gap (5200-0.1)** prohibits motor vehicles on our trail. After following an old, dead-end, lookout-access road 200 yards north, we join the

Green Divide Road (#195) (5200-0.1). This road is gated, so motor-vehicle traffic is rare. Road 195 is unusual among backcountry roads in that it is a pleasure to walk along. Neither deeply eroded nor brutally graveled, it is comfortably packed dirt. We follow this road northeast as its grade lessens. Rolling with the terrain, and shaded by a largely Douglas-fir forest, the road turns east and guides us rapidly past a nonfunctional shelter. One hundred yards farther, the signed

Upper Green Trail (#1034) (4870-3.1) heads north to descend into the valley of the upper Green River. Extra care to avoid starting a fire or polluting the water is warranted, since the Green River supplies Tacoma's water. Views of Mt. Rainier highlight our trek along this east-west jog in the Cascade's backbone. The PCT leaves the north side of **Green Divide Road (4960-1.3)** at a prominent sign. A roadside campsite is across the road here. South from the campsite, a trail, worn and maintained by hopeful water seekers, heads downhill, following the stream beds from two springs (sometimes dry) to an elk-and-deer-watering mudhole at the confluence of the streams. Leaving the road, the PCT parallels it for 0.2 mile, until it abruptly ends. A traverse through Douglas-fir forest with views to the south highlights the hummocky hike to **Green Pass (4894-1.7),** which is reached 150 yards east of a trailside campsite. In late season, water may be a long hike downhill. A few lonely white pines and alpine firs are the only trees on a virtually timber-free climb up Blowout Mountain. In August and September huckleberries abound on these open slopes and those higher on the mountain. Nibbling from bush to bush, we make slow progress up the well-graded trail. Where our trail curves east, the well-camouflaged but signed **West Fork Bear Creek Trail (#943) (5360-1.0)** branches south toward the Naches River. The PCT switchbacks northward **110** through another huckleberry patch, approaching the junction with the **Granite Creek Trail (#1326) (5600-0.6).** A faint trail **111** heading east-southeast is barely discernible here. Very soon we reach

Blowout Mountain (5750-0.2). Our trail skirts about 50 feet below the summit along its west slope. From here we have an outstanding view of the terrain we've crossed. Mt. Rainier's graceful bulk raises the southern skyline. Also to the south the east-west zag in the Cascade ridge and Pyramid Peak stand in relief and bring the topo map to life. Beyond the summit grove and a grassy field is an exposed campsite with no late-season water. The best huckleberry patches on Blowout Mountain are on this north ridge. After zigzagging quickly down a steep section, we find ourselves on a nearly knife-edged ridge, where we meet the **Blowout Mountain Trail (#1318) (5220-1.0)** (Big Creek Trail on the map). The small lake on the eastern bench of Blowout Mountain is reached by forking south from this trail. In late season this lake has the best camping between Government Meadow and Tacoma Pass.

Contouring near the divide, we hike from notch to gap. The country between Blowout Mountain and Yakima Pass was once very lovely climax timberland, supporting prime forests of Douglas-fir and western hemlock. Now huckleberries, fireweed and mountain ash cover the treeless slopes. We grit our sensibilities to the less beautiful hike ahead. Being northbound, we are lucky, for we must stumble down, rather than struggle up, the clear-cut acreage. Logging operations are currently active, so this trail description will soon be out of date regarding logging roads and forest. Weekday hikers here may hear the drone of the bulldozer and the whine of the chainsaw, and so experience a part of "wilderness" that weekend hikers miss.

Our well-graded path descends easily along the crest to the first pass (4760-1.5). This gap, like several to come, has a sign indicating *water* downhill to the east. The quality of the water and its distance from the trail depend on the season. Traversing, we glimpse a clear-cut to the east, and switchback down into a second *water* (west) notch (4390-1.4). Beyond, after contouring above a logging road, we begin the long zigzag descent to forested

Tacoma Pass (3500-2.7). Water and a campsite are east of the trail in the Wenatchee National Forest. Recent "patterns of use" from the northeast encroach on the pass and the trail. After crossing a good gravel logging road through the pass, we climb to meet the westbound **Tacoma Pass Trail (#1033) (3600-0.1).** Ten yards earlier, we passed a trail signed to descend east to Cabin Creek Road. Climbing now, we regain the divide and view more clear-cuts to the east. Bunchberry, vanilla leaf and Oregon grape lightly cover the forest floor as we near **Sheets Pass (3700-1.0).** Camping here under Douglas-fir and western redcedar would be inviting if there were a convenient water supply. Beyond the pass and up the trail, we cross a creek (4000-0.5) which probably carries some water through September. After traversing around the south slopes of Bearpaw Butte, the PCT switchbacks up to the ridge to meet the obscure but signed **Bearpaw Butte Trail (4500-0.9)** at the crest. Following the divide above a growing clear-cut, we reach the **Snowshoe Butte Trail (#1036) (4640-0.7),** which descends south to meet logging roads. Before climbing to traverse the east side of Snowshoe Butte (5135), we acknowledge signs (4640-0.3) pointing southwest to *water and camp.* Descending northward from the east slope of Snowshoe Butte, we zigzag across the section line, into and out of a clear-cut, and cross a logging road. In the clear-cut, the PCT joins the old road. In 200 yards we reach a PCT sign at a bend in the road, where we duck back into the forest (4300-1.4) on a trail. Exposed to the onslaught of westerly winds, many trees at the edge of the logging cut have been victims of these winds. After our route swoops down to and out of a pass, we turn east to follow a subtle, woods-edge road into another clear-cut (4400-1.1). Because this

111
112

area was being harvested in 1973, the trail was covered with debris. When the devastation is completed, the PCT route will be marked with emblems and the logging scar will be easily negotiated. Currently the trail crosses a gully and contours initially east-southeast up the barren slope. It soon curves northeast and re-enters forest (4600-0.6). Enjoying the luxury of unbutchered woods, we descend easily to a small pass and another clear-cut (4300-1.4). After crossing the level, windswept crown of the hill, we start a switchbacking descent. The PCT crosses and follows logging roads with abandon, and would be impossible to follow precisely if snow-covered. Leaving the last clearcut (4100-0.5), but not the overgrown road cuts, we descend into a lovely, forested gap. After climbing out of the miniature valley, we cross under power lines (4000-0.6) and descend along a *no vehicles allowed* road to a **parking area (3970-0.3)**. The PCT route is well marked as it negotiates the spaghetti network of roads in the Stampede Pass area. Following Road 2190A we reach the Stampede Pass Weather Station driveway near a large Cascade Crest Trail wooden map. Beyond the map we intersect another power line and its access road, then turn left (west) at an obvious, well-marked fork. After passing under the last set of power lines, we reach an important, signed junction (3600-0.8). From it we follow signs northeast to *Cascade Crest Trail North* **112** and *U.S. Highway 10*. (Southbound hikers start east on Road 2190A, which bears signs *Stampede L.O.* and *U.S. Weather Bureau Station*.) Signed Lizard Lake (3590) lies west of the road as we approach **Stampede Pass and Road 212 (3680-0.3)**. Interstate 90 (U.S. 10) is about 5 miles east down this graded gravel road.

Stampede Pass is historically significant to the development of the pioneer West, as it was the first Washington pass through which a railroad route went. George B. McClellan, sent by Governor Isaac Stevens to evaluate Snoqualmie Pass as a railroad route, reported negatively. Several years later, in 1880, Northern Pacific could not waste any more time looking for a route. If it didn't complete construction before 1884, it would not receive some millions of acres of federal land offered to help finance railroads as part of a land-grant act. In 1881 Virgil Bogue was assigned the task of locating a feasible route. He selected Stampede Pass and work began. The checkerboard pattern of federal and private ownership of land, with the resultant checkerboard of clear-cuts, is due to the railroad's receiving alternate sections on both sides of the track laid.

At Stampede Pass we cross gravel Road 212 and ascend the far bank near a sign that directs southbound hikers. Climbing west, we cross huckleberry clearings and then turn north to follow the divide. Our forested trail next takes us west through a pass (4140-1.1) and down into the glaring devastation of a clear-cut. A traversing, southward descent leads us across one logging road (0.6 mile) and then another (0.2 mile). Then, in about 85 yards, we merge onto a road, heading roughly southeast, to pass a PCT emblem within 50 yards. We follow the road as it winds westward downhill until it passes a second PCT shield and approaches a "dead-end" turnaround (3740-0.4). About 40 yards before the dead end we head west, downhill, from the southwest-bound road and descend into

Dandy Pass (3700-0.1). From the clear-cut we have just negotiated, one has a fine view of Mt. Rainier framed by Dandy Pass. Just north of the pass we re-enter typical forest and traverse north and west around the north side of a minor hill. Then we amble into an older, huckleberry-rich clear-cut (3700-1.7) and meet a passable road (3650-0.2) at a wooden Cascade Crest Trail sign. This sign marks the trail for south-bound hikers, who might otherwise continue too far along the road. We follow the road north 150 yards, then our brushy trail continues north and finally leaves the old clear-cut (3560-0.3). After contouring northwest, the trail joins the

Meadow Creek Trail (#1338) (3450-0.8). Camping and fishing are available at Stirrup Lake (3560), one-half mile southwest on Trail 1338. In 15 yards we cross Stirrup Creek and fill our canteens from this reliable stream. Angling northeast, we climb easily out of the little valley, cross a logging road (3550-0.2), press northward, and then bend on a northwest traverse far above Meadow Creek. Devil's club and occasional redcedar add variety to the steady floral array, and our thighs are caressed by underbrush as we tread the comfortable path. Bending north-ward, our route approaches another road, crosses it (3670-1.9) and continues 200 yards to ford the headwaters of Meadow Creek. An overgrown trail, marked *abandoned,* heads west from here. Climbing easily northwest, we cross to the west side of the divide and continue up to a crest at a national-forest boundary sign (4000-0.8), where we enter an odd-numbered (clear-cut) section. Descending northeast above the headwaters of North Fork Cedar River, we cross a shaven hillside, then cross one minor logging road and traverse down to

Yakima Pass (3575-0.6), where Twilight Lake was thoughtfully left a forest curtain. Here the trail follows the edge of the clear-cut northwest, passing several signs that forbid trespassing in the Cedar River watershed, Seattle's water supply. In 200 yards we leave the clear-cut and return to healthy forest as our trail mean-

112

113

114

Mirror Lake *Bev Hartline*

ders north to reach Mirror Lake at its outlet (4195-1.0). Tinkham Peak (5395) guards the west shore of the clear, turquoise-blue lake. We hike north along the east shore, 150 yards past the main Mirror Lake Campground, to a junction with the eastbound

Mirror Lake Trail (#1302) (4220-0.4). The heavy use and popularity of Mirror Lake are explained by Lost Lake Road's being only 1 mile down the Mirror Lake Trail. Our path trends northwest as it switchbacks quickly up a flank of Tinkham Peak to a saddle and the **Twin Lakes Trail (#1303) (4500-0.5).** Here the PCT turns west to contour the slopes of Tinkham Peak. Soon the topography forces us to arc north, then west to a small basin with permanent tarns (4320-0.8). Then we switchback briefly to gain some elevation for our traverse of Silver Peak (5605). Views of Red Mountain (5890) north of Snoqualmie Pass, of Tinkham Peak behind us, and of Twin Lakes below dominate the scenery. We descend obliquely north-northeast to cross a pass (3840-1.9) and drop easily to the south tip of **Olallie Meadow (3650-0.3).**

114

Hiking north along the west edge of the marshy green meadow, we pass campsites and paths to other campsites before crossing **Olallie Creek (3610-0.2)** at the north tip of the meadow. Our route traverses north across Mt. Catherine rhyolite and under some power lines to join the power-line **access road (3378-0.5)**. Traveling east along the road, fireweed, scrub maple and huckleberry are our familiar companions in the clearings. Under the power lines again, we fork downhill (east) off the major road onto an overgrown road cut (3240-0.4). Shortly after the brushiness is replaced by boulderiness, our trail splits northeast (3200-0.1) to cross an unnamed creek and begin a scree traverse. We pass over the Snoqualmie (railroad) Tunnel and under some more wires (3250-0.4) as we traverse above the valley of South Fork Snoqualmie River and Interstate 90. The river has worked little physiographic change on the glaciated valley, but highway construction is having a significant effect. Our trail arcs north to the northbound **Silver Peak Trail (#1020) (3150-0.8)**, where we head northeast, cross a bench to a small lake and a trail curving northwest to Interstate 90 (3180-0.2). In about a hundred yards, we approach a campsite and a trail through it to **Lodge Lake (3180)**. A climbing traverse brings us north through a gap to **Beaver Lake (3500-0.9)**. Then we pass under a chair lift among some foxglove and start descending a groomed ski slope. Reflectant white diamonds mark the trail route as it follows selected jeep roads. Initially we travel northeast, curving gradually more easterly. Then we T onto a northwest-southeast-heading road, and choose southeast. In 200 yards, we reach a large gravel road near ski-school huts and turn left (3020-0.7). This road curves east to reach the Snoqualmie Pass "business road" at a wooden PCT map and a **Forest Service Information Center (3004-0.2)**.

Snoqualmie Pass, served by Greyhound Bus, is one of the standard stops on the Seattle-Walla Walla run. The bus station in Snoqualmie Pass is at the Pancake House, across the street from and 200 yards southeast of the Forest Service Information Center. Gasoline, candy bars, restaurants and overnight accommodations are available in this winter-resort community. More-general supplies are obtainable in North Bend, 22 miles west, or Cle Elum, 32 miles east. *Your next en route supplies will be at Stevens Pass, 68 miles distant.*

From the Forest Service Information Center, you hike northwest along the road, following it under the Interstate 90 overpass and beyond as Forest Service Road 2305 to a junction with the **Cascade Crest Trail (#2000) (2920-0.2)**. Here you must select your route to the valley of Middle Fork Snoqualmie River. The

PCT route is more evenly graded, longer, and preferable in bad weather or early season. The CCT is more scenic, more challenging, shorter, impassable for stock, and dangerous before about the end of July if you aren't a skilled snow mountaineer equipped with an ice axe.

If you choose the PCT, continue up the road, crossing Commonwealth Creek and the creek that will grow to be South Fork Snoqualmie River. Soon you pass the plush cottages and condominiums clustered close to Alpental Ski Resort. The route recrosses the infant South Fork and climbs to a parking-lot

Trailhead (3140-1.3) for the PCT and the Snow Lake Trail (#1013). Turning northeast up the hill, we plunge into the woods and climb about 200 yards to the point where the old PCT used to run down the valley before the resort usurped its position. Here we turn up the valley toward the very headwaters of the South Fork at Source Lake. Traversing the valley wall, the route alternates between open timber and more or less open talus slopes, with views of Chair Peak (6238) ahead and Snoqualmie Pass behind. The wildflowers become even more entrancing as we break free of the woods for a high alpine traverse most of the way around Source Lake. Continuing along the rugged side of Chair Peak, we soon re-enter woods just west of a pass. After crossing into the Middle Fork Snoqualmie drainage at this pass (4360-3.4), we switchback abruptly down to Snow Lake and arrive at an inlet stream flanked by an old stone foundation at the edge of Snow Lake (4016-0.8). The PCT continues around the lake to the **115**

Gem Lake Trail (#1012) (4040-0.4), where we turn east to traverse and switchback down the steep talus of the headwall of Roaring Creek's source basin. Wildflowers are abundant, as are insects in the proper season, and the slope may be quite hot in the late afternoon. Gradually the forest becomes more venerable, with stands of Douglas-fir and spruce, and occasional old cedar monarchs. Now the trail plunges down a very steep, densely "reforested" slope that abruptly bottoms out at a junction with the

Middle Fork Trail (#1003) (1620-3.6). This route enters from the west on an old logging road that the PCT here usurps. Rock Creek and an excellent wooded campsite are about 300 yards west down Trail 1003. The PCT turns east on the old road to climb gradually but steadily up the valley. We cross seasonal streams, parade through deep stands of bracken fern with occasional maidenhair fern, tarry among wildflowers, and are serenaded by wrens and wood thrushes, as we arrive at **Burntboot Creek Crossing (1740-2.5).** Here we turn upstream 70 yards to a footlog, where we rejoin the CCT 2000 alternate, which has just completed its steep descent from Red Mountain.

North of Interstate 90, the **Cascade Crest Trail** heads east and then north to circumtour the trailhead parking area. We climb gently through dense climax forest to a junction with the pre-Interstate 90 crest-trail route (3020-0.2). Southbound, this cross trail dead-ends in a half mile at the freeway; northbound it is soon lost among the vacation chalets in the Alpental resort. Leisurely switch-backs guide us into the glaring heat of an old clear-cut (3050-0.1). Here we must climb steeply, zigzagging through mountain ash, huckleberry, bunchberry, fireweed, blackberry and scrub maple. Briefly, we follow a very old logging road and enjoy views of the Snoqualmie Pass ski areas and Denny Mountain (5519). Eventually we exit from the clear-cut near its northeast corner (3220-0.2). The grade slackens almost immediately, and the babbling of Commonwealth Creek soon drowns the traffic noise. Guye Peak (5168), a guardian of Commonwealth Basin, looms above us to the north. Soon we descend to the stream bed and log-cross it (3530-0.6). Don't take the side trail on the southeast bank. The moderately open creek-side forest flatland is riddled with paths and dotted with inviting campsites. We bear east, crossing seasonal creeks on bridges of logs, then briefly parallel Commonwealth Creek before log-crossing it near a blazed tree (3580-0.2). Our trail now switchbacks up the valley wall and crosses a seasonal tributary as we arc northward. After passing a **Trail (3770-0.5)** that trends northeast, we come to a puncheon-crossed marsh. A log over the ponded creek at the end of the puncheon path guides us to the east bank and through some large campsites. In 100 yards a cross trail (3840-0.4) heads north-northeast and west-southwest, giving access to more campsites. Still heading generally north, we reach an arm of Red Mountain (5890) and begin to climb tight switchbacks through thinning woods. Delightful paintbrush, lupine and huckleberry embroider the slope as we pant upward. Soon the path levels off in an idyllic upper **Alpine cirque (4850-1.1).** Scrub timber contains small, quiet campsites near the basin's large tarn. We skirt far above the tarn, traversing the lower scree of Red Mountain's nearby summit, and then switchback vigorously to the Red Mountain-Lundin Peak (6057) ridge.

115

Turning west-northwest to follow the saddle toward Lundin Peak, we reach the westernmost notch (5300-0.5), from which our trail switchbacks steeply down a north-facing couloir, which is likely snow filled until early August. Due to the high angle of the snowfield, descending it ill equipped or inexperienced can be dangerous. As the gully opens out, we traverse northeast beneath the debris-shedding cliffs of Lundin Peak, then arc north to mount a scrub-timbered arm. Our path switchbacks steeply along this minor ridge in its descent into the lushly timbered and copiously harvested valley of Middle Fork Snoqualmie River. Numerous downed trees may make the long downhill romp a somewhat gymnastic feat. Eventually we turn northwest to parallel Burntboot Creek as subtle whiffs of hydrogen sulfide announce minor springs near the valley floor. A campground where our trail finally levels off at the edge of the clear stream is the nicest site between here and Crawford Creek (6.2 miles ahead). At the far end of the campground we rejoin the current, official **PCT** (1750-3.3-7.3).

115
116
118A

Merged together, the PCT and the CCT cross the creek to and pass through Goldmeyer Hot Springs (private property—no camping). During the summer months guards camp in the semipermanent shelters beside the creek. Treading the earthen path, we amble through thick woods to the south bank of
Middle Fork Snoqualmie River (1740-0.2) and continue up this bank to an active mining area. Two hundred yards into the bulldozed complex we cross a road-bridge over the Middle Fork (1960-1.3), then hike up the mining road until it unites with the
Middle Fork Road (#241) (2040-0.2). Turning north-northeast on this road, we continue our trek up the valley, enjoying roadside fireweed and foxglove, to a Y-junction (2620-1.5). Taking the left branch, we work up the logged hillside, top a small rise, and drop into
Hardscrabble Creek Camp (2960-0.6). This camp may or may not be an inviting site. In 1973 considerable road construction had largely reduced it and the road we've followed to a mud wallow. However, one can hope it will soon be reclaimed. After crossing Hardscrabble Creek the PCT continues along the road for about 10 yards before splitting southeast to re-enter woods. We work up the north bank of the Middle Fork, hiking mostly beneath mature timber on a trail that may be extremely muddy in early season. When the path breaks briefly out of the forest to cross steep meadow, brush or scree slopes, views of the rugged

Cascade crest compete for attention with trailside columbine and bleeding heart. We soon arrive at a pleasant campsite (3310-2.4) on the banks of Crawford Creek. Continuing, the PCT crosses numerous springtime streams, passes occasional camps, and winds through early-season marshes as it climbs along the Middle Fork to

Pedro Camp (4120-2.9). This large, flat site, a favorite of fishermen, is nestled unobtrusively among occasional large conifers, alpine gardens, and ruggedly inviting granitic cliffs. Here we bridge the Middle Fork and work east and a bit south through the subalpine terrain to meet

La Bohn Gap Way (4360-0.8). This trail branches northeast to climb toward Williams Lake (4600), while the PCT jumps a small branch of the Middle Fork to prepare for the steep ascent into Dutch Miller Gap. We climb steeply beside the creek, zigzagging to recross it, and work toward the pass. Finally the grade lessens and we amble through idyllic splendor to

Dutch Miller Gap (5000-0.8), probably snow covered until early August. From the gap we plunge abruptly down among weather-torn spruces and large, crumbling sedimentary slabs toward Lake Ivanhoe (4652). Just below a waterfall and a small, cool pool, we cross a tumbling creek and within 150 yards meet the

118A
118B
119

Lake Ivanhoe Loop Trail (4740-0.2). Here we must decide which side of the lake to skirt. The more direct route continues southeast to cross the steep slopes above the lake. When snow lingers, this route ranges from dangerous to impassable. The longer route turns sharply north-northeast to round the lake on its north side. From either trail it is easy to appreciate the beauty of this scenic, clear-blue, sparkling lake, which fills a steep valley between rugged alpine peaks. The largest campsites are at the southeast end of the lake where the two trails rejoin. In 200 yards we reach the

Summit Lake Cabin (4580-0.6) (0.9 by the north-shore route). From this memorial shelter we continue southeast to cross the Lake Ivanhoe outlet on a wooden bridge, and start a long traverse. From a viewpoint overlooking Chief Creek's gorge (4240-0.6) we double back for the first of several switchbacks that deliver us gently into the Waptus River valley. The trail descends on semi-arid, grassy-meadow slopes through paintbrush, lupine, beargrass and occasional white pine, gradually becoming more wooded and passing a sandy-floored camp next to a

Waptus River ford (3075-1.3). Here we wade or rockhop, depending on the season, and turn east to pound the wooded valley bottom toward Waptus Lake (2963). After crossing Spade

Creek (3040-1.1) on boulders or downstream on tenuous, natural log-jam bridges, we soon find ourselves on an open ridge over-looking Waptus Lake. Mountains and hills tower above on all sides, and a campsite below on the ridge invites the weary hiker to cease his day's toil and rest amid this scenic splendor. Around the corner and 200 yards farther, we cross a stream and arrive at more wooded

Waptus Camp #3 (2990-1.0), surrounded by huge conifers, trillium, Devil's club—and mosquitoes in season. Continuing down the PCT-Waptus Lake Trail, we pass a junction with the **Spade Lake Trail (#1337) (2990-0.5)**, which heads initially north-east before turning up-valley toward Spade Lake (5210). In 200 yards we cross a creek and arrive at

Waptus Camp #2 (2990-0.1), a lovely camp right on the lake shore. Then, beyond an unnumbered large camp we climb briefly away from the lake, before a *Public Horse Corral* sign an-nounces the

Waptus Camp #1 (2990-0.6). From the corral, the PCT bears east, while a branch of the Waptus River Trail forks south-southeast to a "horse ford." Presently we come to a second branch that leads to the horse ford, and almost immediately to the foot-traffic branch of the

Waptus River Trail (#1310) (3040-0.3). Now the PCT (2173A) begins to arc to the north-northeast and climb, while the Waptus River Trail heads east-southeast to bridge Spinola Creek. As-cending first steeply, then more gradually, we begin our long trek up Spinola Creek to Deep Lake. Water, except from seldom accessible Spinola Creek, may be scarce on this section, but wildflowers are not: bluebells, vanilla leaf, columbine, trillium and many others gracefully spread under fir, spruce, hemlock and cedar. The forest is frequently gladed in lower Spinola Creek valley, but it becomes more dense as we climb, though also more interrupted by avalanche tracks, stream cuts and rocky scree shoulders. Below us the stream performs acrobatic feats as the PCT steepens and switchbacks up the western valley wall (4000-2.4). After much sweating and panting, relieved by tan-talizing glimpses ahead of Cathedral Rock (6724), we burst out onto a flower-covered alpine meadow and arrive at a ford of the

West branch of Spinola Creek (4260-0.7). The trail doubles back slightly, climbing around a rocky promontory to enter a meadow on the east branch of Spinola Creek. Beyond a nice camp on the very edge of the creek (4340-0.2), we stroll up-valley, ignoring the numerous branching trails and bearing gen-erally north-northwest along the western meadow fringe, keep-ing the creek in view. Then we arc to cross Lake Vicente's

119
120A
120B

outflow creek and continue, through now patchy forest, to approach campsites by

Deep Lake (4390-0.8). A trail around the west shore splits northward and the PCT turns east to skirt the south shore of the lake and cross the outlet stream in 100 yards. In 1973 logs 100 yards downstream kept the early-season hiker's feet dry. Rounding a knoll to the south, we begin a grueling climb to Cathedral Pass. Water may be scarce and thirst intense, so canteens had better be full. Gradually we switchback out of the forest, gaining better and wider views until finally we break out onto steep, meadowy huckleberry slopes with spectacular views to the west. With determination we slog the last few long, gently graded switchbacks to reach the crest at

120B

Cathedral Pass (5610-3.1). Shifting out of low gear and throttling back, we coast with increasing speed into a small, alpine hanging valley, complete with lakes and tarns. The PCT will eventually—perhaps by 1978—turn north up this valley to traverse far above the Cle Elum River to Deception Pass. Now, though, we must turn south-southeast and descend a steep, eroded trail—sometimes nearly a creek—to

Cathedral Rock   *Bev Hartline*

Squaw Lake (4841-1.6). Crossing its outlet, we pass a scenic campsite on the shore and resume our southeastward course in a downward traverse. Upon meeting the old Squaw Lake Trail, we arc north and switchback down to a junction with the

Trail Creek Trail (#1322) (4520-0.8). This trail takes off uphill and soon drops down to Squitch Lake. The PCT itself switchbacks down the heavily timbered slopes of the Cle Elum River valley. Twice we come within earshot of the tumbling stream from Squaw Lake before we cross it as the trail flattens out on the valley bottom and shortly arrives at a bridge over the Cle Elum River which deposits us in the heart of

Cle Elum River Camp (3350-2.3). From the campground we proceed along the gravel access road north and east until it T's into Road 2405 (3380-0.1), where the PCT bears northwest to

Skeeter Creek Camp (3400-0.2). This camp frequently serves as a jumping-off point for backpackers, hunters and fishermen heading into the north-central portion of the *de facto* Alpine Lakes wilderness. The trailhead is reached from Cle Elum by driving about 20 miles north on State 903 to Salmon La Sac, then motoring an additional 14 miles north along the Cle Elum River on the "all weather" gravel Forest Service Road 2405. This stretch of road is steep and occasionally tortuous, as well as very muddy in spring; it also requires fording a tributary of the Cle Elum which might be dangerous in high water, especially with the wrong car.

120B
121

From Skeeter Creek Camp we proceed north-northwest up the heavily timbered Cle Elum River valley. Occasional open areas afford views across the valley to the west as we work our leisurely way to the shores of

Hyas Lake (3448-1.7). Numerous camps may be found on this and little sister Hyas Lake (3450-1.0). Continuing on our way, we and the trail soon (3540-0.7) become tangled in the very headwaters of the Cle Elum: stream beds, both dry and full; swampy growth and swampy ground; and avalanche tracks as well. Breaking free, we climb steeply north-northeast out of the valley to the edge of a ravine cut by a stream (4000-0.4). Here a faint trail leads east-northeast up the bank, climbing arduously to scenic Tuck and Robin lakes. Crossing the ravine and continuing steadily upward, we traverse slightly to the west into a small valley draining the area around Deception Pass. One hundred yards before the signed pass, Trail 1066 angles westward off the PCT to cut around the west side of Deception Creek toward Marmot Lake (4930) and Lake Clarice (4530). Just beyond

Deception Pass (4450-0.9), Trail 1059 continues north, dropping into Deception Creek valley, while the PCT Y's north-northeast to traverse on the east slope of the valley. Soon we

Cathedral Rock and Mt. Daniel *Hartline*

angle sharply north again, cross a stream that is eroding back along a prominent fault, and continue our wooded traverse to

17 Mile Camp (4480-1.4). This is the first established camp north of Deception Pass on the PCT with reasonable late-season access to water. Continuing our traverse toward Deception Lakes, we soon leave the forest for the barren slopes of an old burn, but we are afforded spectacular views back toward Mt. Daniel (7899) and Cathedral Rock (6724). Shortly, we round a northeast bend to reach a junction with a northward-branching

Lateral trail (5020-1.4) to the Deception Creek Trail. In a scant 0.2 mile we cross the outlet stream of Deception Lakes, then hike along the west bank of the smallest lake and arrive at a lovely, but overused, camp on the shores of the middle lake of

Deception Lakes (5053-0.3). From here the old Cascade Crest Trail skirts the shore of the lake to climb into Surprise Gap (5780-0.9) before rejoining the PCT (5130-0.6-1.5) in the northern cirque of Surprise Mountain (6330). The PCT, on the other hand, cuts west-northwest away from Deception Lakes to traverse more gradually around the west side of Surprise Mountain before switchbacking abruptly up to

Pieper Pass (5920-1.6). From this pass we descend switchbacks to a snow-swept alpine tarn flanked by jagged granite boulders and a lovely alpine meadow. Traversing farther east we catch a lingering glimpse of clear, blue Glacier Lake (4806) below, enhanced by ghostly Glacier Peak (10,541) on the northern skyline, before we zigzag down into the rugged cirque of Surprise Mountain. In the level bottom of the cirque, the PCT rejoins the CCT (5130-1.6) and both turn northward, soon to arrive at

Glacier Lake Lean-To (5000-0.3) (capacity four to six persons). To avoid small nocturnal creatures and somewhat shabby accommodations here, one may go one-quarter mile down the trail and round some large boulders to a spot only a few hundred feet from clear, clean Glacier Lake, and there spend a memorable —though perhaps damp—night beside a wild and beautiful lake. From Glacier Lake we continue north and soon traverse the wooded west shore of a skinny little lake (4900-0.5). Descending somewhat and veering east, we part company with the **Surprise Creek Trail (#1060) (4810-0.3),** which continues north to Surprise Lake and beyond, following Surprise Creek to the town of Scenic. We arc farther east and then southeast, crossing the outlet stream of the skinny lake in 100 yards, before resuming our northward traverse. After crossing two large talus slopes and re-entering forest, we abruptly join the old PCT (now the Trap Pass Trail 1060A from Surprise Lake) (5000-1.0) and follow it as it switchbacks east up to

Trap Pass (5800-0.5). From the pass we continue north and east, traversing high on the rock-and-meadow shoulder above Trap Lake. Where the route becomes more wooded, a well-defined trail (5360-0.5) branches acutely south-southwest, to descend 180 vertical feet in one-quarter mile to Trap Lake. Proceeding along the PCT, we soon swing north for a high-angle alpine traverse, with views behind the crest near Thunder Mountain and Trap Pass. Our generally gradual descent is interrupted by a forced climb to a gentle pass (5210-1.8) separating the drainages of Trapper Creek and Basin Creek before we plunge down east and then north to

122A
122B

Hope Lake Forest Camp (4400-1.2). From here an old trail (#1061) forks over the divide to descend along a tributary of Tunnel Creek. The PCT remains on the east side of the crest only a little longer before crossing west into the meadow-and-forest flatlands around Mig Lake (4661-0.7). Then we recross the divide four times in a half mile, circle around a small, unnamed lake, and again begin to climb. The trail crosses the crest above Swimming Deer Lake, traverses northeast, and then angles down to an

Outlook (4950-2.4) above Lake Josephine. A few yards beyond the outlook, the Icicle Trail (#1551) branches north-northwest before circling Lake Josephine (4681) and descending south down Icicle Creek. At this junction the PCT turns west-northwest toward Lake Susan Jane. After traversing east above this lake, we plunge almost due west and pass campsites near the northern lip of Lake Susan Jane (4595-0.5). Here we begin an undulating walk on a fir-and-hemlock-dotted hillside at the head of Mill Creek, where views down the valley are expansive. Many runoff freshets tumble down this slope. None presents any ford-

ing difficulties, but they do boast a profusion of wildflowers, including mountain bluebells, swamp whiteheads, whorled penstemon, shooting stars and white heather. A botanical key would come in handy here. Then we leave the beauty of the gardens for the bold and energetic handiwork of man: an extensive power-line cut. Just before we come into range of the humming, buzzing, crackling signature of our consumptive culture, we tarry awhile in a small, grassy glade with an infant stream, seemingly far removed from what is just around the corner. Leaving the glade, the trail runs west-northwest, climbing slightly as it enters the power-line cut. We swing north to rejoin the access road (4720-1.0), and turn left up the road. In 400 yards the PCT breaks north away from the road. Here we must climb steeply to cross the Cascade crest one last time before descending to Stevens Pass. From this minor pass (5080-0.5) we head down two short sets of switchbacks and then follow the poorly marked, often boggy PCT through open forest to a small lake (currently being destroyed by the Stevens Pass ski industry, for which it serves as a water supply). Continuing past a rope tow, a chair lift and a ski school, we emerge into a parking lot on the south side of

Stevens Pass (4056-1.7). John F. Stevens, explorer for the Great Northern Railway, recommended this pass for a rail route in 1890, and the railway was completed in 1893. Today, a gas station and cafe, with seasonally varying business hours, serve skiers, hikers and the vehicles traveling U.S. Highway 2. Leavenworth, 36 miles east on Highway 2, and Skykomish, 16 miles west, are the nearest supply towns. Traffic is fairly continuous on Route 2 in both directions the year around, especially during the ski season and the fall-color season.

122B
123

From the trailhead atop Stevens Pass at the Stevens Pass Ski Area, you walk 100 yards northeast to Summit Inn, which is a small cafe with a Texaco station. *There are no more stores along the 184-mile stretch of PCT between here and Manning Provincial Park* in Canada, so be prepared for a rugged two-week adventure. Seventy yards northeast of the cafe are public restrooms, and 35 yards north of these is our trailhead, by the northeast corner of the Chelan County Power Summit Substation. A temporary notice instructs us not to camp within 100 feet of the more popular lakes and to keep our horses—if we have any—at least 200 feet from their shores. This measure is to preserve the scenic beauty and water purity of these lakes. Our trail on Mesozoic granite, starting north as a closed road, contours a bushy slope past an assortment of aster, bleeding heart, bluebells, columbine, fireweed, lupine, monkey flower, paintbrush, parsnip and Sitka valerian before curving west into

Left: Thunder Mtn. and Trap Lake *Hartline*

a forested environment. We reach a 3-yard-wide tributary (3850-2.5) of Nason Creek, beside which one could camp, but elect to continue up to a

Meadow (4220-1.0), through which Nason Creek flows. Here among the cinquefoil, shooting stars, red heather and grass are good campsites. Mosquitoes and several species of biting flies, common in northern Washington through midsummer, will not bother you if the day is cold or misty. We climb up the trail to a second meadow, where one could camp, then switchback up to a saddle (5030-1.7), from which we can look down at beautiful Lake Valhalla and across it at the challenging west face of dark gray Lichtenberg Mountain (5844). Descending north from the saddle, we reach meadow campsites and a

Spur trail (5100-0.3) that descends southeast 200 yards to the northwest shore of deep, cool, sparkling Lake Valhalla (4830). Our trail now climbs east to a saddle, snowbound through late July, then steadily descends northeast to Union Gap and a junction with the

Smithbrook Trail (#1590) (4700-1.8), which descends eastward. From the gap, our trail descends northwest along a lower slope of Union Peak (5696) before turning north and ascending to a delightful, singing cascade (4200-1.8). Tree frogs and evening grosbeaks join in a dusky chorus as we approach the large

123
124A
124B

Janice Cabin (4150-0.4) beside shallow Lake Janus (4146), which is somewhat disappointing after Lake Valhalla. The warmer temperatures of this semiclear lake, however, do allow you a comfortable dip. Just northwest of the shelter is the clear outlet creek, but, judging by all the horse manure around the lake—despite the posted 200-foot restriction against horses—we feel you should treat the water before drinking it. Beyond this creek, the PCT switchbacks west up to the crest (5180-1.6), traverses a short, northeast slope with a view due north of distant, regal Glacier Peak (10,541), and then reaches a saddle. A moderate descent northwest takes us to a meadow (5070-0.8), from which a faint trail leads 40 yards northeast, then descends a moderately steep gully toward Glasses Lake (4626). At the west end of the meadow, our trail passes a good, designated campsite, then follows a winding crest route up past outcrops of mica schist before it reaches the upper

West shoulder (5580-2.1) of Grizzly Peak (5597). From it we hike north along the ridge, round another summit, then come upon a designated but poor campsite on a saddle. Leaving it behind, we descend moderately across a west slope, pass well above shallow Grizzly Lake (4920), cross the crest (5120-1.4) and reach a good but shadeless campsite (5030-0.2) on a grassy

Glacier Peak, from atop Grizzly Peak

flat. Descending north on a moderate-to-steep, sometimes soggy trail, we reach the crest again, then switchback down it to broad, forested **Wenatchee Pass (4230-1.0),** where there is another good campsite. Climbing north to a flat, we reach a junction with the

Top Lake Trail (#1506) (4570-0.6), which curves east one-half mile to that lake (4590). You can camp 50 yards southwest of this junction, but with Pear Lake next on the itinerary, you'd be foolish to stop here if you can still make it to that lake by dusk. Your trail heads west to a gully whose west side is composed of large boulders. Gushing from them is the outlet of Pear Lake, which is dammed behind them. We climb several short switchbacks to a saddle, a few more to a ridge, and then descend west toward Pear Lake (4809). Following the trail to the lake's northwest corner, we reach the very good

Pear Lake campsite (4830-1.0) by a few trees 35 yards from the shore. Our trail climbs above the west shore of this granite-lined lake, passes a good campsite beside a huge boulder, then soon switchbacks up to Frozen Finger Gap (5250-0.6). Looking back, we can see how Pear Lake got its name. Now we descend about 20 short switchbacks on a slope rich in mica schist which contrasts with the cliff of granitic rocks across the gully. Arriving at lower Fortune Pond, we bridge its outlet creek and meet a junction with the

Meadow Creek Trail (#1057) (4670-0.7), which bears west before descending south toward Rapid River. Above this junction are two very good campsites. Our trail starts beside the outlet creek, curves north before crossing it, and then climbs

steadily north to a large, subalpine meadow. Here, in addition to
the flower species mentioned just north of Stevens Pass, this
slope contains bistort, corn lily, elephant head, heart-leaved
arnica, ligusticum, spiraea, thistle and tiger lily, all living har-
moniously within a community of ferns. On a misty day, this
meadow becomes saturated with droplets, and you become
soaked from the waist down. We crest the west ridge (5220-1.3)
of Summit 5504, then make a steep northward descent past
seasonal creeklets before the trail eases its gradient and crosses
two permanent creeks. Thirty yards upstream from the second
one (4700-0.7) is a small but good campsite. Beyond the crossing,
the PCT makes a short climb, then contours north before its final
climb to

Saddle Gap (5060-1.3). We follow our northward-curving path
down to a junction with the unsigned **West Cady Ridge Trail
(#1054) (4930-0.3),** which climbs north-northwest. After descending north toward a prominent knob of metamorphic rock,
we follow long switchbacks down to a fair campsite west of
three-yard-wide Pass Creek. Immediately after crossing it on
stepping stones, we meet the **Pass Creek Trail (#1053) (4200-1.0),**
which descends north alongside the creek. Our trail climbs
northeast and shortly arrives at Cady Pass, where the

125
126

Cady Creek Trail (#1501) (4310-0.4) departs northeast before
dropping to that creek. At this forested pass is a dumpy, dry
campsite that we would recommend for emergency bivouac
only. A long ascent—a taste of what's to come—now begins as
the PCT switchbacks north up to a metamorphic ridge and
reaches an exposed campsite at its crest (5470-1.9). This strenuous ascent does reward us, near its top, with scenic views to the
south and east. After descending slightly to a granitic saddle, our
trail rounds the east slope of a knob (5642), then reaches another
saddle. Beyond it, trailside snow patches last well into August.
We contour across the east slope of rugged Skykomish Peak
(6368), then descend to icebound

Lake Sally Ann (5479-1.7). On the ridge just northeast of its
outlet creek are several lovely campsites of excellent quality
once the snow melts. If there is still snow or there are too many
campers, continue northeast down to a junction with the

Cady Ridge Trail (#1532) (5380-0.4), on which you can descend east 200 yards to suitable campsites on an open saddle.
Beyond this junction, our often-snowbound trail climbs northwest across a slope of greenish mica schist, glistening white-vein
quartz and speckled adamellite before it switchbacks up to
Wards Pass (5710-0.7). Turning north, we then hike along a crest
route that takes us down to the soggy, volcanic soils of Dishpan
Gap, where the

Bald Eagle Trail (#650) (5600-0.6) veers left and contours northwest. Our route veers right and crosses the southeast slope of Peak 5892 to a ridge-crest campsite (5450-0.5) on an open slope of grass, cinquefoil and fawn lilies. Should you camp here or at a similar open site, don't be surprised to see deer come around and graze beside your tent. Following the crest east across this glaciated country, we quickly arrive at a junction with the

Little Wenatchee River Trail (#1525) (5440-0.3), which contours southeast. We diagonal up the northwest slope of a triangular summit, then reach a saddle where a spur trail (5500-0.2) contours south to Trail 1525. The PCT heads north toward Kodak Peak (6121), then climbs east across its flowery, picturesque south slope of metamorphic rocks to a ridge from where both Mt. Rainier and Glacier Peak are plainly visible on clear days. Along this ridge, a footpath called the

Little Wenatchee Ridge Trail (#1524) (5660-0.7) strikes east-southeast across a long saddle. Here, too, we sign a register along this ridge crest southern boundary of Glacier Peak Wilderness. Our trail turns northwest and descends across waning snowfields before it curves north, enters forest and arrives at a fenced-in pasture at

Indian Pass (5020-1.3). Although the ground may be damp here, fresh water is lacking; hence the camping is only fair. Ascending from the southeast is the **Indian Creek Trail (#1502).** From its junction with the PCT, we arc northwest up to a southwest spur of Indian Head Peak (7442), then climb northward to an adequate campsite at the north end of shallow, semi-clear Kid Pond (5320-1.0). The location of this pond and the nature of its surrounding rocks of garnet-graphite-mica schist both indicate that it fills a slight depression behind avalanche deposits. Our trail proceeds north to a ridge and is joined by an older trail, then it descends to

126

Lower White Pass (5378-0.7), from which the old Cascade Crest Trail once descended northeast. Nowadays, the trail is called the **White River Trail (#1507).** An adequate campsite lies 30 yards east of this junction. Our trail climbs a ridge north to good campsites on the west and southwest shores of pensive Reflection Pond (5560-0.3), then traverses across snowbound northeast slopes up to a junction with an unsigned trail that we can see curving northeast from

White Pass (5904-1.9). Here, a 270-yard-long trail descends steeply southwest to a three-sided shelter on a small, open bench. The open side faces toward the slope, so you won't get a view, but neither will you get chilled by the strong, sometimes-misty winds. Back on the PCT, we follow its contouring path west-northwest to a fork where the

North Fork Sauk Trail (#649) (5950-0.6) descends steeply westward. The meadow here has such an abundance of flowers and insects, it's no wonder that birds fly north to feast on them. Flycatchers hover and snatch insects from midair as we start a steady climb west-northwest. The trail becomes dusty as we approach a small summit (6650), then turns north and shortly reaches the gray, garnet-biotite gneiss rocks of

Red Pass (6500-1.3), where one could spend a night with the marmots at a windy campsite. The view from here is nothing short of spectacular. Above us and five miles to the northeast is a towering volcano, Glacier Peak (10,541). Below us is the perennially snowclad upper canyon of the White Chuck River. To the distant south is lofty, glistening Mt. Rainier (14,410), cloaked in snow, giving it the appearance of a giant stationary cloud that reigns eternally over the distant forest. If you're heading south, you'll definitely remember your climb up to this pass. Our trail first switchbacks, then descends along the base of the east ridge of Portal Peak (6999). Since this trail is usually snowbound, most hikers slide directly down the steep, but safe, upper snowfield, then head east down-canyon until they reach the visible trail. Keeping north of the headwaters, the PCT descends toward a lone, three-foot-high cairn (5700-1.4) on a low knoll, turns northward, and then descends to campsites at a

126

127

Saddle (5500-0.3) between a 20-foot-high hill to the east and a high slope to the west. Better sites are on the hill. Just 230 yards north, we pass another campsite; then, farther down, we can see numerous campsites along the banks of the rumbling White Chuck River, below and east of us. We may spot a blue grouse and its chicks as we descend alongside a swelling creek that we cross three times via log bridges. Hikers have camped beside each crossing. Leaving the last crossing (4700-1.5), our trail switchbacks down toward the White Chuck River, parallels it above its west bank, and then crosses it (4000-1.0) eastward via a wide, planked horse bridge. We leave the river's side, follow an undulating route north, then descend to a good campsite just before a log crossing of cold, roaring

Baekos Creek (3880-1.0), whose north bank contains much green mica schist. We follow the base of its high north bank downstream a short way, switchback over it, then descend to level ground and a number of log crossings over small creeks. Mountaineers intent on climbing Glacier Peak (10,541) usually leave the PCT between Baekos and Kennedy creeks. Should you try, bring rope, crampons and ice ax. Near a campsite beside the north bank of Chetwot Creek (3730-1.2), the vegetation opens enough to give us views southwest to broad Black Mountain glacier, which spreads across the upper rim of a deeply glaciated side canyon. Continuing northward, we reach Sitkum Creek, make a precarious log crossing of it, then find ourselves at an excellent campsite with a raised fire ring and an isolated pit toilet. From this site the

White Chuck Trail (#643) (3852-0.9) descends northwest to Kennedy Hot Spring (3275-1.8). Many hikers used to skinny-dip in this small spring, but its increasing popularity led to a ban on this sport. Rather than backtrack from the spring, you can return to the PCT by descending the White Chuck Trail north for half a mile to the Kennedy Ridge Trail (#643A), then climb north up it one-and-three-fourths miles to your PCT reunion.

From Sitkum Creek, a long climb lies ahead of us. After an initial 250-yard climb north, we reach an adequate campsite. One-quarter mile later, we reach a better one beside Sitkum Creek, then we cross an unmapped creek just before reaching a morainal ridge. Enjoying a short-lasting descent northeast, we pass by small outcrops above us that are composed of quartz-and-biotite-rich Miocene adamellite intrusions. The slopes above them are composed of andesitic lava flows from Glacier Peak. We reach chilly, glacier-fed

Kennedy Creek (4050-1.2), a 10-yard-wide torrent that in 1973 had to be forded since its bridge had been washed downstream. Another bridge is scheduled to be built. After crossing the creek, we climb southwest up a path cut through unstable morainal material that is in turn being undercut by the creek. Soon we reach a junction with the

127
128A

Kennedy Ridge Trail (#643A) (4300-0.4), down which you can head west toward Kennedy Hot Spring. Its warm water indicates that molten magma is relatively close to the surface. Now the real climb begins as we ascend six short, steep switchbacks past huge andesite blocks to the lower crest of Kennedy Ridge. This we struggle upward, stopping several times to catch our breath and to admire the scenery around us. In spots, this crest is no wider than the trail. The gradient eases off and we eventually reach an excellent campsite by

Glacier Creek (5640-1.9), which recently had an avalanche roar down its canyon, destroying all the trees in its path. Leaving the creek, we switchback north, then climb northwest past adamellite boulders to a junction with the unsigned

Glacier Ridge Trail (#658) (6050-0.7), which is a six-inch wide footpath that descends that ridge westward. After a short, steep descent northeast, we contour in that direction to jump-across Pumice Creek (5900-0.5), whose bed contains metamorphic, granitic and volcanic rocks. You might try to identify all three

**Kennedy Glacier (left) and Scimitar Glacier (right)
on Glacier Peak**

types and decipher their stories. A fair campsite is beside the north bank. Our trail descends west, then contours over to a ridge (5770-1.6). North of it, we descend even more, then cross an unmapped creek (5370-0.8) on logs that are just below its fork upstream. On an open meadow atop a bluff 20 yards north of it is your last good campsite this side of Fire Creek Pass. Now we make one final effort, and *voila!* a magnificent panorama of the North Cascades unfolds around us as we gain access to

Fire Creek Pass (6350-1.7). The North Cascades of Washington contain 756 glaciers, which account for about half of all the glacier area existing within the conterminus United States. The range's great number of fairly high summits coupled with a year-round barrage from storms accounts for its vast accumulation of ice and snow. Chances are that you'll encounter at least one storm, lasting only a few days if you're lucky, before you reach the Canadian border. At Fire Creek Pass, the trail goes between two large cairns 30 yards northwest of an emergency campsite. Our usually snowbound route switchbacks down a ridge north-northeast to a ford of the outlet of perpetually frozen

Mica Lake (5430-1.1), whose cirque wall of dark metamorphic schist is intruded by light pegmatite dikes. From its shore, you can see dozens of unappealing switchbacks you'll have to climb to surmount the next ridge. As we descend farther, we must boulder-hop across wide, shallow Mica Creek, just east of which is a good, but open, campsite (5110-0.5) on a small bench. We continue to switchback eastward and reach a basin, another creek and a good, obvious campsite (4400-1.1). From it our unrelenting descent takes us down to deep, 5-yard-wide Milk Creek. A log crossing existed in 1973, but it was scheduled to be replaced with a "permanent" bridge. As you'll discover along this trail, nothing endures but change. Just 35 yards past this crossing, we meet the unsigned

128A

Milk Creek Trail (#790) (3800-1.3), descending north, which the old Cascade Crest route used to follow before the train of switchbacks to the east of us were constructed. Snowfields and avalanche hazards probably prevented the construction of a trail that would contour around Glacier Peak at the 6000-foot level. Take your time switchbacking up the east wall of this canyon. If the day is drizzly, you'll find that the "fog drip" on the flowers of this heavily vegetated slope will saturate you from the thighs down. Ahead of you grow miles of this inconsiderate vegetation that you must switchback through. Rationalizing your fate, you can observe that in this weather there are no flies or mosquitoes around to bother you. When you finally finish your creekless ascent and reach the

Ridge crest (5750-2.5), you may be greeted by a marmot. If not, at least you can expect a rest at an open campsite near a small pond. The summit due south of us is not Glacier Peak but Kennedy Peak (8384), which is a resistant high point on Glacier Peak's north ridge. Now, after a short, negligible climb, we contour the east slope of our ridge and leave behind its outcrops of densely clustered, light-colored Miocene dikes, sills and irregular masses. As we enter the deeply glaciated East Fork Milk Creek basin, these outcrops give way to pre-Tertiary metamorphic rocks. Along the south wall of this basin, our trail passes just below a small knoll (5860-1.5), 100 yards below which is an adequate campsite. Beyond this point, we shortly cross a hundred-yard-wide boulder field that is laced with creeklets. Our route now climbs gently northeast to another ridge (6090-0.6), from which we can see an open campsite at the base of a ridge knoll 10 feet below and 100 yards north of us. Our route switchbacks slightly up the ridge, contours southeast across it, then starts the first of 59 switchbacks down to Vista Creek. After a few of these, we reach the

Dolly Creek campsite (5830-0.7) beneath a few, protective mountain hemlocks. A pit toilet is immediately north; water is about 100 yards downslope. From the campsite, our path switchbacks northeast down through open forest to a saddle (5380-0.5) on Vista Ridge, where we reach a dry, open campsite. Northeast of us this resistant ridge is composed of Miocene intrusive rocks that are capped with remnant Quaternary andesite flows from Glacier Peak. Starting down into deep, glaciated Vista Creek canyon, we're grateful that we're descending the last 38 switchbacks rather than ascending them. By the time we reach the last one, 50 yards from the creek, we've left most of the "rain forest" behind, and we hike 100 yards northeast to a large, signed

128A
128B
129A

Campsite (3650-2.6) beside Vista Creek. From it, our trail descends into a Douglas-fir forest that has an understory of huckleberry, ferns and Oregon grape. The trail curves east and the gradient eases as we approach a log crossing of wide, silty Vista Creek (2877-2.1). On its southeast bank is a good campsite with a fire ring. Now we contour east across a gentle slope to a crossing of Gamma Creek (2910-0.8). Part of its flow is derived from the 140°F., sodium-chloride-bicarbonate-rich waters of Gamma Hot Springs (5000), about three miles upstream. Our trail gradually curves southeast and arrives at a junction with the

Suiattle River Trail (#798) (3028-0.7), which first bears southeast before climbing south up-river. The PCT descends north, switchbacks down to a 50-yard-long horse bridge across the silty-gray Suiattle River, then immediately reaches a junction with the

Suiattle River access trail (2860-0.8). If you turn right (south-east) and follow this trail one-third mile upstream to the aluminum Lyman Camp shelter, you'll find it no longer offers protection from the elements. One of the elements, a giant red-cedar, recently flattened it! Its large, flat site, however, is still a nice place to camp, once you get used to the horse manure. If you turn left (northwest) and follow this trail downstream, you'll pass by some campsites, then after 330 yards reach a good shelter and a separate toilet both above the south bank of Miners Creek. Our new trail segment, straight ahead, makes long, easy switchbacks up to the lower edge of Middle Ridge, then climbs east up its north slope to a junction with the

Buck Creek Pass trail (4580-4.4), which climbs five miles south to that pass. We make an initial steep descent north, bridge a nearly stagnant creek, and then quickly arrive at a very good campsite on the south bank of Miners Creek (4440-0.4). Like all large campsites we've encountered, this one suffers from horse pollution. We bridge the creek, then start up an old, northwest-curving trail that becomes horrendously steep well before its switchbacks end at the level

Suiattle Trail (#784) (5549-1.0). The old route we've just ascended is quite a contrast to the new one we ascended along Middle Ridge. If you walk 130 yards west on Trail 784, you'll encounter a popular campsite: a 15-by-20-foot roofless cabin with a 10-by-10 roofed anteroom. A small creek is immediately west of this structure. Just after we start east on our level trail, we cross a creek that contains small, green grains of malachite (copper ore) that have washed down from the mines above. These mines are located near the contact of the granitic, Miocene Cloudy Pass pluton and the pre-Cretaceous Swakane biotite gneiss. Minerals were concentrated at this contact zone when the pluton intruded and metamorphosed the overlying rocks. This area has seen some logging—very likely for the mines and their associated structures—but eastward the forest condition improves until we reach a granite-lined, 3-yard-wide creek, down which there has been noticeable avalanche damage. A hundred yards beyond it, we come to a maze of broken-down, littered, mining shacks (5500-1.3). Miners still use the only standing one, so please respect their property. Now, our trail makes a steady climb up to a junction with the

129A
129B

Suiattle Pass Foot Trail (#1279) (5920-1.0), on our right (east). After four short switchbacks, our trail crests at Suiattle Pass (5983), descends north through snow patches, crosses a gully with a spur trail north (5760-0.3), then switchbacks east down to a meadow from where the

Railroad Creek Trail (#1256) (5550-0.4) heads east over

Cloudy Pass and descends to Holden. We now start a lengthy descent north alongside South Fork Agnes Creek, and after 120 yards reach a very good campsite that has a table, fire pit and toilet. A few parts of our descent are steep, but most of the route is moderate until we reach a large, bushy meadow (4400-1.8), where the gradient eases and the views temporarily open up. Beyond it, we enter forest and reach a flat, spacious campsite (3850-1.4) between the trail and the creek that is complete with table, benches and toilet. At this campsite, and similar ones downstream, you might spot a small, stubby-tailed winter wren picking away at a fallen log in its search for insects. An interesting feature of our route north *down* the South Fork Agnes Creek canyon is how much trail we've got to climb! The trail shoots straight up every little ridge along our way down; it doesn't attempt to contour at all. We make a log crossing of 5-yard-wide Glacier Creek (3580-1.4), then quickly reach

Hemlock Camp (3560-0.2), a large flat site sunk deep between Saddle Bow Mountain (7410) to the west, and Dark Peak (8504) to the east. It comes equipped with benches, a table and a fire ring. Continuing north along our near-the-creek route through a forest of western hemlock, Engelmann spruce, western red-cedar, Douglas-fir and western white pine, we descend past Mt. Blankenship (5926) to the west and Needle Peak (7885) to the east before reaching

129B
130
131A

Spruce Creek Camp (2900-2.7). On the topographic map, this site is identified as *Cedar Camp*. Both species of trees exist here. At this site, you'll find only log stumps around a fire pit, but it's still quite a nice camp. Our canyon grows ever deeper as we trek northward, catch a glimpse of the blue-green waters of the South Fork, and then contour over to the well-equipped **Swamp Creek Camp (2780-1.3).** Here, beside the seven-yard-wide torrent, the **Swamp Creek Trail (#712)** begins a three-mile climb up the creek toward Dark Glacier, which is tucked in a deep amphitheater below Dark Peak. Leaving this very good campsite, we cross the creek on a sturdy horse bridge, progress north to the rim of the inner gorge of the South Fork (2570-1.6), then gradually curve down to a junction with the

West Fork Agnes Creek Trail (#1272) (2160-1.4), which descends west-northwest to that creek. Several fair campsites are just west of this junction, but much better ones are at the Fivemile Camp, about 100 yards east, above the west bank of Pass Creek. These are the last campsites we'll see within Glacier Peak Wilderness. Hiking northeast, we'll soon leave the granitic rocks of the Cloudy Pass batholith behind and walk upon schist and gneiss that date back to Jurassic times or earlier. The overpowering canyon which we hike through bears a strong resemblance to deep Kings Canyon in the Sierra Nevada of California, except that this one supports a much denser growth of flowers, shrubs and trees. We pass by seasonal Trapper Creek (2070-1.1), then approach Agnes Creek, which, like its South Fork, possesses an inner gorge. Our undulating trail goes right out to its brink at several spots, then descends to switchbacks that take us down to a massive bridge 40 feet above roaring

Agnes Creek (1550-3.6), which, at this point, is larger than most rivers we've seen along the Pacific Crest Trail. Now within the Lake Chelan National Recreation Area, we cross the 27-yard-long bridge, climb a low ridge, then contour northwest to a trailhead at a bend in the

Stehekin River Road (#3505) (1650-0.2). You can descend it 200 yards to the High Bridge Ranger Station, which is immediately northeast of a bend in the Stehekin River. During the summer, shuttle buses from the Stehekin resort area, 10.6 miles downstream, depart daily at 8 A.M., 10 A.M., 2 P.M. and 4 P.M., arriving at the High Bridge Ranger Station about an hour later. The 8 A.M. and 2 P.M. buses continue from this station north to Cottonwood Camp, 11.3 miles up-river, before returning to Stehekin. You can take a bus up to the PCT Bridge Creek trailhead if you don't want to hike 4.6 rocky miles up the road to it. In 1973 this taxi service cost 50c per person and 25c per pack. Of course, you can take the bus over to the Stehekin Resort, and if its supplies are insufficient for your tastes, you can take a 46-mile boat ride ($7.50 round trip in 1973) along sinuous Lake Chelan to the resort town of Chelan. If you take a shuttle bus north to the Bridge Creek trailhead, you'll bypass some little-used campgrounds and some excellent fishing spots.

131A
131B
132

From our trailhead near the High Bridge Ranger Station, we start hiking north and after 35 yards reach the **High Bridge Campground.** It has a shelter and outside tables. Water can be obtained by walking back down the road to the high bridge and then descending steep, short switchbacks northward to the west bank of the Stehekin River. About 80 yards north of the campgound's entrance, we pass a trail on our left (west) that ascends toward upper Agnes Gorge. Farther along our closed road, we enter North Cascades National Park before reaching

Tumwater Campground (1750-0.8), which has a table and two outhouses, but no shelter. In 250 yards we bridge the Stehekin River, climb above good fishing spots along its east bank, and then arrive at **Dolly Varden Campground (1850-1.0),** more spartan than the two preceding campgrounds. Next on our itinerary is **Shady Campground (1950-1.5),** near a roadside pipe spring. Nearing our trailhead, we reach the **Bridge Creek Ranger Station (2105-1.0),** and just beyond it pass **Bridge Creek Campground**

with its shelter. After a few more minutes of walking, we arrive at the

PCT Bridge Creek trailhead (2180-0.3), located 240 yards southeast of Road 3505's crossing of Bridge Creek. Glad to be back on a trail again, we climb up a wandering path that takes us past a small lily-pad pond, on a bench, then winds to the edge of the Bridge Creek gorge and climbs its slopes to jump-across Berry Creek (2720-1.7). Watching out for western toads, we climb a little higher on the slope before we descend to a side-planked horse bridge above wild, roaring

Bridge Creek (2540-1.0). Climbing a few yards north of the bridge, we reach the dusty, rustic **North Fork Camp** atop a rocky bluff that overlooks the junction of the North Fork with Bridge Creek. The camp's resident landlords—golden-mantled ground squirrels—may exact "rent" from your backpack while you're not looking. From this site we switchback east up to a junction with the

North Fork Bridge Creek Trail (#1233) (2810-0.3), which climbs northward. We climb east up a bushy, aromatic slope, reach a point several hundred feet above Bridge Creek, and take in gorge-ous views below us as we descend slightly to a small, stonewall campsite immediately before a saddle. Beyond it, we descend north to a challenging ford across wide, alder-lined Maple Creek (3070-1.5). Successfully completing a tricky ten-yard boulder-hop across it, we then follow our level, relaxing path east and come to a 250-yard-long **spur trail (3130-1.7)** that descends southeast, steeply at first, through a meadow of tall cow parsnips, to **Six Mile Camp**, a well-furnished site designed with horseback riders in mind. Not far beyond this spur trail, the

132
133A
133B

Rainbow Lake Trail (3240-0.7) peels off from the PCT, descends southeast, and climbs up South Fork Canyon to Pass 6230, immediately west of domineering Bowan Mountain (7895), and Rainbow Lake south of the pass. From the junction, our route continues east through alternating forest and brush cover, then reaches a junction with a 110-yard-long **spur trail (3510-1.5)** that descends first southwest, then southeast to the loveliest Bridge Creek campsite: **Hide-Away Camp**. Strictly for backpackers, this shady, creekside campsite has a table, log stumps and a fire ring. Continuing east within hearing distance of the creek, we leave this campsite and eventually turn northeast just before reaching a junction with the

Twisp Pass trail (#1277) (3635-0.9), which curves east and bridges Bridge Creek after 70 yards. Forty yards east-northeast from this crossing, a right fork veers southeast 30 yards to the large, flat, dusty, but well-furnished Fireweed Camp. Our trail climbs moderately northeast, passes an old log cabin, on our left,

View up South Fork Bridge Creek

(west), leaves North Cascades National Park, and reaches a shallow, wide ford of Bridge Creek (4145-2.2). Now we climb north to a junction with the little-used

Stiletto Peak Trail (#1232) (4250-0.2), which leads east-northeast. After a few minutes' walk, we make a log crossing of State Creek, pass an adequate campsite on its west bank, and then continue north toward the traffic we hear on the highway above us. We quickly encounter the abandoned **Washington Pass Trail (#1275) (4420-0.5),** on our right (east), which was desecrated when the North Cascades Highway was paved over it. This new road, completed in 1972, lessened the wilderness experience at least to the same extent that the new Tioga Road in Yosemite National Park diminished that park's High Sierra wilderness character. Our trail arcs northwest up to a

Spur trail (4510-0.5) that forks right (west) 50 yards to a parking lot beside the highway at a point 0.1 mile below its crossing of Bridge Creek. Our trail, also called the **Bridge Creek Trail (#419),** bears west-southwest 35 yards to a tricky ford of Bridge Creek, then parallels the highway west up to the outlet creek (4705-0.7) of Rainy Lake. From it, our path climbs gently north,

levels off and strikes a course through the soggy headwaters of
Bridge Creek before reaching a junction with the

Rainy Lake Trail (#310) (4830-0.8), which climbs gently
southward before descending to that lake. In about 60 yards, we
reach a very short spur trail that immediately crosses over Bridge
Creek and reaches a large roadside parking lot. The PCT, under
construction during the summer of 1973, was being extended
north a quarter mile so that it would cross the

North Cascades Highway (State 20) (4855-0.3) at Rainy Pass.
Here our trail leaves the North Cascades Highway at the Skagit
County boundary sign. To reach this point from the Pacific Crest
Trail parking lot, hike north along the highway past the Rainy
Pass sign, then turn east into Douglas-fir forest at the county-line
sign. Bearing north almost immediately, we begin a climbing
134 northward traverse. One creek, draining Cutthroat Peak (7865),
cascades across our path even in September and October.
Numerous other streams are of nuisance value early in the season, but typically dry up by late August. The grade levels as we
near

Porcupine Creek (5080-1.5). After bridging the creek, we turn
northeast to parallel it and resume our ascent. A pair of switchbacks lift the path away from the stream bed and guide us onto a
steep, open slope where avalanches sweeping down from Peaks
7004 and 7762 may threaten May and June hikers. After traversing higher to contour around the headwaters bowl of Porcupine
Creek, we switchback up the steep, glacier-formed basin wall.
Deciduous larches, the poetic tamaracks, add foreground to the
rugged panorama unfolding before us. Black Peak (8970) and
Corteo Peak (8100), across the highway, front the more distant

Lewis Glacier and Black Peak   *Bev Hartline*

Cutthroat Pass *Bev Hartline*

North Cascades. Scrub huckleberry and heather compose the basic ground cover which "springtime" (July) flowers eloquently embroider. We pass campsites which are inviting, though lacking late-season water, as the PCT levels to the west of grassy, granitic

Cutthroat Pass (6820-3.6). Here the unsigned Cutthroat Lake Trail (#483) forks east to begin its traversing descent to Cutthroat Lake (4935), visible in the valley below. Liberty Bell Mountain (7720), a favorite rock climb, peaks above the ridge across the lake. We head northeast to arc around two bowls, contouring across steep scree slopes beneath precipitous cliffs. Before leaving the second cirque we choose the upper and more traveled of two trails. The lower trail dead-ends on the ridge 100 yards ahead. Climbing slightly, we reach a crest and pause to enjoy a picturesque view of Tower Mountain (8444). Our route continues northward, balancing precariously across a precipice before executing several short, tight switchbacks down the rugged north ridge. Avoiding the rock walls above Granite Pass, we descend south to zigzag above beautiful, glacier-carved Swamp Creek valley, Then, at

134

Granite Pass (6290-2.4), we reach "terra flata" and are welcomed into a sheltered camp. Don't expect convenient late-season water here. From the camp our route to Methow Pass makes a long traverse of the open lower slopes of Tower Mountain. Scrub alpine fir, western white pine, mountain ash and heather provide little protection for sun-beaten or windswept walkers. Outcrops of the Golden Horn granodiorite are clearly exposed by the trail cut. Upon reaching the bowl below Snowy Lakes, we lose some precious elevation as we drop into an idyllic park, where a bubbling stream, grassy flowerlands, larch and spruce all recommend a large campsite (6300-2.2). Shedding our packs and donning our sweaters, we settle in. Firewood in this delicate alpine valley is in limited supply, and is better left unburned. A cross trail from the campsite heads north, up-valley, to Upper and Lower Snowy Lakes in a higher cirque. From the camp a pair of switchbacks help us climb out of the bowl to set up the approach to

Methow Pass (6600-0.9) (pronounced MET-how). Views of Mt. Arriva (8215) and Fisher Peak (8050) are the last we'll have of the mountains west of Granite Creek. Mt. Hardy (7197), just west of the pass, and Golden Horn (8366), to the north, will stay with us during our trek down the valley of the Methow River's West Fork. Like most high-elevation "campsites," Methow Pass is waterless when it is not swampy. Leaving Methow Pass on a northward traverse, we spy below us on a level bench a back-packers' campsite with an uncertain water supply. Now zigzag-ging into the valley, the PCT crosses a few infant streams, then straightens to parallel the West Fork of the Methow. At sunset, Golden Horn glows spectacularly against the deep blue-black of the eastern sky. A long, slight but steady downgrade brings us to Golden Creek and **Willis Camp (4570-4.2)**. Nimbly rockhopping the stream, we have only a short stint before bridging the

134
135

West Fork Methow River (4390-0.7). A small camp by the bridge on the east bank is the best trailside camp between here and Brush Creek. Within 200 yards the level path enters the first of several avalanche paths. At a PCT mileage sign we merge onto the route of the old Cascade Crest Trail (#756) (4380-0.8). This overgrown trail climbs west out of the Methow Valley via Mebee Pass to descend along East Creek, pass the Gold Hill Mine, and meet Granite Creek and Washington Highway 20. This trail also extends diagonally 0.2 mile downhill to riverside Horse Heaven Camp. The PCT, bending east and crossing what the map calls Jet Creek, reaches a junction with the

Mill Creek Trail (#755) (4380-0.2), which looks like a rocky stream bed in the grass of the clearing. Almost immediately we cross signed Jet Creek, dry in late season. Douglas-fir, western hemlock and western white pine form stands of trees between avalanche paths. The scree fields change in character and com-position as we head east out of the granodiorite body and into a zone of lower Cretaceous graywackes ("muddy" sandstones), conglomerates, slates and shales. Then our trail turns northeast to enter the mouth of Brush Creek's canyon. Passing a small campsite, we cross Brush Creek on a bridge and in 50 yards meet the

West Fork Methow Trail (#480) (4280-1.9). Here we zig once and start climbing in earnest along steep, brushy Brush Creek. A few small campsites line the trail in this fairly hospitable and picturesque valley, and high in the west some small glaciers cling between the rugged upper cliffs of Azurite Peak (8400). A few switchbacks ease the grade of the final climb to

Glacier Pass (5520-2.8), where campsites without nearby late-season water are found in the forest-sheltered gap. Two trails, the first heading north, the second trending west, are separated by 100 PCT trail yards. Ambling on, we gear down for a long, zigzagging climb to a grassy pass. Dwindling scrub alpine fir, spruce and larch accompany us up the slope. Pausing for breath, we appreciate the view of three little lakes nestled near the head of South Fork Slate Creek's glacial valley, as well as the broadening panorama of the North Cascades. At last we top off the climb and descend slightly along the ridge into an alpine-garden pass (6750-2.6) above South Fork Trout Creek. Here the trail begins a long traverse northeastward. Beyond the first ridge we round is a pleasant trailside campsite with water (6600-1.0). Continuing, we climb to a windy, viewful pass (6900-0.9) on the southwest shoulder of Tatie Peak (7386). As our trail contours around the peak we pass stratified outcrops of alternating shale and conglomerate, then approach a knife-edge saddle above Ninetynine Basin, beyond which the Slate Peak Lookout Tower (7440) is prominent. A descending traverse guides us around Peak 7405 through a gap in a side ridge. Both the Harts Pass Road and the Brown Bear Mine house remains can be seen from here. Angling down, we pass below the sites of the mine tunnels, not obvious from the trail, and approach dirt Road 3739. Twenty yards short of the road (6440-2.8), PCT emblems guide us onto a new stretch of trail that avoids it. In 150 yards we cross the jeep-trail access to the Brown Bear tunnels, and then continue to traverse above Road 3739. A trail from the road joins us as we approach and then thread a minor gap (6390-0.7). Beneath exposed outcrops of banded slate and gray sandstone, we traverse north along a steep hillside before our trail turns to traverse down to

135

136

Harts Pass (6198-1.3). A Forest Service Guard Station, manned during the summer, is on the east side of Harts Pass Road (#374) across from a parking lot and car-camping area. The small community of Mazama is 18.7 miles east on Road 374. Also at the pass, Road 3730 branches east-northeast from Road 374 to parallel the PCT for 1.3 miles before switchbacking up to Slate Peak Lookout.

The Slate Creek mining district was a relatively rich mining area in the State of Washington. Boom camps were fairly populated in the early 1890s until word of the Klondike bonanza lured all the miners away. Del Hart, who owned some mines near Slate Creek, commissioned Charles H. Ballard in 1895 to survey a road from Mazama to the mining area. The pass through which the road was routed now bears Hart's name. The road today is a favorite summer-recreation route and one of the best access **136** roads to the Pasayten Wilderness, which we will soon enter. Gold, silver, copper, lead and zinc are among the metals whose ores were mined in the Slate Creek District. An interesting sidelight to the history of this area is that the first hydroelectric power plant in the high Cascades was installed here. O.B. Brown designed, paid for and supervised construction of the 350-kilowatt plant that he located on the South Fork of Slate Creek.

From the PCT crossing of Road 374, a scant 35 yards north-northwest of the pass proper, we proceed east-northeast through partly open spruce-fir woods parallel to Forest Service Road

Silver Star Mtn. above Harts Pass   *Hartline*

Windy Pass   *Fred Hartline*

3730 and about 100 feet below it. Beyond a meadow our trail switchbacks up onto a small shoulder with an adequate camp, where we come to a

Junction (3560-1.6) with a spur trail to Road 3730. It is about 0.1 mile east-southeast down this spur to parking spaces. Continuing west-northwest on the PCT, we ascend gradually past scattered Lyall larches, common on this small shoulder. Soon the shoulder gives out, leaving the trail hanging on the side of Slate Peak, with spectacular views down the Slate Creek valley, dominated by Mt. Baker (10,778) and other peaks to the west. Passing occasional outcrops of gray and green slate, we descend gradually to the

Pass (6700-2.2) just above Benson Creek Camp. Still on the west side of the divide, we climb up around an arm and descend past Buffalo Pass (6550-0.7) to

Windy Pass (6257-0.9), from where a trail crosses ours to descend south-southwest to Indiana Basin. In about 35 yards we pass a sign heralding our entrance into the Pasayten Wilderness. The PCT continues north-northwest, leading us out of true-to-its-name Windy Pass and around to the northeast cirque of Tamarack Peak (7290)—clad in tamarack, or larch. After crossing a small basin with water and an adequate camp, the trail switchbacks up and over an arm of Tamarack Peak, descends the open north cirque, and finally traverses the northwest arm of the mountain to

Foggy Pass (6180-2.2). From this pass we cross to the west side of the divide for a brief wooded hike to Jim Pass (6270-0.7). Then, back on the east side of the divide, we traverse around Jim Peak (7033) to the rocky shoulder called Devils Backbone (6180-1.3). Descending into the north cirque of Jim Peak, the PCT crosses the head of Shaw Creek and ascends gradually for

136

137

138

about a mile before plunging down switchbacks to a junction with Trail 752 at

Holman Pass (5050-4.4). This pass is heavily wooded and not particularly nice for camping, although wildlife abounds in the vicinity. We climb northwest out of Holman Pass, crossing the outlet stream from Goat Lakes in about a mile, and switchback up a grassy knoll to a never failing spring (6200-2.4) and a good but much used camp. From here the trail traverses up the steep, grassy slopes bounding Canyon Creek to

Rock Pass (6491-1.2). A good early-season bypass of the precipitous east-wall traverse of Powder Mountain (7714) climbs over the divide about 300 yards southeast of Rock Pass and descends into the avalanche-swept valley of Rock Creek. The PCT stays high on the rugged east wall of Powder Mountain for the most exposed hiking of this last leg of the PCT. Descending gradually, we rejoin the bypass trail just beyond an unreliable creek (and/or snowfield) draining the northeast cirque of Powder Mountain. We then climb the beautiful garden slopes of a small ridge, past nestled camps and a trail leading via Coney Basin down to the Pasayten River, as we follow the PCT into misnamed, rock-strewn

138
139

Woody Pass (6624-1.8). From here the trail traverses open slopes with a few wooded fingers, the least spectacular side of Three Fools Peak (7930), until it rounds the south arm of the cirque that cradles Mountain Home Camp, a flat, grassy bench with good camping. Beyond, the trail begins to climb steadily as it traverses the grassy headwall of the cirque. Shortly after we arc to the north, climbing through occasional stands of scrub conifers, a faint trail (6800-2.5) takes off down a more or less open gully to the flat bench of Mountain Home Camp, now 400 feet directly below us. Continuing on the PCT, a short switchback brings us to the crest of Lakeview Ridge, on which a short spur trail takes us to an enticing view of a nestled lake 1000 feet below, and the valley of Chuchuwanteen Creek beyond. The PCT continues along the crest for a short distance before it is forced to the west just long enough to switchback once more before climbing to an

Unnamed summit (7126-0.7) on Lakeview Ridge. From here we have views on all sides, weather permitting: to the south, the very rugged Three Fools Peak; to the north our first glimpse of Hopkins Lake; and farther north and west, the rugged Cascades of Washington and Canada. Now heading down toward Hopkins Pass, we stick to the ridge crest most of the time until we are forced by Peak 6873 on the ridge to pass east of it. Then our route switchbacks around the north side of the amphitheater for which Hopkins Lake is the "stage." Several short switchbacks and two longer ones bring us down nearly to the level of the lake, to where a trail (6220-1.7) to dependable campsites at Hopkins Lake (6171) takes off to the southwest. We continue almost eastward for a few hundred yards to

Hopkins Pass (6122-0.2), where the old trail down Chuchuwanteen Creek linking up with the Boundary Trail is marked *abandoned.* The Pacific Crest Trail continues north-northwest from Hopkins Pass, traversing the mostly wooded west slopes of Blizzard Peak (7622). After a mile we reach a stream and its clearing, then re-enter woods and continue our traverse about 0.4 mile before starting a gradual descent toward Castle Pass. Shortly before the pass we join the Boundary Trail (#749), turn sharply left and follow it around a small hummock to

Castle Pass (5451-2.5), where we might lunch in the sunshine of a small open area. Then, after meandering northward down a quarter mile of lush alpine gardens, the trail becomes firmly established on the east slope of the Route Creek watershed. We cross two seasonal streams and two avalanche paths, one from the east and one from the west. A reasonable camp lies 200 yards off the trail on the edge of one avalanche track; don't stay there if there is still much snow on the slopes above. Continuing the traverse, we come to two reliable streams in about a mile, then leave the woods for more-open slopes with rounded granite outcrops. Past two more streams and a stock gate across the trail, we finally pound down the last four switchbacks to

139
140

Monument 78: U.S.-Canadian Border (4240-4.1). After shooting several pictures of the scaled-down, five-foot-high, bronze "Washington Monument," we leave the Pasayten Wilderness for the final leg of our trip. Welcome to Canada! (See the section on border crossing in Chapter 2.) Plunging into the dense, wet valley-bottom woods, we emerge only briefly, in a few hundred yards, to cross Castle Creek's raging torrent or calm burble (depending on season) on a rustic log bridge. Back in the woods, the trail winds through dense, young, spruce-fir forest, climbing steadily upward. Occasionally the undergrowth gives way to partly open glades with white-barked birch trees. As the path climbs, we cross from granite to slate and back again, plod up a single pair of switchbacks, cross a few ravines, jump a few creeks and arrive at the west base of Windy Joe Mountain (5987). Here the PCT takes a sharp turn to the left; to the right is a hunters' camp, the last camp before the civilized roar of Route 3, Canada's main east-west thoroughfare. Continuing northwest 0.3 mile on the PCT brings us to a junction with the

Mt. Frosty Trail (5130-4.3). From here the PCT continues to traverse, with a little climbing, around Windy Joe Mountain to a junction with the **Windy Joe Jeep Road (5300-0.5).** This road

leads from the summit of the mountain down to Route 3 very near
Manning Park Headquarters. We turn down the road and pound
the last miles of generally well-graded—but sometimes remarkably steep—road into the Similkameen River valley. Crossing an
ample bridge over the river, we climb just a little to enter the

Parking lot (3680-2.5) that marks the end of the long trail—or
the beginning, if you are going south. Our trail is signed in re-
verse as *Frosty Mtn. Trail, Windy Joe Trail.* Hikers arriving on
Highway 3 may have trouble finding the parking lot, as it is
140 marked only by a small brown sign on the south side of the road,
saying *Windy Joe, Mt. Frosty, Mon. 78.* The lot is about 0.2 mile
east on Highway 3 from Manning Park Headquarters, or 0.4 mile
east from Manning Park Lodge. Hikers arriving on the trail can
turn west on Highway 3 and go 0.4 mile to the lodge, where food
and lodging are available, as well as bus service to and from
Vancouver, B.C.

We hope you arrived warm, dry, happy and healthy. If you
hiked all the way from Mexico to Canada, won't you please write
us and tell us how things went for you.

Manning Park, British Columbia   *Hartline*

6

The Maps

The 140 pages of topographic maps which follow cover the entire Oregon-Washington PCT route and our suggested alternate routes. Some maps have shaded portions, because they were photographed from topographic maps available only with green overprint. 138 maps, which are portions of U.S. Geological Survey 7.5' or 15' quadrangles, have been reduced or enlarged to a scale of 1:50,000, or about 0.8 mile per inch. On these maps there is no border overlap; the next page continues exactly where the preceding page left off. Two maps, at a scale of 1:250,000, or about 4 miles per inch, show an alternate route along State Highway 96 in northern California. All but these two are oriented so that north is at the top of the page; on the two, a north arrow and a graphic scale are printed on each. The graphic scale for the 1:50,000 maps is reproduced below.

LEGEND

U.S.G.S. map symbols		Wilderness Press symbols	
Heavy-duty road	⸺	Freeway	▬▬▬
Medium-duty road	═▬➤	* Major roads	══➤
Light-duty road	══	* Minor roads	═══➤
Dirt or jeep road	======	* Trail	▬ ▬ ▬➤
Trail	------	PCT	⸺
R.R.: single track	┼─┼	Proposed PCT	· · · · · ·
R.R.: multiple tracks	╫═╫	Alternate routes	▬ ▬ ▬

(*An arrowhead means the route continues in that direction.)

0	1	2	3 miles

Mt. McLoughlin, southern Oregon; Glacier Peak Wilderness, northern Washington; Mt. Washington, central Oregon.

To see these stereopairs in three dimensions, hold the book in front of you about 18 inches from your eyes. *Relax* your eyes. Stare blankly *through* the page at some imaginary object far away. *Do not focus on the page.* You will first see two fuzzy images, but these will gradually overlap into one fuzzy image—if your eyes are relaxed. *After* you obtain one fuzzy image, focus on it.

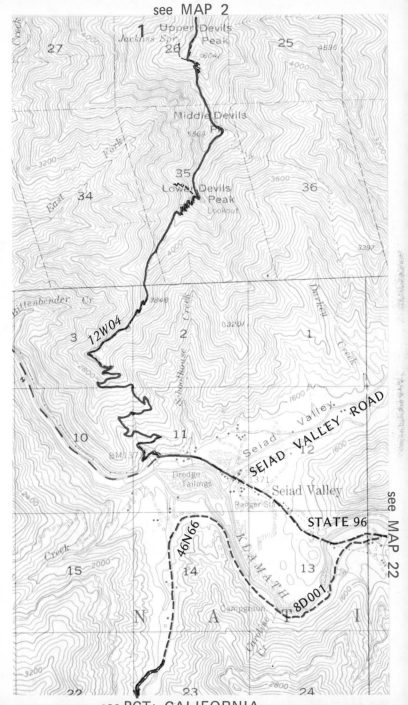

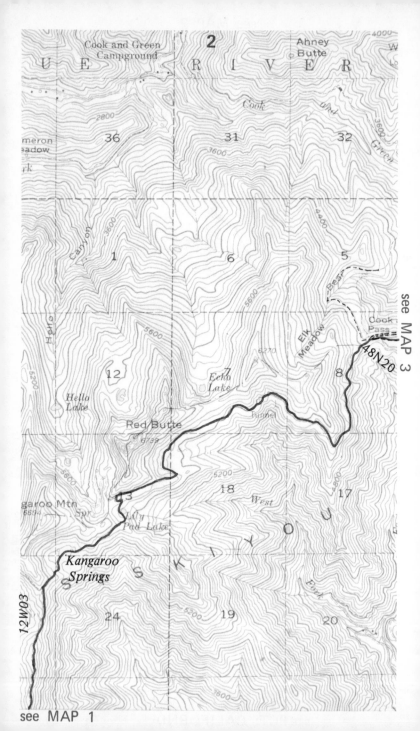

Cook and Green
Campground

Ahney
Butte

U   E   R   I   V   E   R

meron
meadow
rk

Cook

36   31   32

Cook Green

1   6   5

Bear

Cook
Pass

48N20

Elk
Meadow

12   7   8

Echo
Lake

Hello
Lake

Red Butte

Tunnel

18   West   17

garoo Mtn
Spr

Lily
Pad Lake

Kangaroo
Springs

S   K   I   Y   O   U

24   19   20

Fork

12W03

see MAP 3

see MAP 1

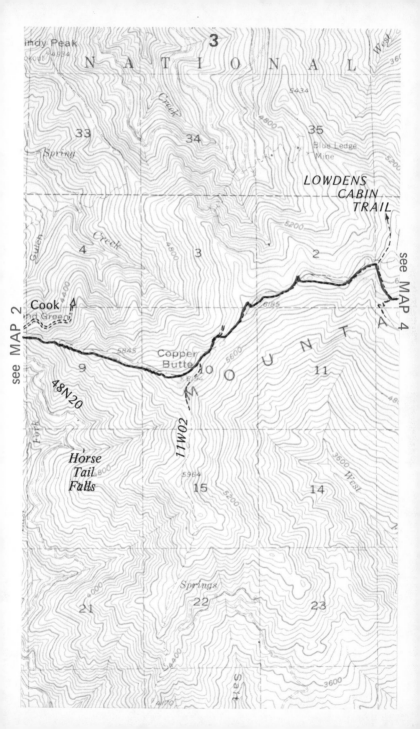

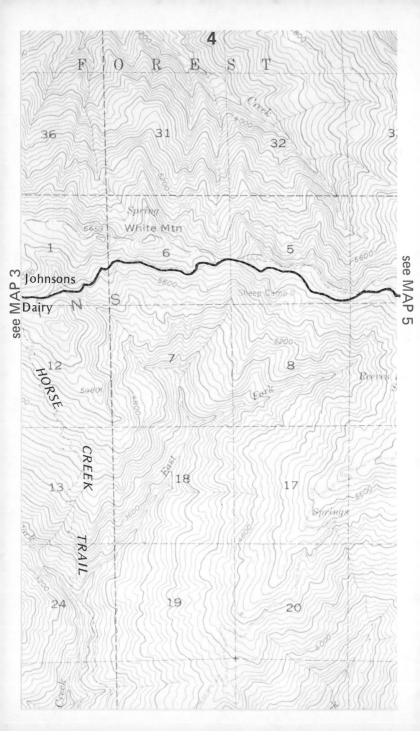

FOREST

Creek

36   31   32   3

Spring

White Mtn

1   6   5

Johnsons
Dairy

Sheep Camp

N   S

12   7   8   Reeves

HORSE

Fork

CREEK

East

13   18   17

Springs

TRAIL

24   19   20

Creek

see MAP 3

see MAP 5

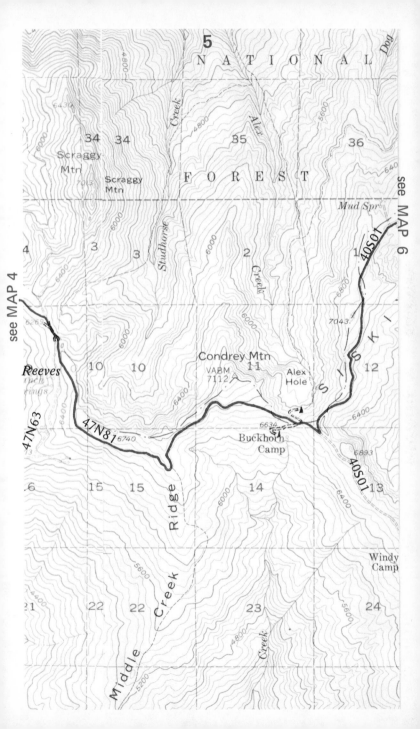

see MAP 4

see MAP 6

N A T I O N A L

Dog

Creek

Alex

34   34

Scraggy
Mtn

Scraggy
Mtn

F O R E S T

Mud Spr

35

36

4   3   3

Studhorse

2

Creek

Reeves

Spch
rings

10   10

Condrey Mtn

VABM
7112

11

Alex
Hole

12

40S01

7043

47N63

47N81 6740

6634

Buckhorn
Camp

6893

6   15   15

Ridge

14

40S01

13

Creek

Windy
Camp

21   22   22

Middle

23

24

Creek

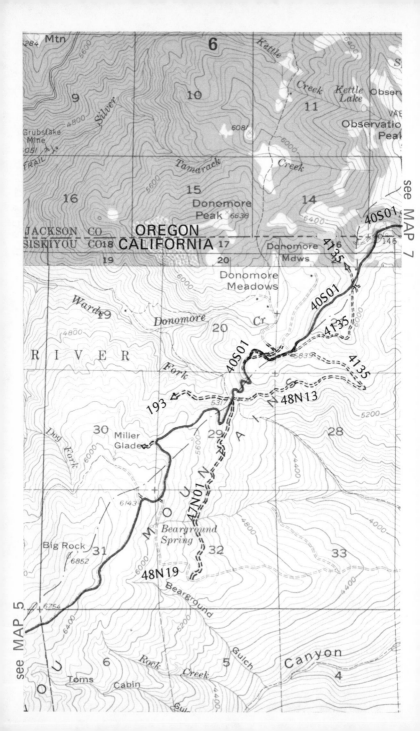

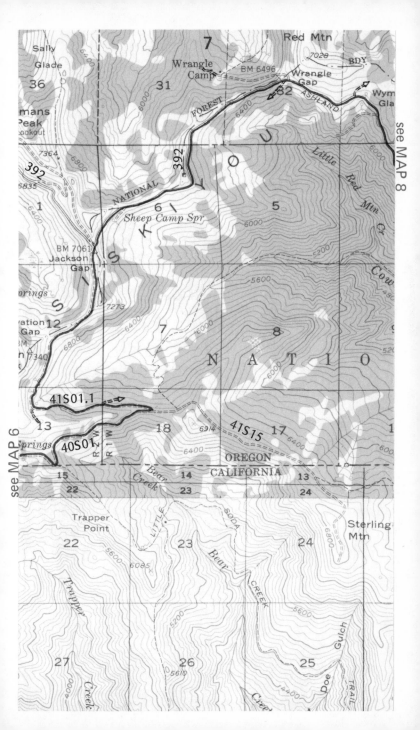

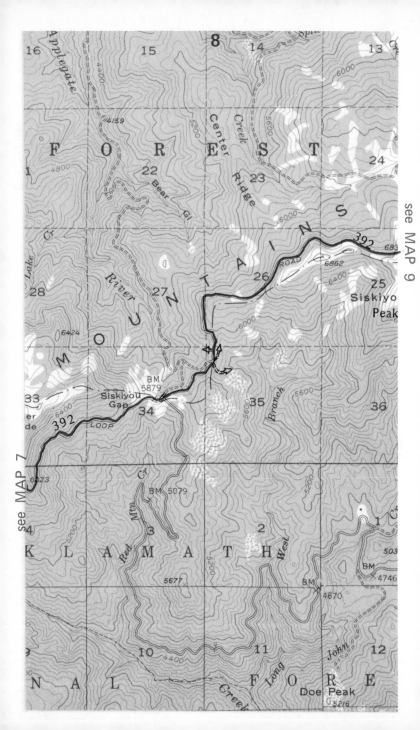

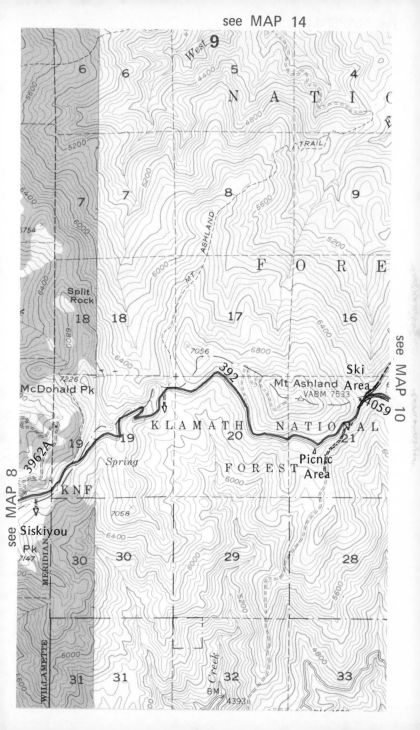

West **9**

6

6

5

4

N A T I O

7

7

8

9

TRAIL

Split
Rock

18

18

17

16

7056

392

Ski

Mt Ashland Area

VABM 7533

McDohald Pk

3962A

KLAMATH   NATIONAL

19

19

20

21

Spring

F O R E S T

Picnic
Area

KNF

7058

Siskiyou
Pk
7147

30

30

29

28

31

31

Creek

32

BM
4393

33

see MAP 8

see MAP 10

1059

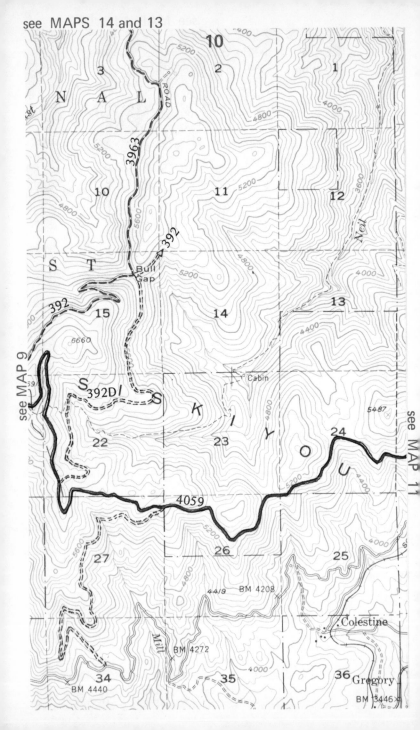

10

3

2

1

N A L

ROAD

3963

10

11

12

Neil

S T

392

Bull
Gap

392

15

14

13

6660

Cabin

see MAP 9

S 392D

S

K

I

Y

5487

24

see MAP 11

22

23

O

U

4059

27

26

25

44/9

BM 4208

Colestine

Mill

BM 4272

34

35

36 Gregory

BM 4440

BM 3446

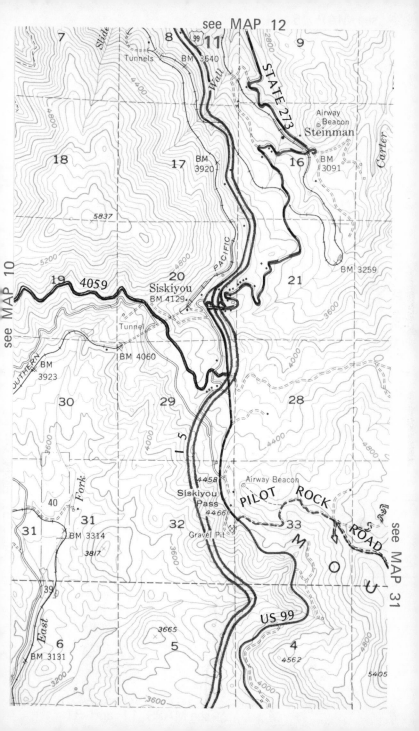

see MAP 12

see MAP 10

see MAP 31

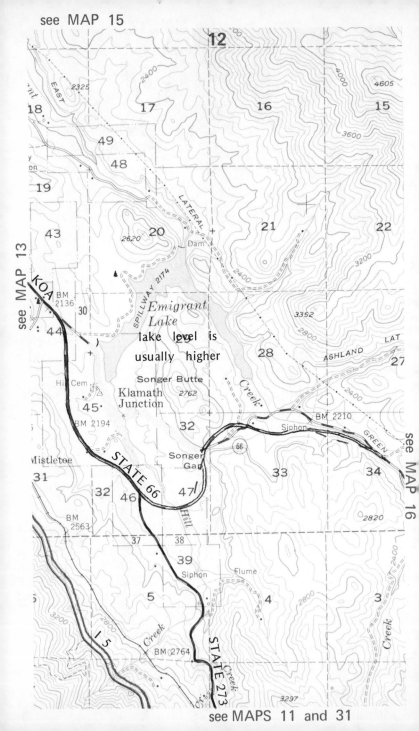

see MAP 15

12

see MAP 13

18

17

16

15

49

48

19

20

21

22

43

KOA

BM 2136

30

44

Emigrant Lake

lake level is

usually higher

28

23

Hi. Cem

Songer Butte

Klamath

Junction

2762

27

see MAP 16

45

BM 2194

32

BM 2210

Siphon

Mistletoe

STATE 66

Songer Gap

33

34

31

32

46

47

Hill

BM 2563

37

38

39

Siphon

Flume

5

4

3

I 5

Creek

BM 2764

STATE 273

Creek

3297

see MAPS 11 and 31

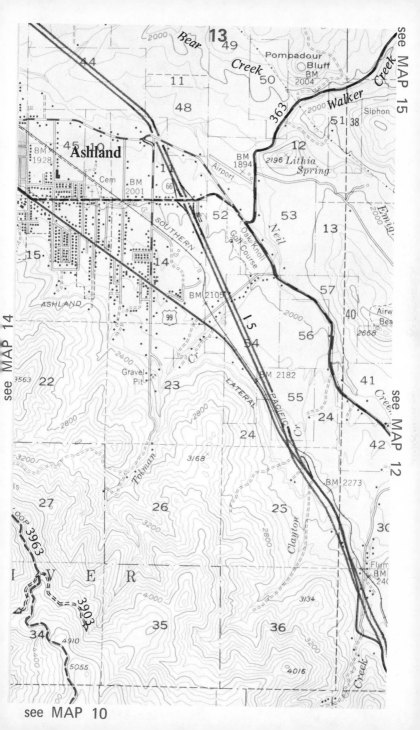

see MAP 15
see MAP 14
see MAP 12
see MAP 10

13

Bear Creek

Walker Creek

Pompadour Bluff
BM 2004

363

49

50

11

48

51 38

Siphon

45 10

Ashland

BM 1928

Cem

BM 2001

66

12

BM 1894

2196 Lithia Spring

52

53

13

Airport

Oak Knoll Golf Course

Neil

Emig

15

14

57

BM 2105

40

Airw Bea

2668

99

56

54

ASHLAND

22

23

Gravel Pit

2400

LATERAL

BM 2182

41

55

PACIFIC

24

42

2800

24

3563

2800

3963 LOOP

27

26

Tolman

3/68

3200

25

2800

Clayton Cr

BM 2273

30

Flum BM 240

3903

34

4910

4000

35

3134

36

3200

5055

4016

Creek

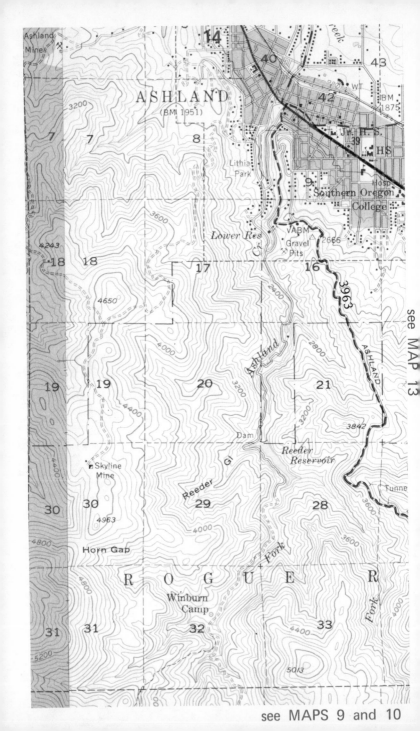

see MAP 13

see MAPS 9 and 10

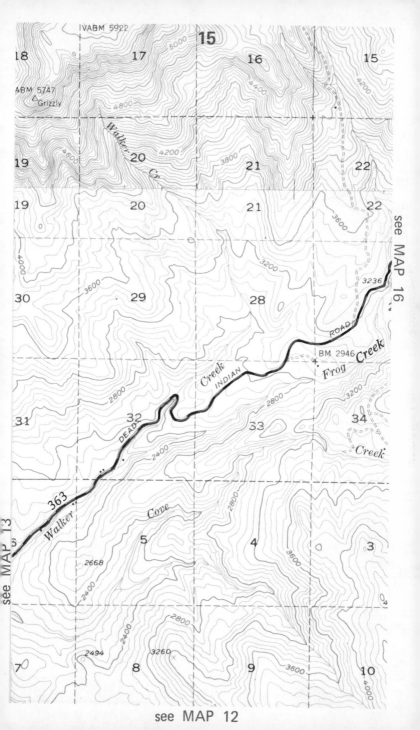

see MAP 16
see MAP 13
see MAP 12

VABM 5922

15

18   17   16   15

ABM 5747
Grizzly

Walker Cr.

19   20   21   22

19   20   21   22

3236

30   29   28

Creek INDIAN

Frog Creek

ROAD

BM 2946

31   32   33   34

DEAD

Creek

363

Walker   Cove

5   4   3

2668

7   8   9   10

2494   3260

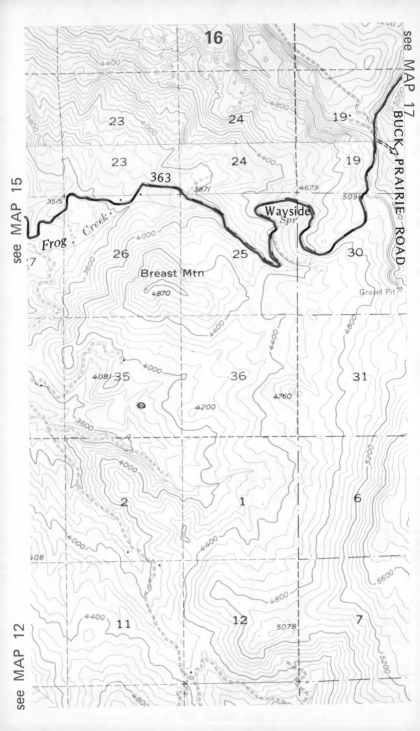

BUCK PRAIRIE ROAD

23
24
19
23
24
19
363
3871
4679
509
Wayside
Spr
Frog
Creek
35/5
26
25
30
Breast Mtn
4870
Gravel Pit
408/ 35
36
31
4760
4200
2
1
6
11
12
7
5078
408

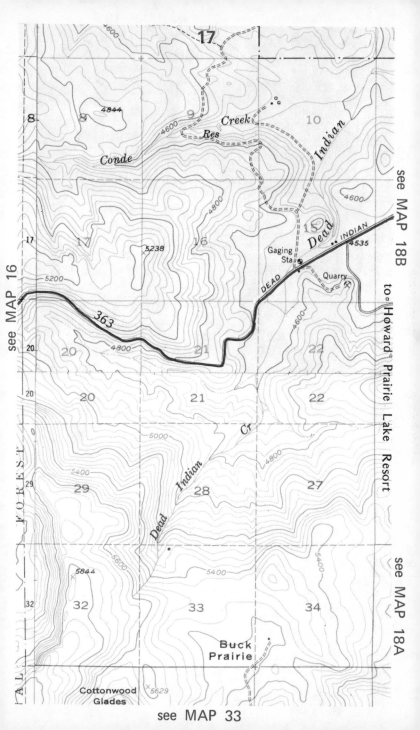

see MAP 17

see MAP 18B

see MAP 16

to Howard Prairie Lake Resort

see MAP 18A

see MAP 33

Conde

Res

Creek

Indian

Dead

INDIAN

DEAD

Gaging Sta

Quarry

4535

363

5238

5200

4800

4844

4600

4600

4600

4600

4800

Dead Indian Cr

5000

5400

5400

5400

5400

5600

5000

5844

FOREST

AL

Buck
Prairie

Cottonwood
Glades

5629

8

8

9

10

17

16

18

17

20

20

20

21

22

29

28

27

32

33

34

29

20

21

22

32

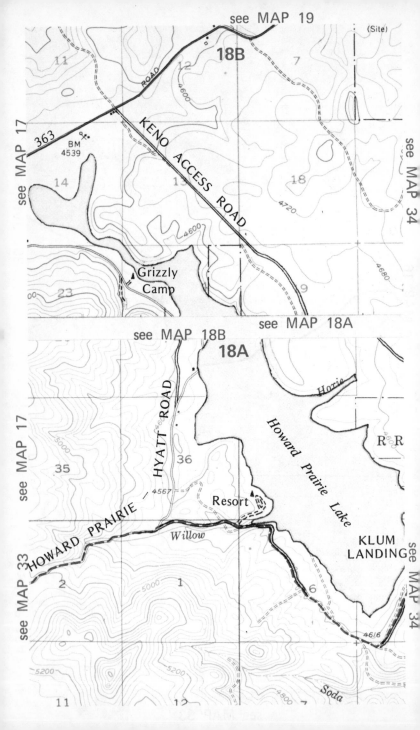

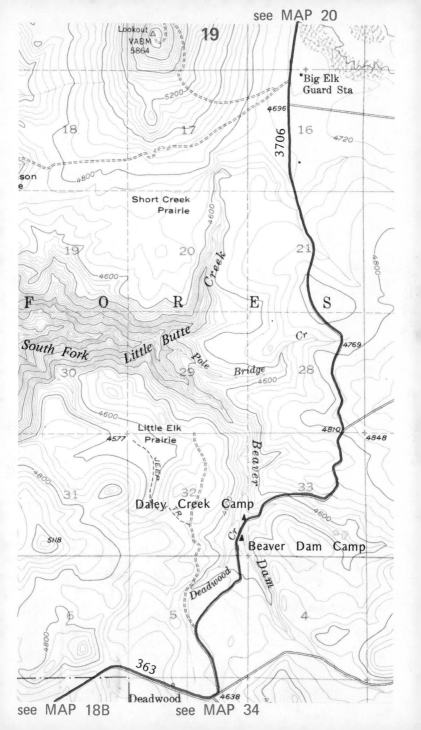

see MAP 20

19

Lookout
VABM
5864

Big Elk
Guard Sta

4696

3706

16

4720

18   17

5200

son
e

4800

Short Creek
Prairie

4600

19   20

Creek

21

4600

F   O   R   E   S

4800

Cr

South Fork   Little Butte

4769

Pole

30   29   Bridge

4600   28

4600

4810

4848

Little Elk
Prairie

4577   JEEP

31   32

Daley Creek Camp

Beaver

33

4600

5118

Cr   Beaver Dam Camp

Deadwood

Dam

6   5

4800

4   4600

363

see MAP 18B   Deadwood   see MAP 34

4638

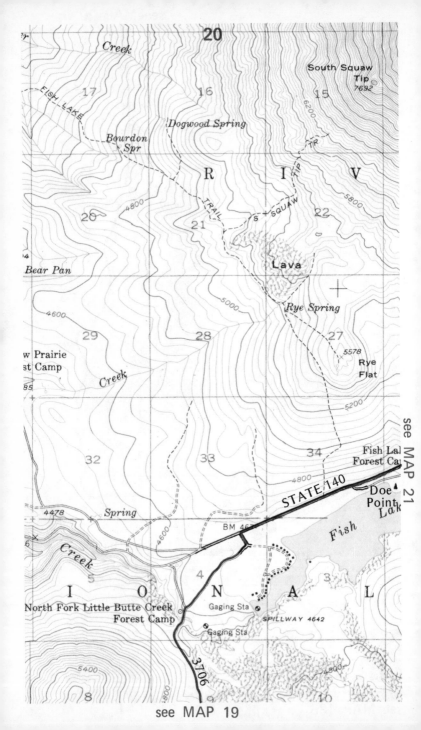

Creek

South Squaw
Tip
7692

17

16

15

6200

FISH LAKE

Dogwood Spring

Bourdon
Spr

R   I   V

TR TIP

20

4800

21

TRAIL

S SQUAW TIP

22

5800

Bear Pan

Lava

5000

Rye Spring

w Prairie
st Camp

29

4600

28

27

5578

Rye
Flat

85

Creek

5200

32

33

34

5200

Fish La
Forest Ca

4800

see MAP 21

Doe
Point
Lak

STATE 140

Spring

4478

4600

BM 46

Fish

Creek

4600

4

3

I   O

5

N

A

L

North Fork Little Butte Creek
Forest Camp

Gaging Sta

SPILLWAY 4642

Gaging Sta

3706

5400

4800

8

9

10

see MAP 19

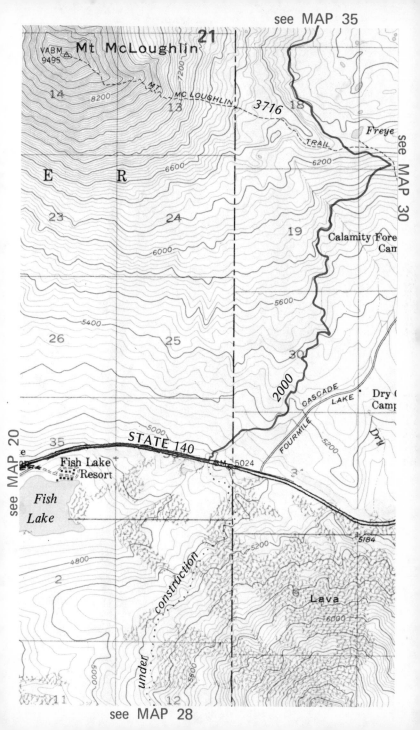

see MAP 35

21

VABM
9495
Mt McLoughlin

14

8200

MT. 13 MC LOUGHLIN

3716

18

7200

Freye

see MAP 30

TRAIL

6600

6200

E R

23

24

19

Calamity Fore
Cam

6000

5600

5400

26

25

30

2000

CASCADE

Dry (
Camp

LAKE

5200

FOURMILE

Dry

5000

STATE 140

35

BM 5024

3

Fish Lake
Resort

e

Fish
Lake

5184

see MAP 20

4800

5200

2

under

5200

construction

Lava

6000

5000

5600

11

12

see MAP 28

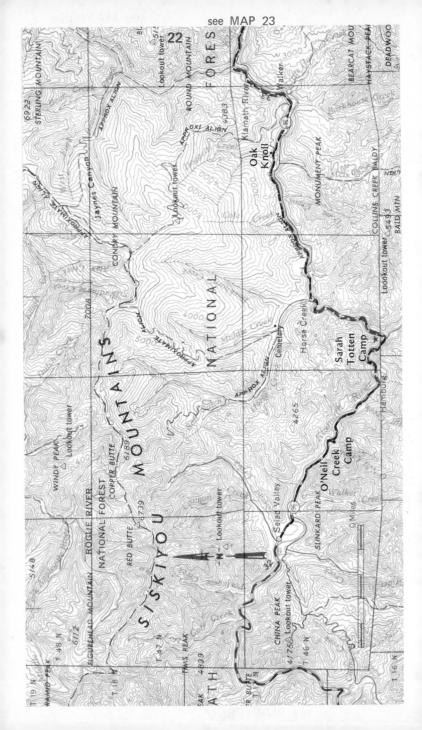

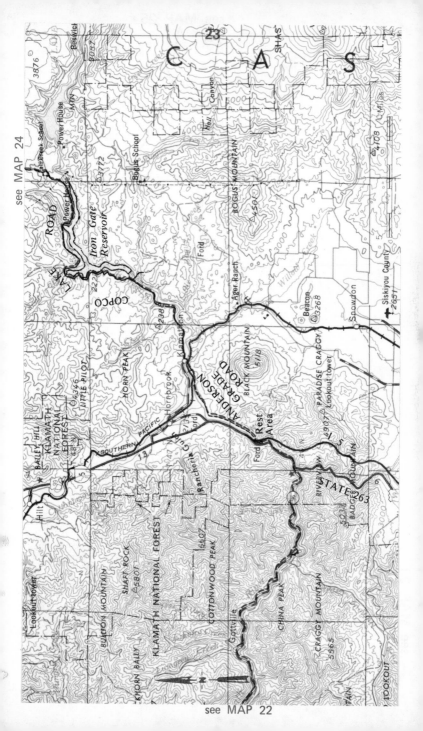

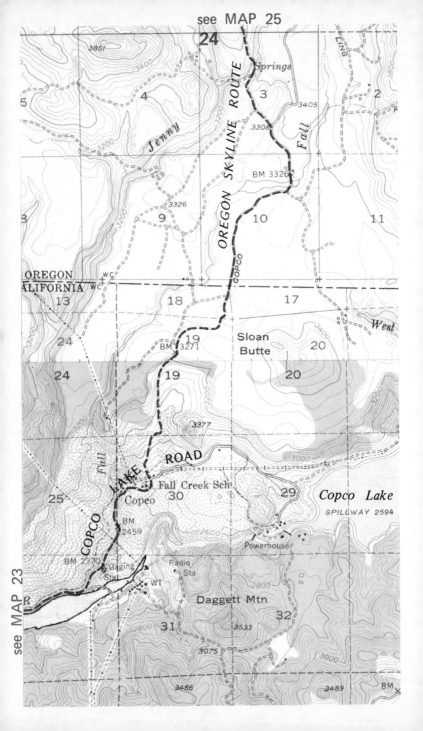

see MAP 23

OREGON SKYLINE ROUTE

Springs

Jenny

Fall

BM 3326

OREGON
CALIFORNIA

Sloan
Butte

West

BM 3271

ROAD

Fall Creek Sch

Copco Lake

SPILLWAY 2594

Copco

COPCO LAKE

BM
2459

BM 2370

Gaging
Sta

Radio
Sta

Powerhouse

WT

Daggett Mtn

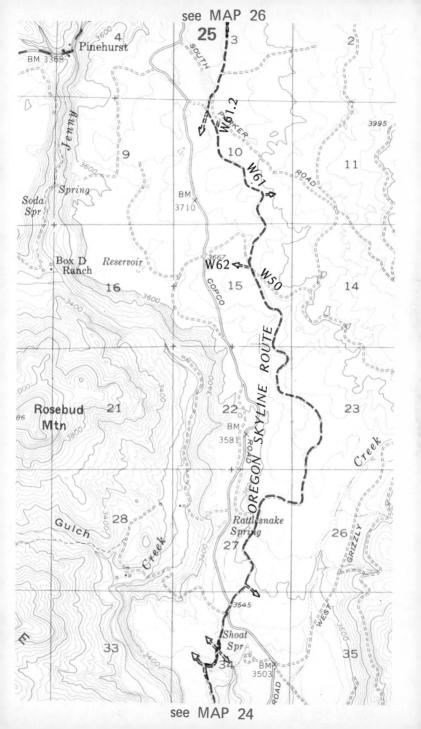

see MAP 26

25

see MAP 24

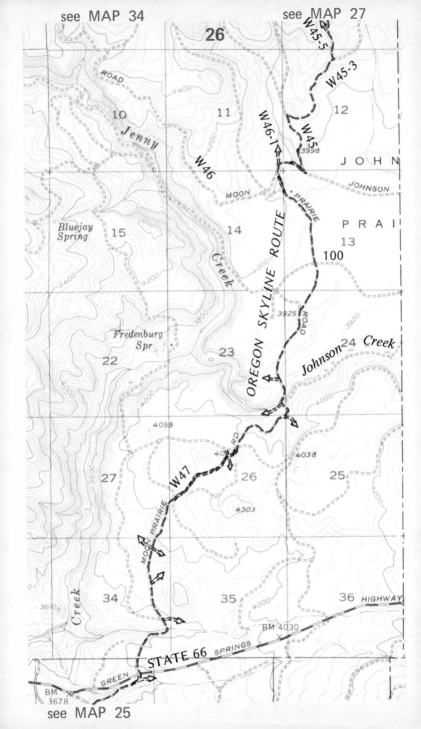

26

W45.5

W45-3

12

10

Jenny

11

W46-1

W46

W45

3998

J O H N

MOON

JOHNSON

Bluejay
Spring

15

14

P R A I

13

Creek

100

OREGON SKYLINE ROUTE

PRAIRIE

3925

ROAD

3920

Fredenburg
Spr

23

Johnson 24 Creek

22

4000

27

4059

40   RD

4038

26

W47

25

4303

MOON PRAIRIE

34

35

36 HIGHWAY

4000

Creek

3610

BM 4030

STATE 66   SPRINGS

GREEN

BM
3678

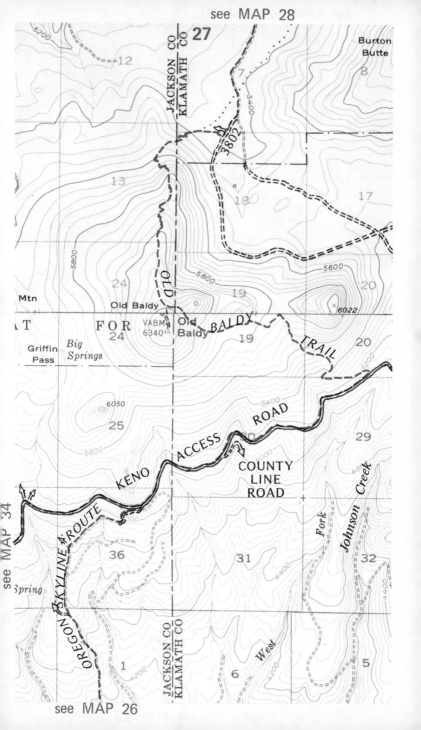

see MAP 28

27

Burton
Butte

7

8

JACKSON CO
KLAMATH CO

3802

12

13

18

17

5200

5400

5600

5800

24

19

20

6022

Mtn

Old Baldy

FOR

24

VABM
6340

Old
Baldy

BALDY

19

TRAIL

20

Griffin
Pass

Big
Springs

6050

5400

ROAD

5200

29

25

ACCESS

5600

KENO

COUNTY
LINE
ROAD

see MAP 34

OREGON SKYLINE ROUTE

Fork

Johnson Creek

36

31

32

Spring

JACKSON CO
KLAMATH CO

West

1

6

5

4200

4400

see MAP 26

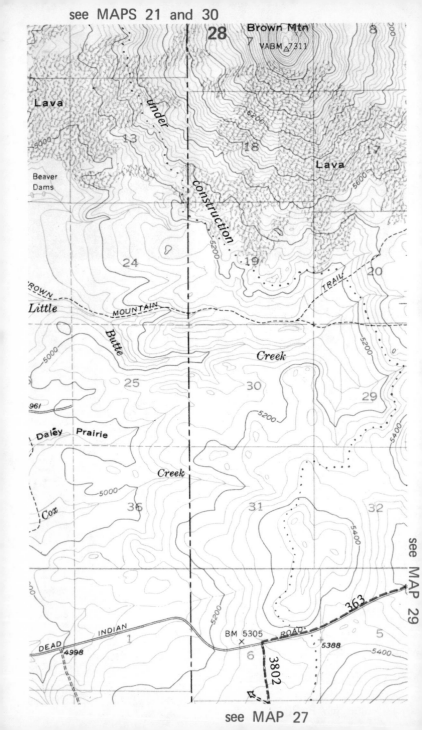

28

Brown Mtn

7 VABM △7311 8

Lava 13

under

construction

Beaver Dams

18

17

Lava

5600

24

19

TRAIL 20

BROWN MOUNTAIN

Little

Butte

Creek

25 30

29

Daley Prairie

961

Creek

Cox 36 31 32

5400

INDIAN 363

DEAD 4998

BM 5305 × ROAD

3802 6 5388 5

5400

see MAP 29

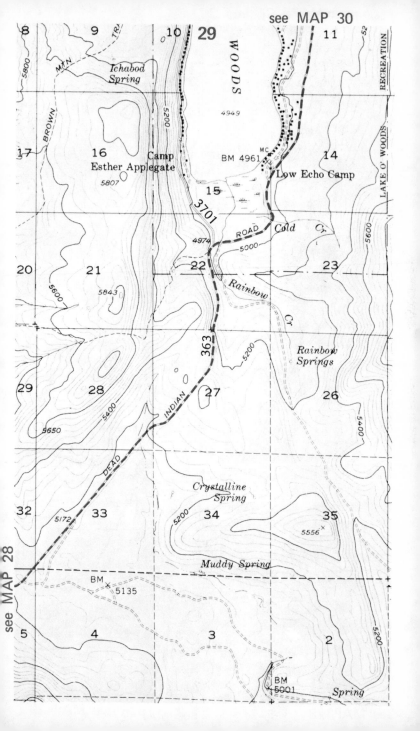

see MAP 28

8
9
10
29
11

WOODS

Ichabod Spring

5800

BROWN MTN TR

5200

4949

52

RECREATION

17
16
Camp
Esther Applegate

5807

BM 4961
MC

14
Low Echo Camp

15

3701

4974

ROAD
Cold Cr.

5000

LAKE O' WOODS

20
21
22
23

5843

5600

5600

Rainbow

Cr.

363

Rainbow Springs

5200

29
28
27
26

5400

5650

5400

DEAD INDIAN

Crystalline Spring

5172

32
33
34
35

5200

5556 ×

Muddy Spring

BM × 5135

5200

5
4
3
2

BM × 5001

Spring

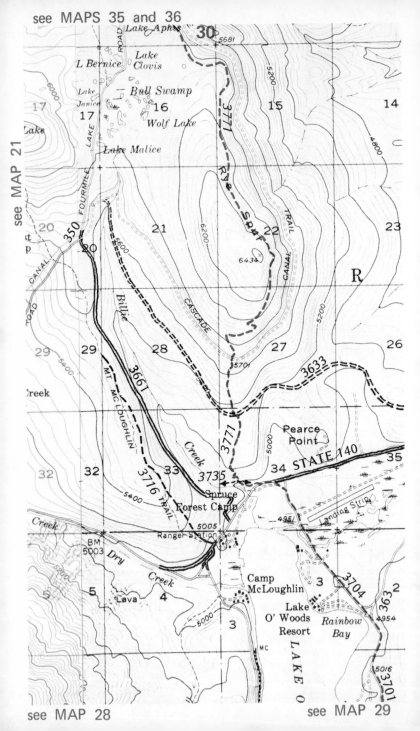

see MAPS 35 and 36

see MAP 21

Lake Aphis

30

5681

5200

Lake Clovis

L Bernice

Bull Swamp

16

15

14

Lake Janice

17

17

Wolf Lake

4800

Lake Malice

5200

6000

FOURMILE   LAKE

ROAD

350

20

21

22

23

R

6200

6434

CANAL

ROAD

CASCADE   TRAIL

CANYON   TRAIL

Rye Spur

3771

5200

5600

Billie

29

28

27

26

29

3661

5400

5200

MT. MC LOUGHLIN   TRAIL

3633

5701

5000

3771

Pearce Point

Creek

32

32

33

3716   TRAIL

34

STATE 140

35

5400

3735

Spruce Forest Camp

5005

Ranger Station

495

Landing Strip

Creek

BM 5003

Dry

Creek

Lava

5

5

4

3

Camp McLoughlin

3

3704

363

2

Lake O' Woods Resort

Rainbow Bay

4954

5000

3

MC

LAKE O

5016

3701

see MAP 28

see MAP 29

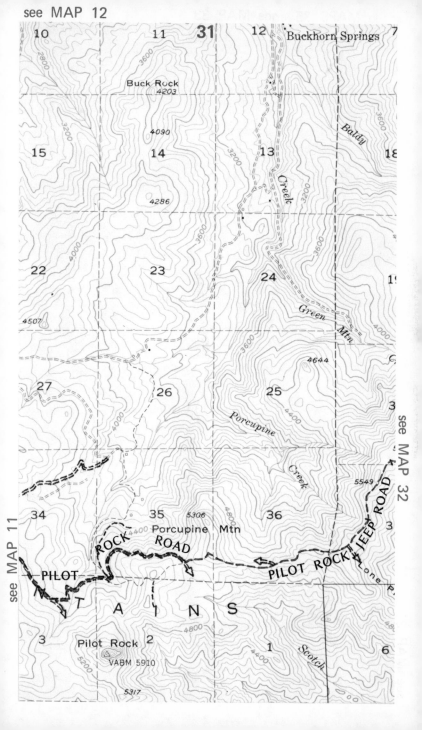

see MAP 12

31

Buckhorn Springs

see MAP 32

see MAP 11

10   11   12   7

Buck Rock
4203

4090

15   14   13   18

4286

22   23   24   19

4507

Green

Mtn

4644

27   26   25   3

Porcupine

5549

34   35   36   3

5306

Porcupine Mtn

ROCK   ROAD

PILOT ROCK JEEP ROAD

PILOT

Lone P.

T   A   I   N   S

4800

3   Pilot Rock 2   1   6

VABM 5910

Scotch

5200

5317

4400

Creek

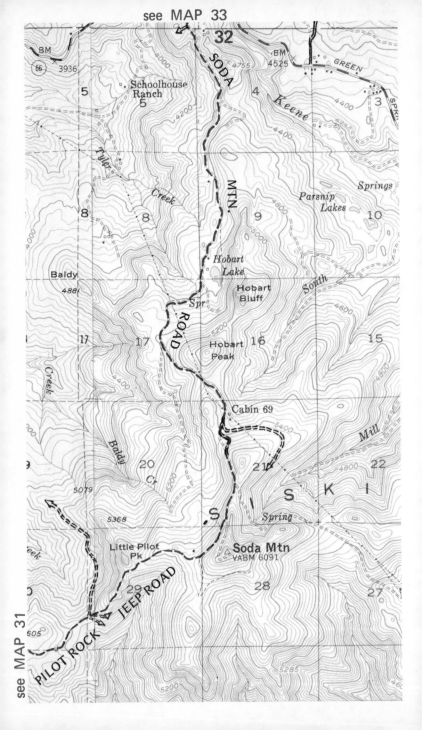

see MAP 33

32

SODA

Keene

GREEN

BM 4525

BM 66 3936

5 5 Schoolhouse Ranch

Tyler

Creek

8 8

Baldy 4881

MTN.

4

4755

3

SPRI

Springs

Parsnip Lakes 10

9

Hobart Lake

Hobart Bluff

South

17 17

ROAD

Spr

Hobart Peak

Hobart 16

15

Creek

Cabin 69

Mill

5079

Baldy Cr

20

21

22

5368

S

S K I

Spring

Little Pilot Pk

Soda Mtn VABM 6091

29

JEEP ROAD

28

27

605

see MAP 31

PILOT ROCK

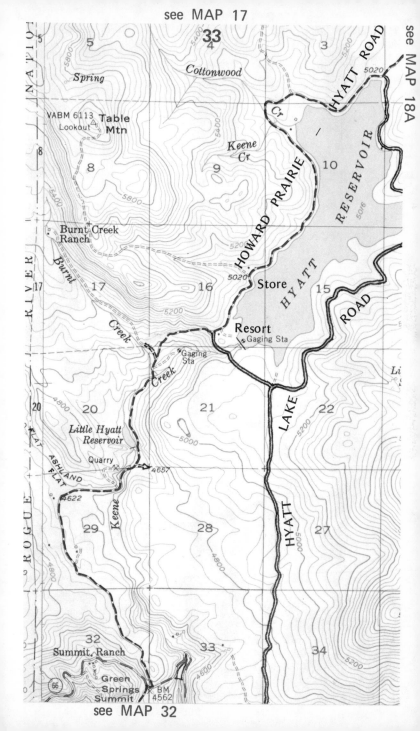

see MAP 17

33

see MAP 18A

HYATT ROAD

5
4
3

Spring

Cottonwood

5020

VABM 6113
Lookout **Table Mtn**

Keene
Cr

HOWARD PRAIRIE

10

RESERVOIR

5006

8
9

RIVER

NATIO

5400

5800

Burnt Creek
Ranch

Burnt

5200

HYATT

Store

Creek

17
16
15
Store

5020

ROAD

Resort
Gaging Sta

Creek

Gaging
Sta

LAKE

Li

20
21
22

HYATT

Little Hyatt
Reservoir

4800

5000

5200

Quarry

ASHLAND FLAT

4657

4622

Keene

29
28
27

4800

ROGUE

32
33
34

Summit Ranch

66

Green
Springs
Summit

BM
4562

4600

5200

see MAP 32

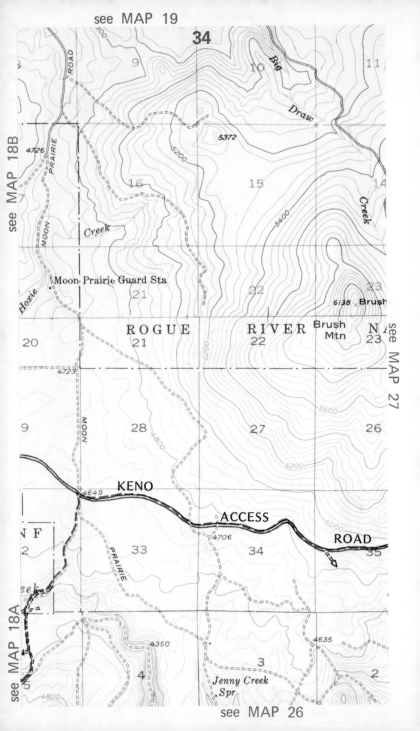

see MAP 19

34

see MAP 18B

see MAP 27

see MAP 18A

see MAP 26

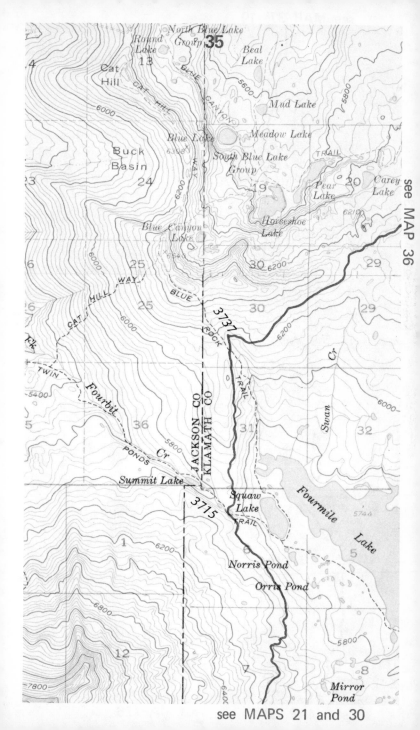

see MAP 36

see MAPS 21 and 30

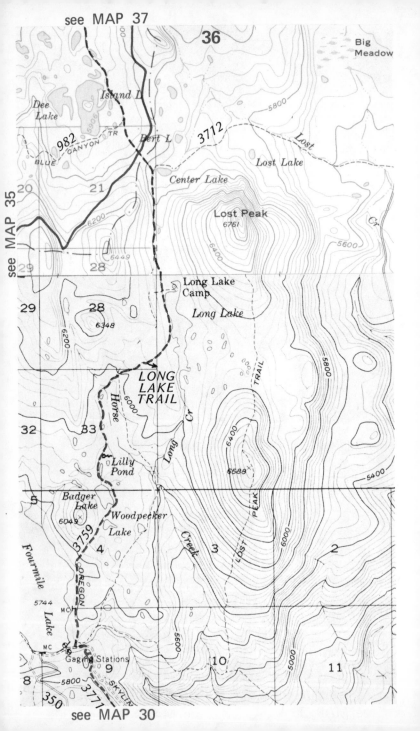

see MAP 37

36

Big
Meadow

Island L.

Dee
Lake

982
CANYON
TR

BLUE

Bert L.

3712

Lost

Lost Lake

Center Lake

Lost Peak
6761

see MAP 35

20

21

6200

5800

5600

29

28

6449

6400

Long Lake
Camp

Long Lake

29

28
6348

6200

6290

*LONG
LAKE
TRAIL*

Horse

6000

Long Cr

TRAIL

5800

32

33

6400

6588

Lilly
Pond

5400

5

Badger
Lake

6049

Woodpecker
Lake

3759

OREGON

4

Creek

3

LOST PEAK

6000

6000

2

Fourmile
Lake

5744

MC

5600

5000

5000

MC

Gaging Stations

9

SKYLINE

10

11

8

5800

350

3771

see MAP 30

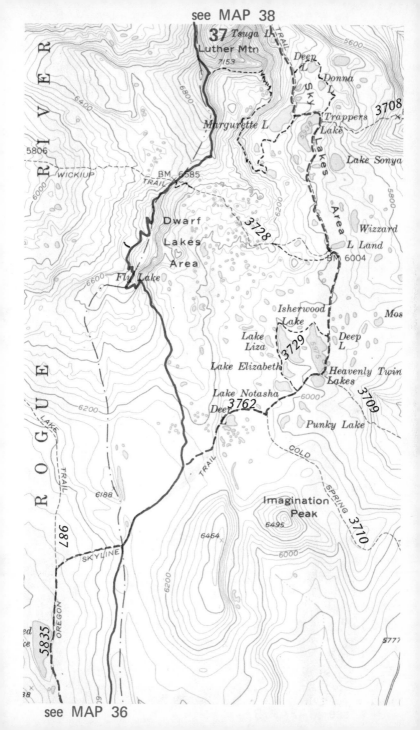

37 Tsuga L.
Luther Mtn
7153

Deep
L

Donna

Margurette L

Trappers
Lake

3708

Lake Sonya

R I V E R

5806

WICKIUP

BM 6585
TRAIL

Sky

Lakes

Area

Wizzard
L Land
BM 6004

Dwarf

Lakes

Area

3728

Fly Lake

Isherwood
Lake

Mos

Lake
Liza

3729

Deep
L

Lake Elizabeth

Heavenly Twin
Lakes

Lake Notasha
Deer **3762**

3709

Punky Lake

R O G U E

COLD

TRAIL

SPRING

Imagination
Peak
6495

3710

6188

6464

6200

987

SKYLINE

OREGON

ed
ce **5835**

5777

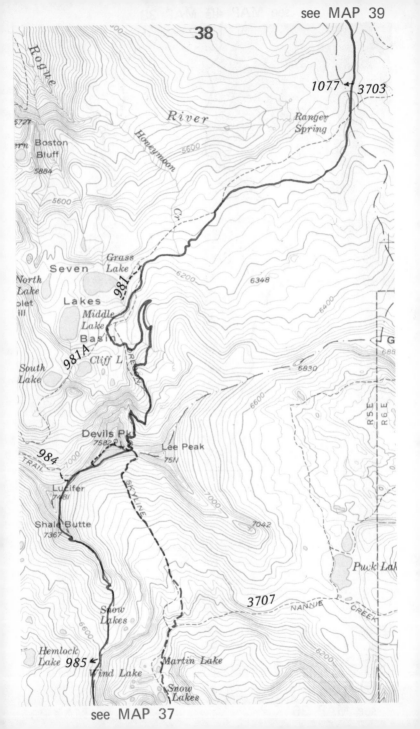

Rogue

River

Boston
Bluff
5884

Honeymoon

Cr.

Ranger
Spring

1077 → 3703

5727

5600

5600

5600

6200

6348

6400

Grass
Lake

981

Seven

North
Lake
let
ill

Lakes

Middle
Lake

Basin

981A

Cliff L

South
Lake

CREEK

6830

G
688

6600

6400

R 5 E
R 6 E

984

TRAIL

7000

Devils Pk
7582

Lee Peak
75N

SKYLINE

7000

7042

Lucifer
7481

Shale Butte
7367

Puck Lake

Snow
Lakes

6600

3707

NANNIE

CREEK

6200

Hemlock
Lake

985

Wind Lake

Martin Lake

Snow
Lakes

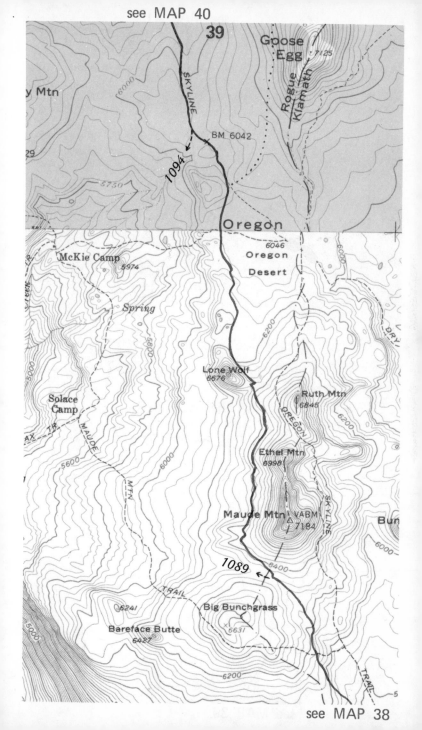

Goose
Egg
7125

Rogue
Klamath

SKYLINE

y Mtn

6000

5750

BM 6042

1094

Oregon

McKie Camp
5974

6046
Oregon

Desert

6000

Spring

5800

6200

5000

5600

Lone Wolf
6676

Ruth Mtn
6845

Solace
Camp

MAUDE

OREGON

Ethel Mtn
6998

SKYLINE

5600

6000

Maude Mtn
VABM
7184

Bun

DRY

6200

6000

1089

6400

TRAIL

6241

Big Bunchgrass

Bareface Butte
6427

6637

5000

6200

TRAIL

5

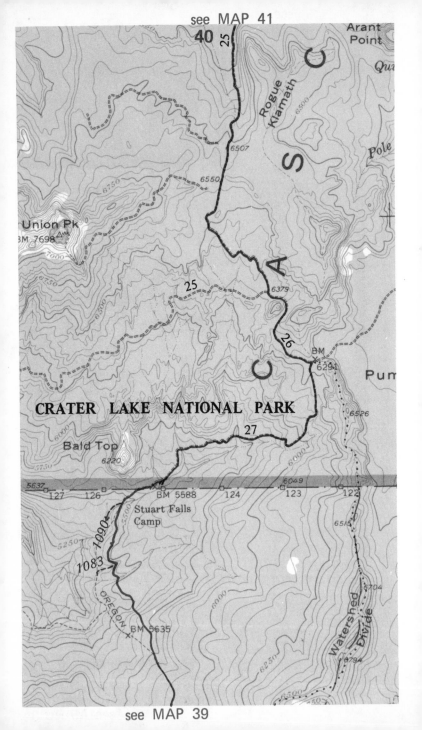

see MAP 41

40

Arant
Point

Rogue
Klamath

Pole

Union Pk
BM 7698

CRATER LAKE NATIONAL PARK

Pum

Bald Top

Stuart Falls
Camp

BM 5588

OREGON

BM 5635

Watershed
Divide

see MAP 39

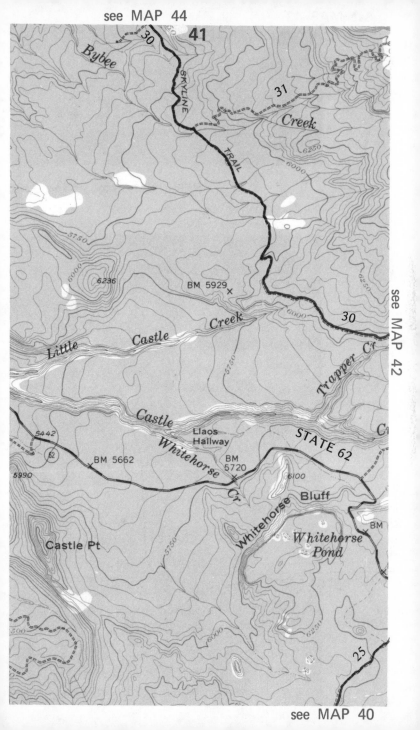

Bybee

SKYLINE

30

31

Creek

6250

6000

TRAIL

5750

6000

6236

BM 5929 ×

30

6000

see MAP 42

6250

Little

Castle

Creek

5750

Trapper Cr

Castle

Llaos
Hallway

STATE 62

Cr

5442

Whitehorse

62

BM 5662

BM
5720

6100

C

5990

×

Whitehorse

Bluff

BM

Castle Pt

5750

Whitehorse

Whitehorse
Pond

×

6250

500

6000

25

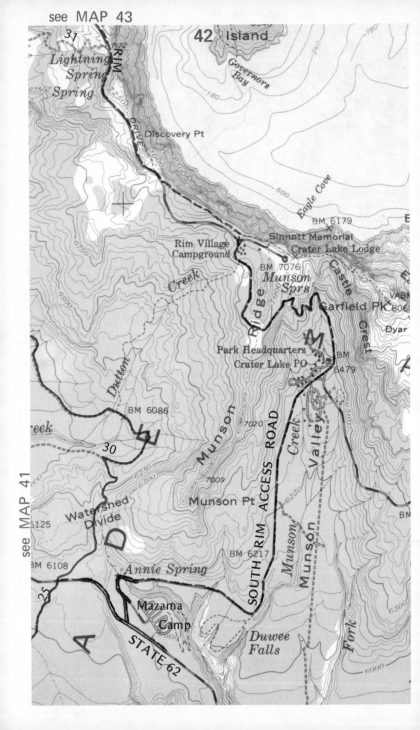

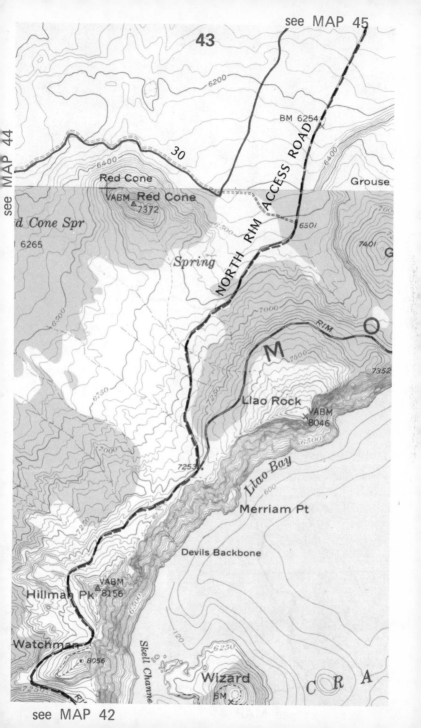

see MAP 45

43

see MAP 44

6200

BM 6254 ×

6400

30

6400

Red Cone

Grouse

VABM Red Cone
△ 7372

d Cone Spr

NORTH RIM ACCESS ROAD

6265

6501

Spring

6500

7401

G

6500

7000

RIM

M

7500

O

6550

7352

7250

Llao Rock

× VABM
8046

6500

7253

Llao Bay

600

7250

Merriam Pt

Devils Backbone

VABM
△ 8156

Hillman Pk

6500

6250

Watchman

○ 8056

Shell Channel

120

7250

R

Wizard

BM
×

C R A

see MAP 42

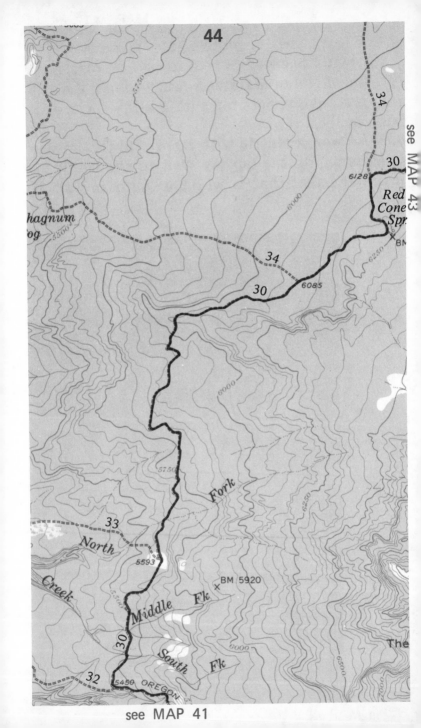

44

see MAP 43

34

30

6128

Red
Cone
Spr.

BM

hagnum
og

5560

34

30

6085

6250

30

6000

6250

6000

5750

Fork

33

North

5593

Creek

BM 5920

Middle   Fk

30

South   Fk

32   5450

OREGON

8000

The

see MAP 41

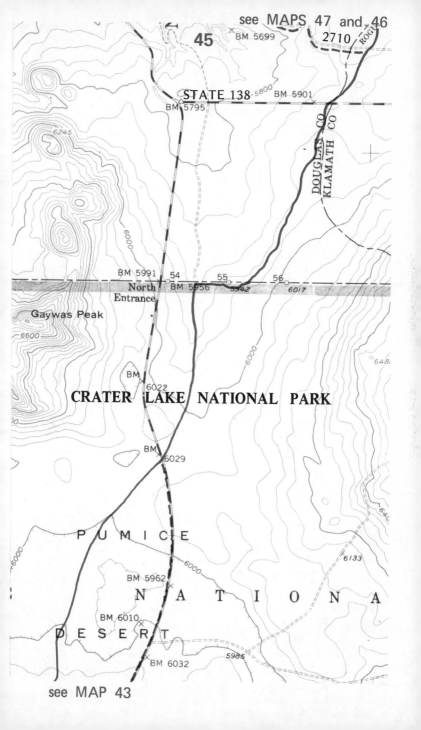

45

× BM 5699

2710

ROGU

STATE 138 5800 BM 5901

BM 5795

6245

DOUGLAS CO
KLAMATH CO

6000

BM 5991   54   55   56
North   BM 5956   5942   6017
Entrance

Gaywas Peak

6600

648

6600

BM
6022

CRATER LAKE NATIONAL PARK

BM
6029

6000

P U M I C E

6000

6133

BM 5962

N A T I O N A

BM 6010

D E S E R T

BM 6032   5985

see MAP 43

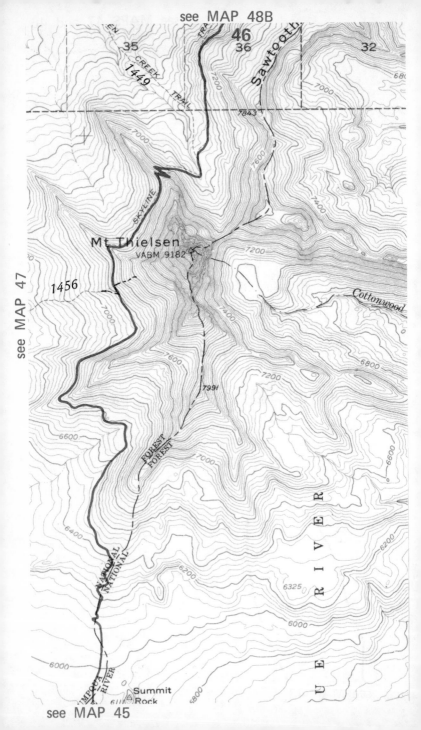

see MAP 48B

46

see MAP 47

Mt Thielsen
VABM 9182

1456

1449

35

36

32

Sawtooth

Cottonwood

SKYLINE

CREEK   TRAIL

FOREST
FOREST

NATIONAL
NATIONAL

RIVER

UE

Summit
Rock

see MAP 45

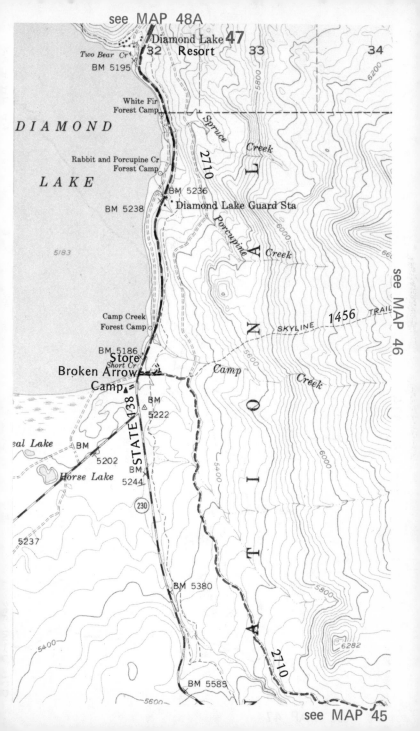

see MAP 48A

Diamond Lake **47**
Resort

Two Bear Cr 32   33   34

BM 5195

White Fir
Forest Camp

DIAMOND

Spruce

Creek

Rabbit and Porcupine Cr
Forest Camp

2710

LAKE

BM 5236

BM 5238 • Diamond Lake Guard Sta

5183

Porcupine

Creek

6000

Camp Creek
Forest Camp

SKYLINE 1456 TRAIL

BM 5186

Store

Short Cr

Broken Arrow
Camp

Camp

Creek

5600

6000

BM
5222

STATE 138

eal Lake BM

5202

BM
5244

Horse Lake

230

5400

5237

BM 5380

6000

2710

6282

BM 5585

5600

5400

see MAP 45

see MAP 46

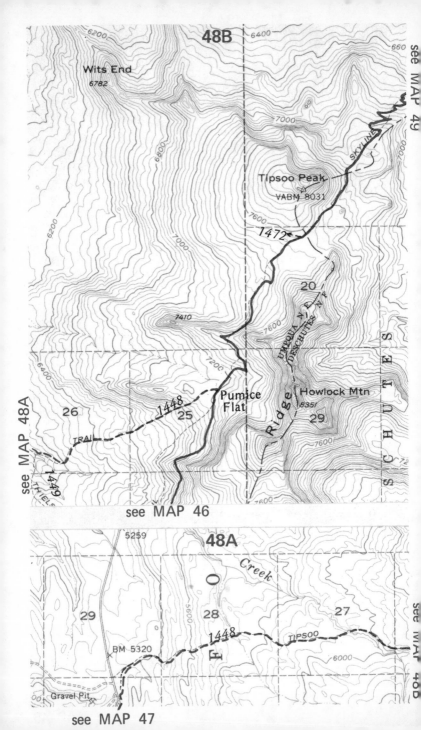

48B

Wits End
6782

Tipsoo Peak
VABM 8031

1472

20

7410

Pumice
Flat

1448

26

25

TRAIL

1449

THIELS

Ridge

Howlock Mtn
8351

29

SCHUTES

UMPQUA N F
DESCHUTES N F

see MAP 49

see MAP 48A

see MAP 46

48A

5259

Creek

29

28

27

BM 5320

1448

TIPSOO

6000

Gravel Pit

see MAP 48B

see MAP 47

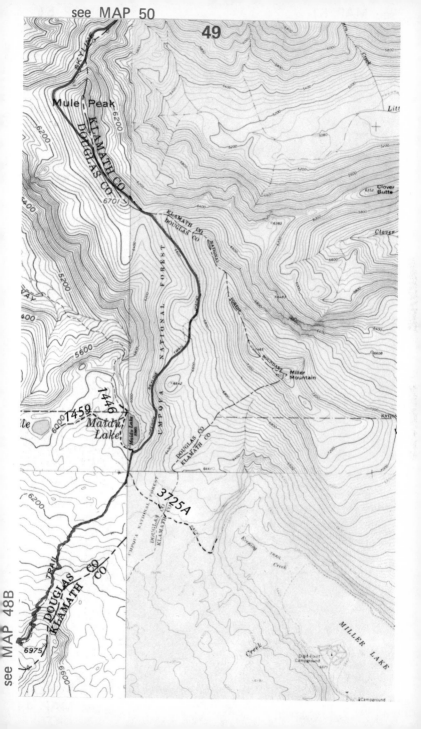

see MAP 50

49

Mule, Peak

KLAMATH CO
DOUGLAS CO

6701

KLAMATH CO
DOUGLAS CO

UMPQUA NATIONAL FOREST

Clover
Butte

Clover

1446

1459

Maidu
Lake

Maidu Lake

Miller
Mountain

DOUGLAS CO
KLAMATH CO

3725A

UMPQUA NATIONAL FOREST
DOUGLAS CO
KLAMATH CO

TRAIL

DOUGLAS CO
KLAMATH CO

6975

MILLER LAKE

Digit Point
Campground

Campground

see MAP 48B

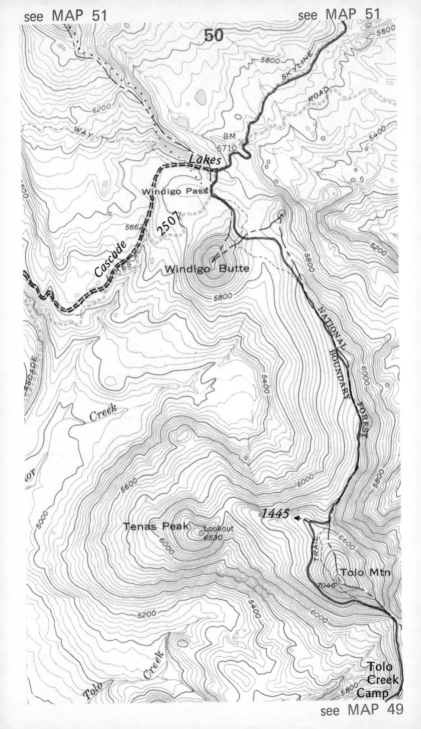

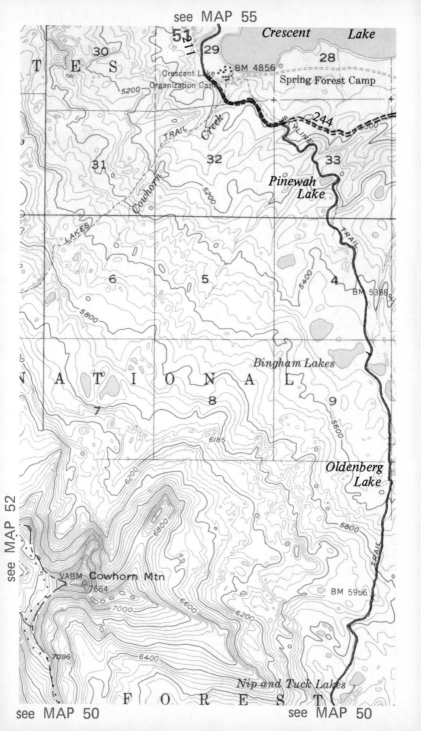

see MAP 55

51

211

29

Crescent   Lake

30

T   E   S

28

Crescent Lake
Organization Camp

BM 4856

Spring Forest Camp

5200

244

LINE

31

32

33

TRAIL

Creek

Cowhorn

*Pinewah
Lake*

5200

LAKES

5400

6

5

4

BM 5388

5800

TRAIL

Bingham Lakes

N   A   T   I   O   N   A   L

7

8

9

6185

5600

*Oldenberg
Lake*

6200

5800

6800

VABM Cowhorn Mtn
7664

7000

6600

6200

BM 5956

TRAIL

7096

6400

6600

Nip and Tuck Lakes

F   O   R   E   S   T

see MAP 52

see MAP 50

see MAP 50

see MAP 53

see MAP 51

Meek Lake

S C H U

25

59.

35

36

6295

EST

3

2

1

WINDY

10

WINDY

Windy Lakes

1

12

Lake

5600

6000

PASS

KLAMATH CO

DOUGLAS CO

6600

Timpanogas
Lake

Forest Camp

6400

WAY

5400

5600

Amos and Andy
Lake

6200

6600

WAY

SAWTOOTH

WAY

6000

6

Indigo
Lake

6200

6885

PASS

6400

Sawtooth Mtn

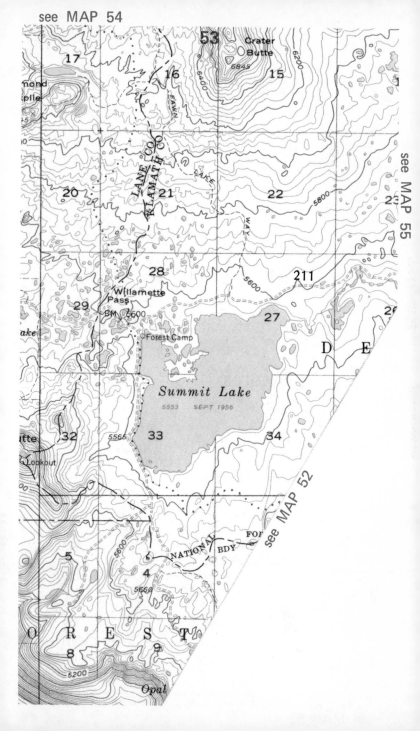

53

Crater
Butte

17

16

15

6845

6200

6400

6400

FAWN

nond
pile

1

20

21

22

LAKE

5800

LANE CO.
KLAMATH CO.

see MAP 55

23

WAY

28

5600

211

Willamette
Pass

29

BM 5600

27

D

E

26

Forest Camp

ake

Summit Lake

5553   SEPT 1956

32

5565

33

34

itte

Lookout

5600

see MAP 52

5

NATIONAL   BDY   FOR

4

5660

O   R   E   S   T

8

9

5200

Opal

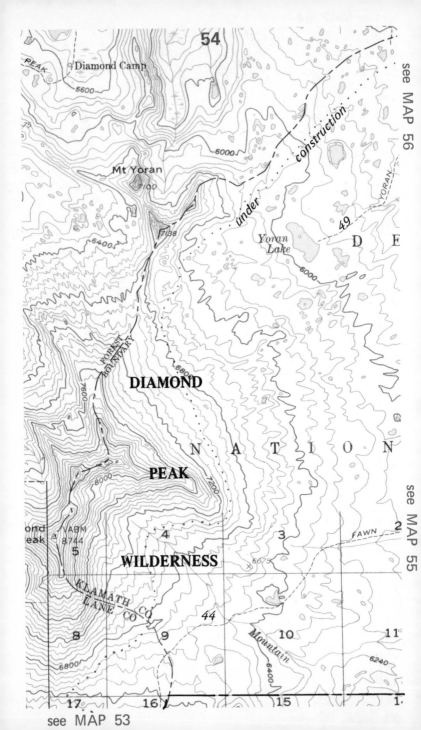

see MAP 56

PEAK

Diamond Camp

5600

75

6000

Mt Yoran
7100

7138

6400

under construction

YORAN

49

Yoran
Lake

6000

D E

FOREST BOUNDARY

6800

DIAMOND

7600

N   A   T   I   O   N

8000

PEAK

7200

see MAP 55

ond
eak

VABM
8744

5

4

3

FAWN

2

WILDERNESS

×6675

KLAMATH CO
LANE CO

44

Mountain

8

9

10

6400

11

6240

6800

17

16

15

1

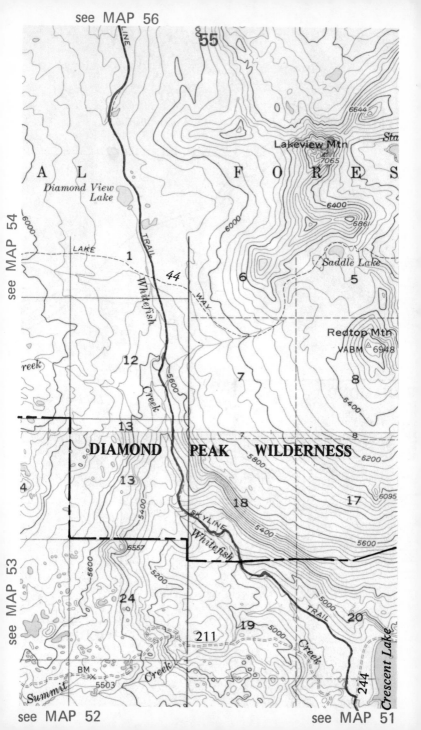

see MAP 56

55

see MAP 54

see MAP 53

see MAP 52

see MAP 51

Lakeview Mtn
7065

6644

Diamond View
Lake

A L

F O R E S

Saddle Lake

LAKE

TRAIL

Whitefish

1

44

WAY

6

5

Redtop Mtn
VABM △ 6948

Creek

12

7

8

Creek

13

DIAMOND PEAK WILDERNESS

4

13

18

17
6095

SKYLINE

Whitefish

5557

24

TRAIL

20

211

19

Creek

244

BM
X
5503

Summit

Creek

Crescent Lake

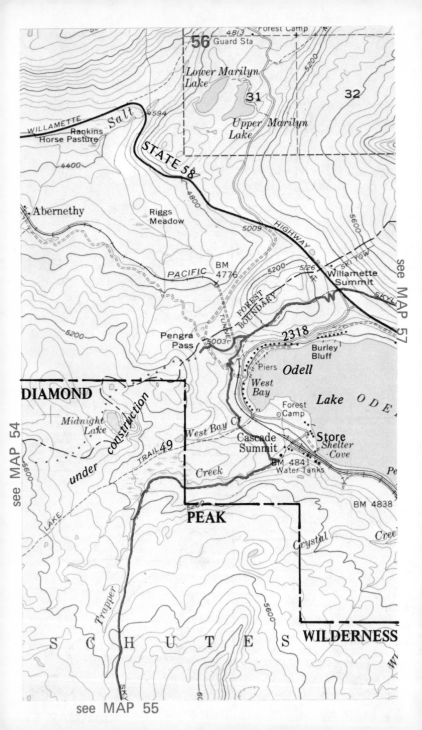

see MAP 57
see MAP 54
see MAP 55

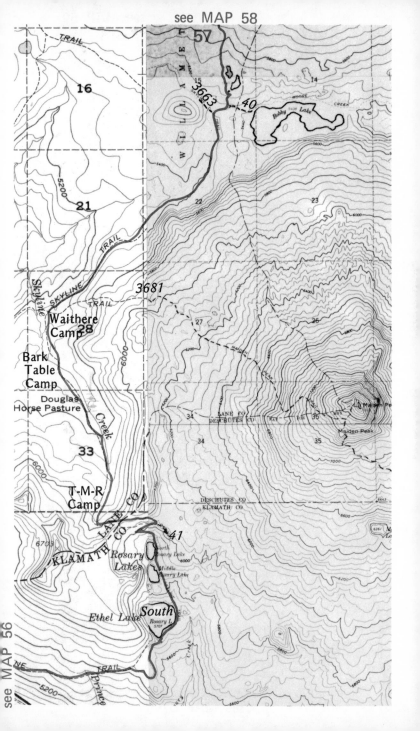

57

TRAIL

16

21

3663

40

Bobby Lake
5408

MOORE CREEK

14

15

22

23

WILLAMETTE

3681

SKYLINE TRAIL

TRAIL

Skyline

Waithere
Camp

28

27

26

Bark
Table
Camp

Douglas
Horse Pasture

33

Creek

34

LANE CO.
DESCHUTES CO.

Maiden Pk

35

Maiden Peak

36

T-M-R
Camp

LANE CO.

KLAMATH CO.

41

DESCHUTES CO.
KLAMATH CO.

North
Rosary Lake

Rosary
Lakes

KLAMATH CO.

6705

Middle
Rosary Lake

Ethel Lake

South

South
Rosary L
5700

TRAIL

Prince

5200

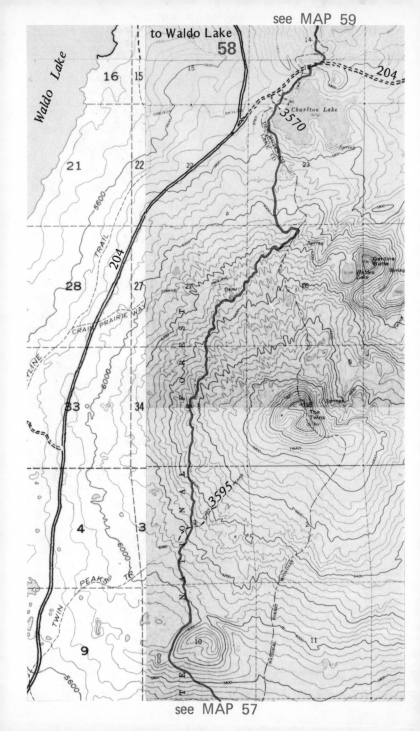

to Waldo Lake
58

Waldo Lake

16 15

OREGON SKYLINE

Charlton Lake

3570

Spring

21 22

TRAIL

204

23

28 27

CRANE

CRAIG PRAIRIE WAY

SKYLINE

6000

Geraline Butte

Walden Lake

Spring

26

33 34

The Twins

3595

TRAIL

4 3

6060

6000

PEAK TR

TWIN

9

10 11

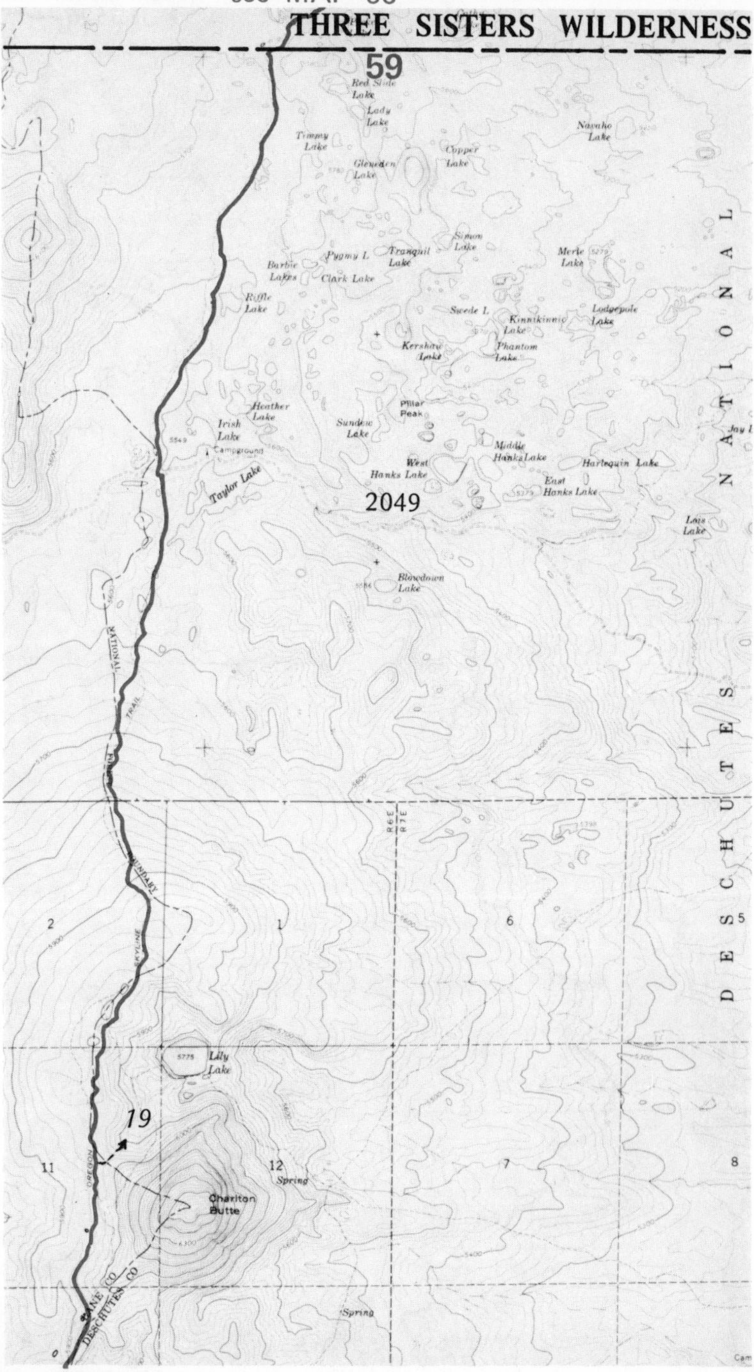

THREE SISTERS WILDERNESS

59

Red Slide Lake

Lody Lake

Timmy Lake

Navaho Lake

Glewiden Lake

Copper Lake

Pygmy L.

Tranquil Lake

Simon Lake

Merle Lake

Barbie Lakes

Clark Lake

Kinnikinnic Lake

Lodgepole Lake

Riffle Lake

Swede L.

Kershaw Lake

Phantom Lake

Heather Lake

Irish Lake

Pillar Peak

Sundew Lake

Middle Hanks Lake

Harlequin Lake

Campground

West Hanks Lake

East Hanks Lake

Taylor Lake

2049

Lois Lake

Blowdown Lake

N A T I O N A L

R6E R7E

2

1

6

5

D E S C H U T E S

Lily Lake

19

11

12

Spring

7

8

Charlton Butte

LANE CO.
DESCHUTES CO.

0

Spring

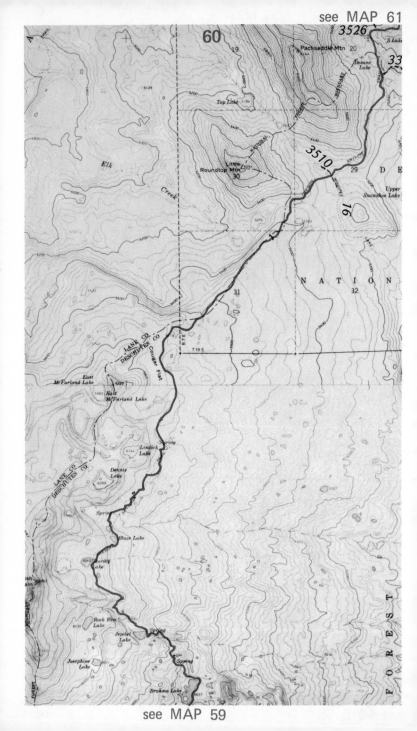

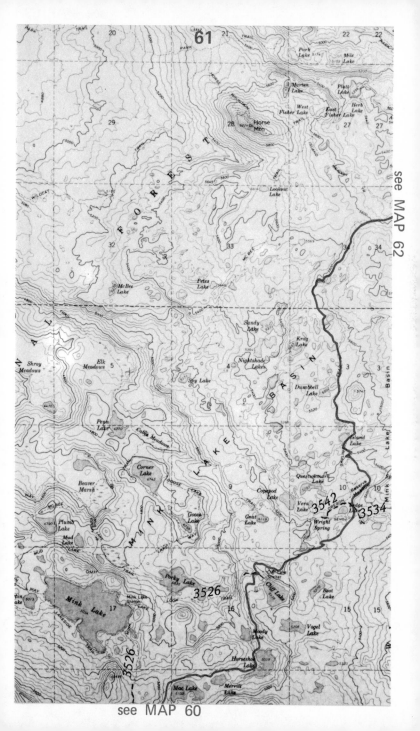

see MAP 62

see MAP 60

F O R E S T

M I N K   L A K E   B A S I N

20
21
22
22

29
28
27
27

32
33
34
34

5
4
3
3

8
9
10
10

7
16
15
15

Horse Mtn.

Pork Lake
Mile Lake
Marten Lake
West Fisher Lake
East Fisher Lake
Platt Lake
Herb Lake

Lookout Lake

McBee Lake
Peter Lake

Sandy Lake
Kraig Lake
Nightshade Lakes
Dumbbell Lake

Shroy Meadows
Elk Meadows
Sky Lake

Wildcat

Peak Lake
Cabin Meadows
Island Lake

Corner Lake
Beaver Marsh
Quaternary Lake
Copepod Lake
Vera Lake
3542
3534

Goose Lake
Plumb Lake
Mud Lake
Gnat Lake
Wright Spring

Porky Lake
3526
Chig Lake
Boot Lake

Mink Lake
17
16
Moody Lake
Vogel Lake

3526

Horseshoe Lake

Mac Lake
Merritt Lake

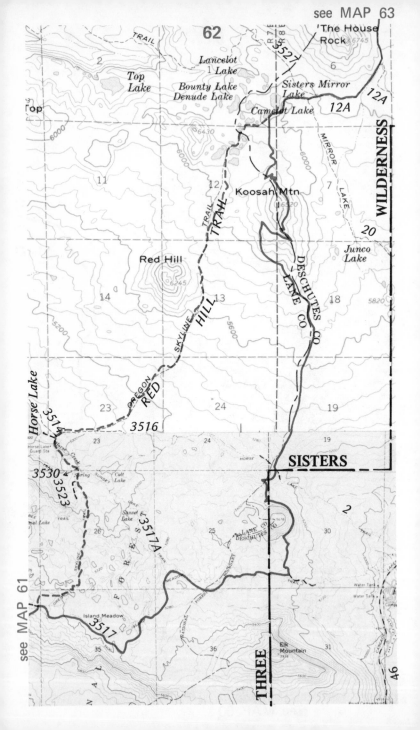

see MAP 63

62

The House
Rock
6745

Lancelot
Lake
Top
Lake
Bounty Lake
Denude Lake
Sisters Mirror
Lake

12A

Top

Camelot Lake

12A

WILDERNESS

6000

6430

6000

11

12

Koosah Mtn

6320

20

Red Hill

Junco
Lake

DESCHUTES

14

6245

13

LANE CO.

18

5820

SKYLINE

RED HILL

5600

5200

OREGON

TRAIL

TRAIL

Horse Lake

23

3514

3516

24

19

SISTERS

23

24

19

Horse Lake
Guard Sta

3530

3523

Spring

Colt
Lake

HORSE

5678

2

Sunset
Lake

3517A

26

25

LANE CO.
DESCHUTES CO.

30

see MAP 61

Island Meadow

3517

35

36

Elk
Mountain
5926

31

THREE

46

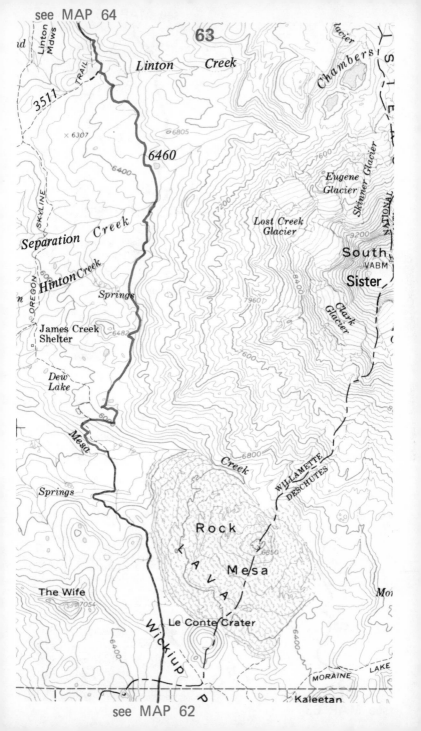

63

Linton Creek

Linton Mdws

TRAIL

3511

×6307

6805

6460

6400

Chambers

lacier

Eugene Glacier

Skinner Glacier

7600

Lost Creek Glacier

7200

9200

SOUTH

VABM

NATIONAL

SKYLINE

Separation Creek

Hinton Creek

Springs

OREGON

8400

Sister

7960

Clark Glacier

James Creek Shelter

6482

7600

Dew Lake

Mesa

Springs

Creek

6800

WILLAMETTE DESCHUTES

Rock

L A V A

Mesa

6850

The Wife

7054

Le Conte Crater

Wickiup P

6400

6400

Mor

MORAINE

LAKE

Kaleetan

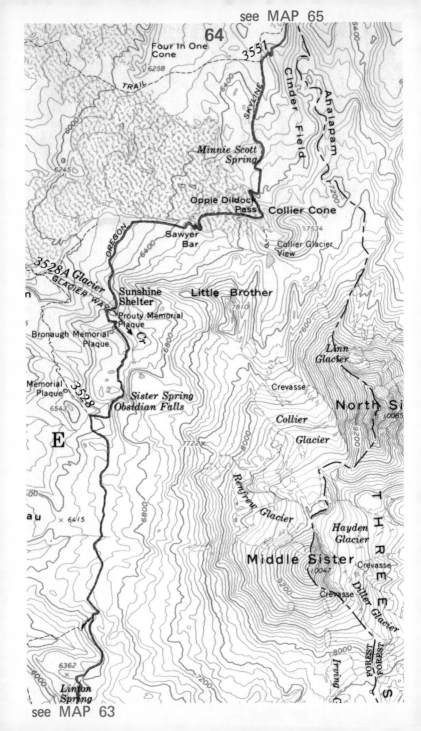

64

Four In One
Cone

6258

TRAIL

3551

SKYLINE

Cinder Field

Ahalapam

6400

6245

*Minnie Scott
Spring*

Oppie Dildock
Pass

Collier Cone

7200

7534

OREGON

Sawyer
Bar

Collier Glacier
View

6400

3528A Glacier

GLACIER WAY

Sunshine
Shelter

Little Brother

7810

*Prouty Memorial
Plaque*

Bronaugh Memorial
Plaque

Cr

Linn
Glacier

6600

Memorial
Plaque

6543

3528

6900

*Sister Spring
Obsidian Falls*

Crevasse

North Si

10085

*Collier

Glacier*

7722

E

8000

6800

Renfrew Glacier

8000

*Hayden
Glacier*

Middle Sister

10047

Crevasse

6400

× 6415

Diller Glacier

9200

Crevasse

T H R E E   S i

6362
×

9000

8000

*Linton
Spring*

7200

FOREST
FOREST

Irving

8000

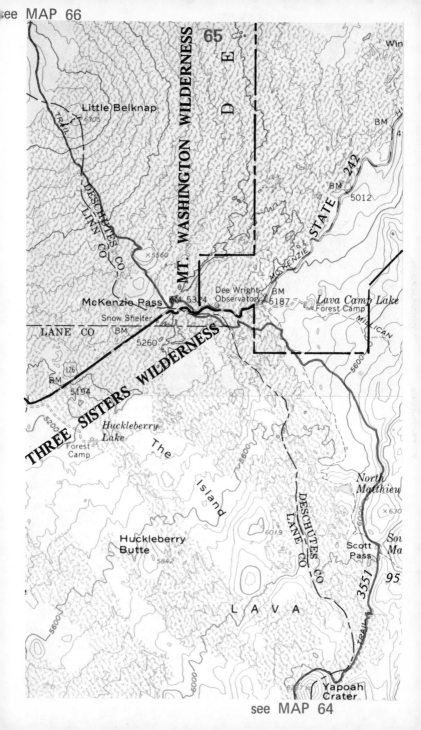

65

Little Belknap
6305

MT. WASHINGTON WILDERNESS

D E

Win

BM
4

STATE 242

5012

BM

Trail

DESCHUTES
LINN CO.

×5560

McKENZIE

Dee Wright
Observatory

BM
5187

BM

Lava Camp Lake
Forest Camp

McKenzie Pass

BM 5324

Snow Shelter

LANE CO

BM

5260

MILICAN

126

BM

5194

THREE SISTERS WILDERNESS

5600

5200

Huckleberry
Lake

The

Forest
Camp

5600

Island

North
Matthieu

DESCHUTES

6019

×630

Huckleberry
Butte

5842

LANE CO

Sou
Ma

Scott
Pass

95

3551

L A V A

TRAIL

5600

6000

5600

Yapoah
Crater

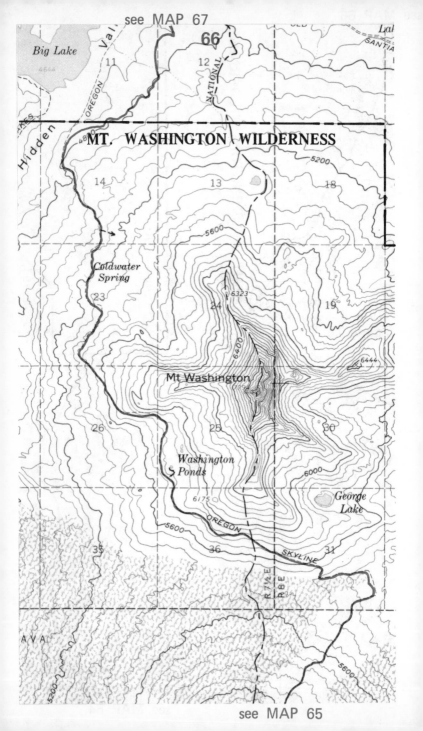

see MAP 67

66

Big Lake

11

12

7

SANTIA

La

OLD

48

OREGON

NATIONAL

Hidden

Val

MT. WASHINGTON WILDERNESS

5200

14

13

18

5600

Coldwater Spring

23

24

6323

19

6400

6444

Mt Washington

26

25

30

Washington Ponds

6000

6175

George Lake

5600

OREGON

35

36

31

SKYLINE

R 7½ E

R 8 E

A V A

5200

5600

see MAP 65

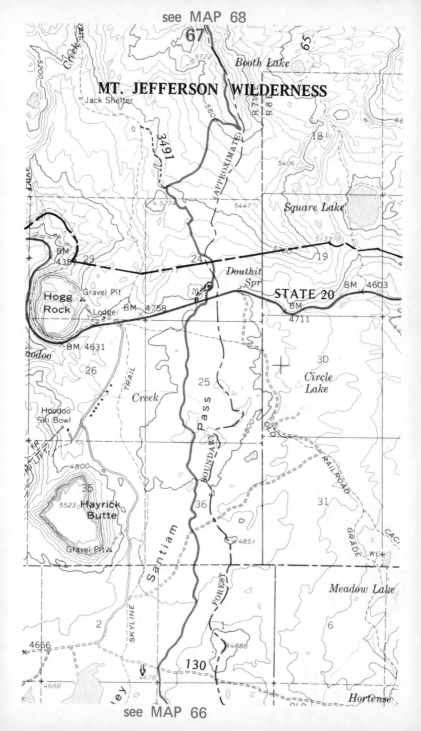

see MAP 68

67

65

Booth Lake

MT. JEFFERSON WILDERNESS

Jack Shelter

3491

18

5406

Square Lake

5447

BM 435

23

24

Douthit Spr

19

STATE 20

BM 4603

Hogg Rock

Gravel Pit

Lodge

BM 4758

BM 4711

BM 4631

Hoodoo

26

30

Circle Lake

25

TRAIL

Creek

Hoodoo Ski Bowl

SKI LIFT

4800

35

5523 *Hayrick Butte*

BOUNDARY Pass

4800

OLD

RAILROAD

31

36

4851

Gravel Pit

GRADE

CAC

WC

Meadow Lake

Santiam

FOREST

4666

2

SKYLINE

1

4888

6

4688

4678

130

see MAP 66

Hortense

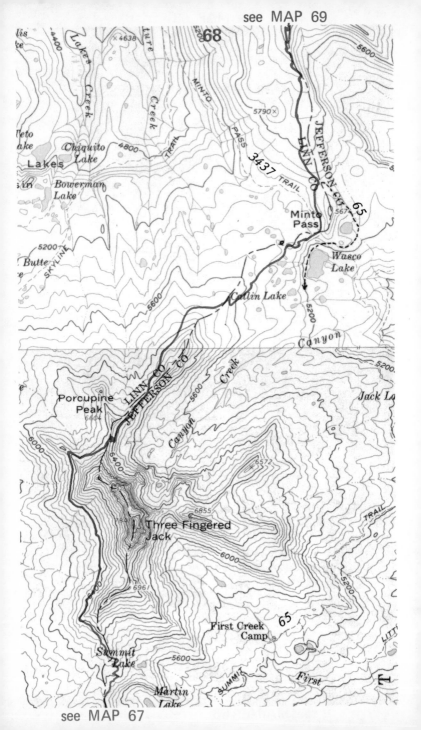

see MAP 69

68

see MAP 67

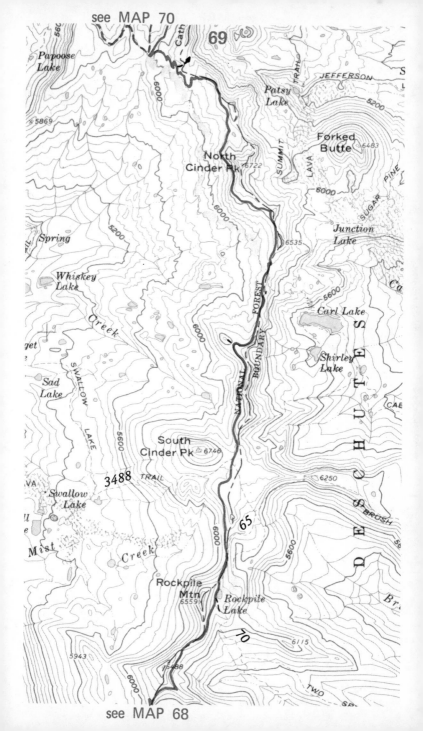

see MAP 70

69

Papoose
Lake

Cath

JEFFERSON

5200

Patsy
Lake

Forked
Butte 6483

North
Cinder Pk 5722

SUMMIT TRAIL

LAVA

SUGAR PINE

6000

Spring

5200

6535

Junction
Lake

NATIONAL

5600

FOREST

Carl Lake

Whiskey
Lake

Creek

6000

BOUNDARY

Shirley
Lake

get

SWALLOW

Sad
Lake

LAKE

South
Cinder Pk 6748

5600

6250

CAE

DESCHUTES

3488 TRAIL

65

BRUSH

Swallow
Lake

LAVA

Mist

Creek

6000

5600

Rockpile
Mtn
6559

Rockpile
Lake

70

6115

Br.

5943

5498

TWO

6000

see MAP 68

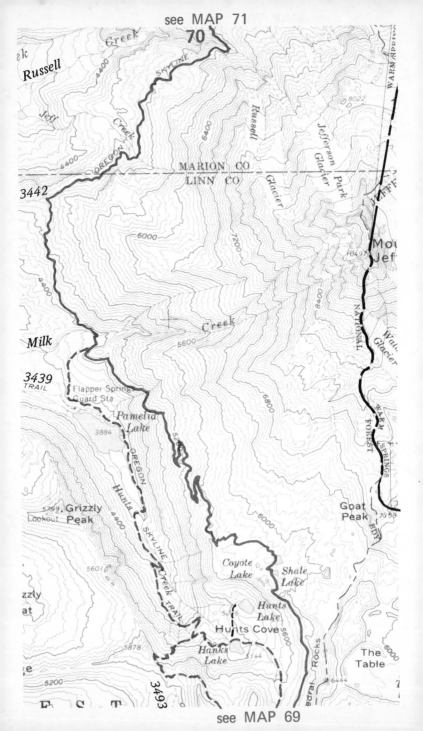

Russell

Creek

SKYLINE

Jeff

Creek

4400

6400

OREGON

4400

Russell

Jefferson Park Glacier

8022

MARION CO
LINN CO

3442

Glacier

JEFF

6000

7200

Mou
Jeff

4400

1849?

Creek

5600

NATIONAL

Glacier

8400

Milk

3439
TRAIL

Flapper Spring
Guard Sta

Pamelia
Lake

3884

WARM SPRINGS

FOREST

6800

5299, Grizzly
Lookout Peak

Hunts

OREGON

SKYLINE

Creek TRAIL

4400

5601

zzly
at

Goat
Peak

6000

7159

Coyote
Lake

Shale
Lake

Hunts
Lake

5486

Hunts Cove

5600

5878

Hanks
Lake

5164

5200

Rocks

The
Table

6000

6444

3493

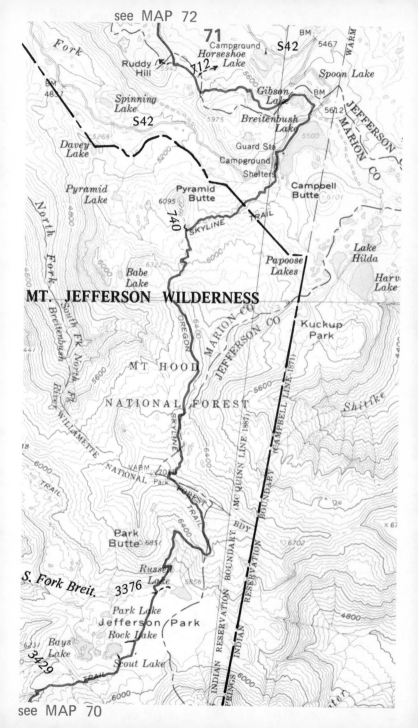

see MAP 72

71

Fork

see MAP 72

Ruddy
Hill

712

Campground
Horseshoe
Lake

S42   5467

WARM

BM

Spoon Lake

Gibson
Lake

BM

JEFFERSON

Spinning
Lake

S42

5975

Breitenbush
Lake

5612

5500

MARION CO.

Davey
Lake

5269

5200

Guard Sta

Campground
Shelters

Campbell
Butte

6101

Pyramid
Lake

Pyramid
Butte

6095

740

SKYLINE   TRAIL

Lake
Hilda

North Fork

4800

5000

6000

Babe
Lake

6322

6000

Papoose
Lakes

Harv
Lake

MT. JEFFERSON WILDERNESS

South Fk. North Fk. North Fork Breitenbush

River WILLAMETTE

441

OREGON

6400

MARION CO.

JEFFERSON CO.

Kuckup
Park

MT HOOD

NATIONAL FOREST

5600

Shitike

418

TRAIL

6000

SKYLINE

NATIONAL

BM

Park

6400

FOREST

TRAIL

McQUINN LINE 1887

CAMPBELL LINE 1871

JEFFERSON CO.

Park
Butte   6851

6400

Po

672

6702

S. Fork Breit.   3376

Russell
Lake

5856

INDIAN RESERVATION BOUNDARY

INDIAN RESERVATION BOUNDARY

BDY

4800

623/

Park Lake
Jefferson Park
Rock Lake

Bays
Lake

3429

Scout Lake

TRAIL

6000

PRINGS

6000

see MAP 70

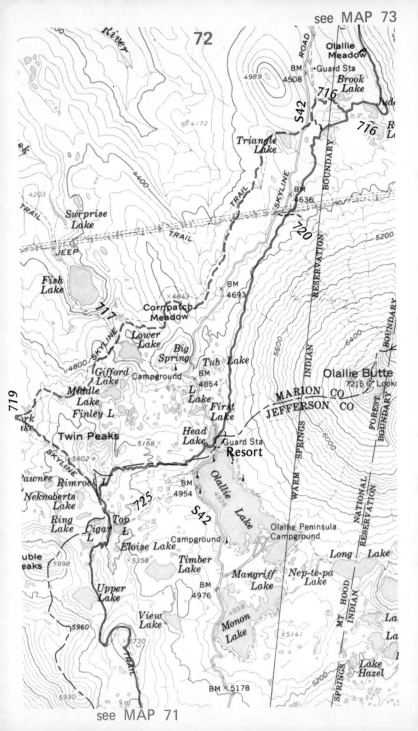

see MAP 73

72

see MAP 71

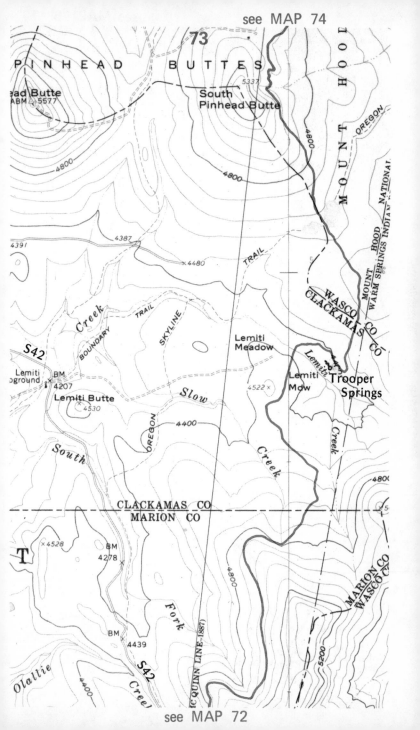

see MAP 74

73

PINHEAD BUTTES

South
Pinhead Butte

MOUNT HOOD

5337

4800

4800

OREGON

4800

4800

MOUNT HOOD NATIONAL

WARM SPRINGS INDIAN

4391

4387

×4480

TRAIL

WASCO CO
CLACKAMAS CO

Creek

TRAIL

SKYLINE

BOUNDARY

Lemiti
Meadow

Lemiti

S42

Lemiti
ogground

BM
4207

Lemiti
Mdw

Trooper
Springs

Lemiti Butte

4530

Slow

OREGON

4522 ×

South

4400

Creek

4800

Creek

CLACKAMAS CO
MARION CO

T

×4528

BM
4278 ×

4800

5

MARION CO
WASCO CO

BM
4439

Fork

S42

5000

Olallie

4400

MC QUINN LINE 1887

Creek

see MAP 72

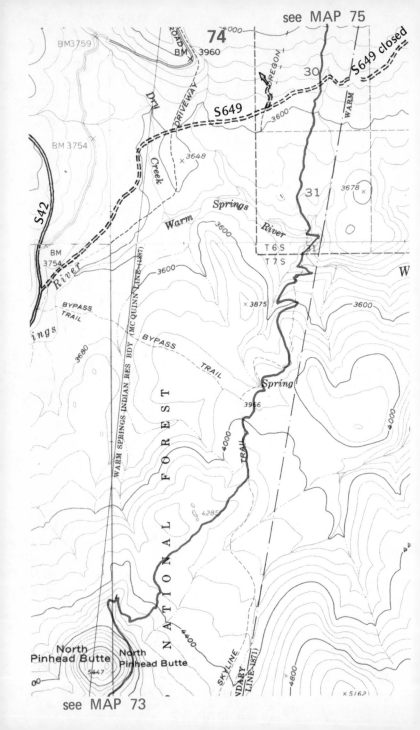

see MAP 75

S649 closed

BM3759

BM 3960

74

ROAD

OREGON

30

S649

DRIVEWAY

3600

WARM

BM 3754

Dry

Creek

× 3648

3678 ×

31

Springs

S42

Warm

3600

River

River

BM
3754

T 6 S

31

T 7 S

W

BYPASS

TRAIL

3600

× 3875

3600

ings

3680

BYPASS

WARM SPRINGS INDIAN RES BDY (MC QUINN LINE)(1871)

3600

TRAIL

Spring

3966

N

3680

A

4000

4000

T

I

O

4285

N

A

L

4400

F

O

R

E

S

T

SKYLINE

BOUNDARY LINE (1871)

North
Pinhead Butte

North
Pinhead Butte

4800

5447

5162 ×

see MAP 73

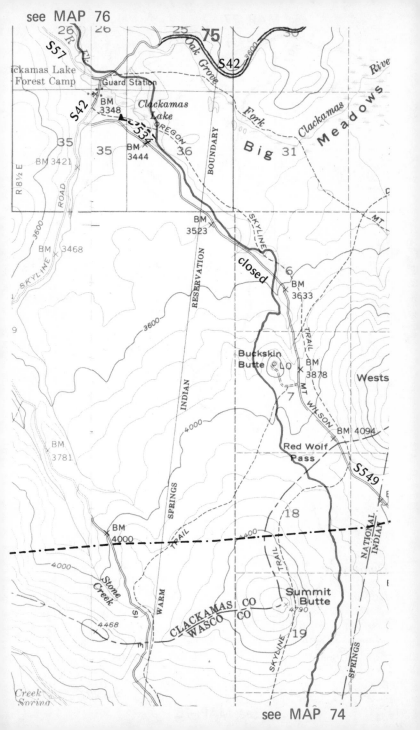

see MAP 76

75

S57

Oak Grove

S42

ckamas Lake
Forest Camp

Guard Station

Fork

Clackamas

River

S42

BM
3348

Clackamas
Lake

Oregon

Big

Meadows

35

35

BM
3444

36

BOUNDARY

31

BM 3421

R 8½ E

BM 3468

BM
3523

SKYLINE

closed

6

BM
3633

ROAD

3600

SKYLINE

3600

RESERVATION

9

3600

Buckskin
Butte

LO

BM
3878

Wests

MT

INDIAN

BM
3781

4000

7

TRAIL

MT WILSON

BM 4094

Red Wolf
Pass

S549

SPRINGS

18

BM
4000

TRAIL

4000

NATIONAL INDIAN

4000

Stone
Creek

WARM

4468

CLACKAMAS CO
WASCO CO

Summit
Butte

4790

19

TRAIL

SKYLINE

SPRINGS

Creek
Spring

see MAP 74

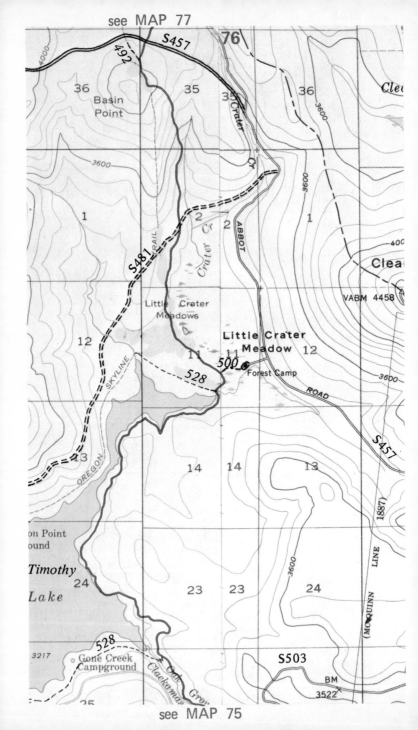

see MAP 77

S457

76

36

Basin
Point

35

35

Crater Cr

36

Clea

3600

3600

3600

400

1

3600

2

Crater Cr

2

ABBOT

1

Clea

S481

TRAIL

VABM 4458

A

Little Crater
Meadows

**Little Crater
Meadow** 12

12

11 11

500

Forest Camp

ROAD

3600

528

SKYLINE

13

14

14

13

S457

OREGON

1887

on Point
ound

Timothy

24

23

23

24

(McQUINN

Lake

3600

LINE)

3217

528

Gone Creek
Campground

Clackamas

Oak Gro

S503

BM
3522

25

see MAP 75

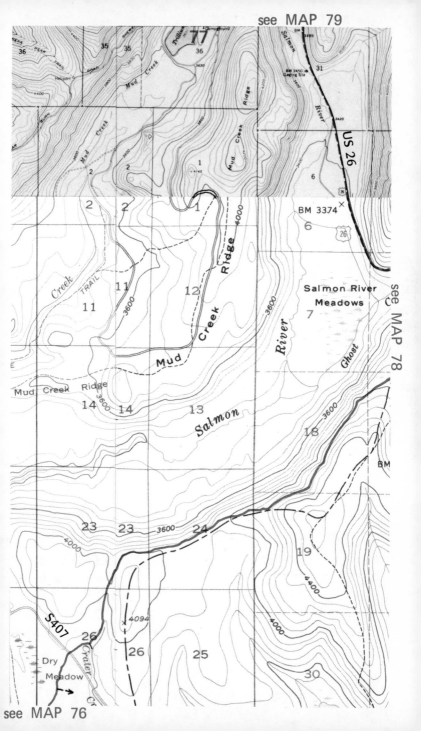

see MAP 79

see MAP 78

see MAP 76

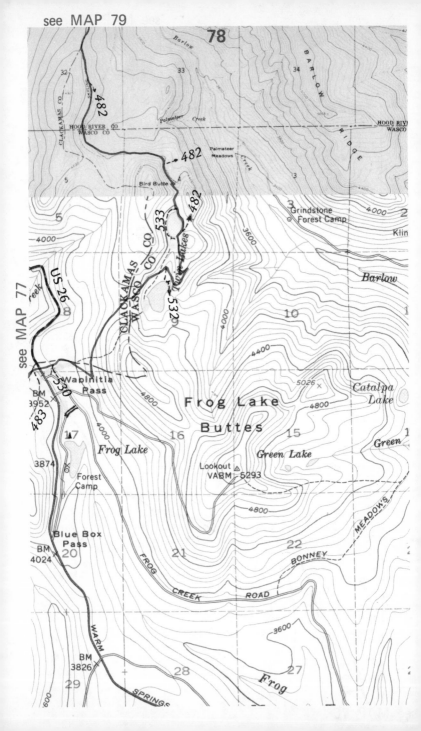

78

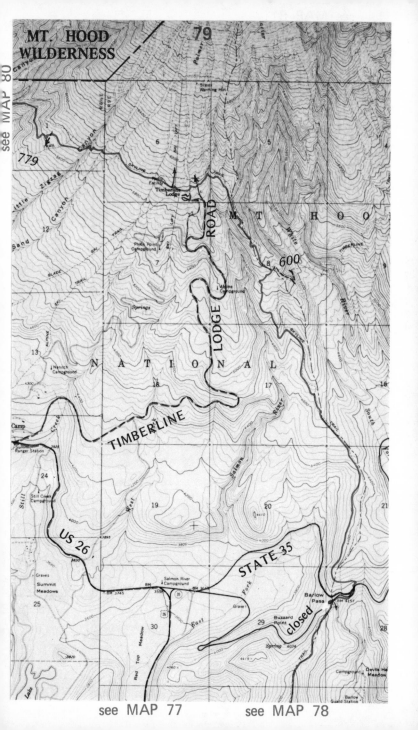

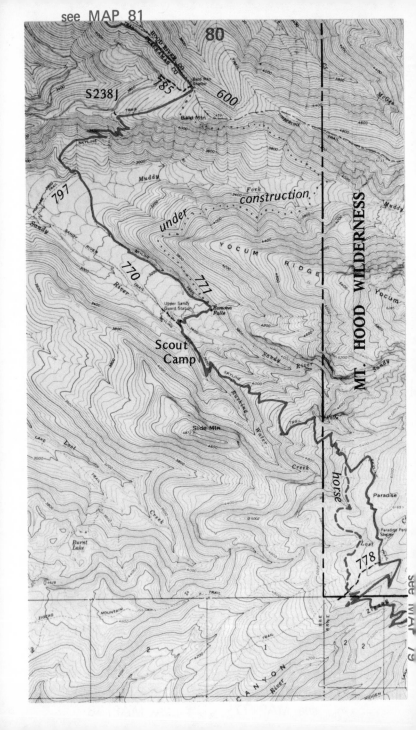

80

MT. HOOD WILDERNESS

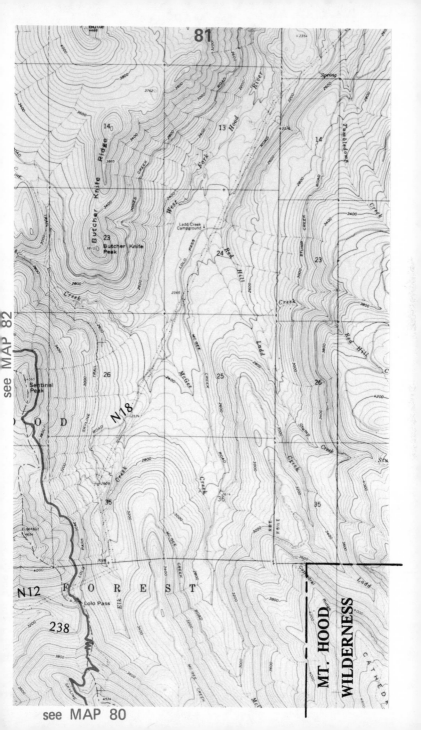

see MAP 82

MT. HOOD
WILDERNESS

see MAP 80

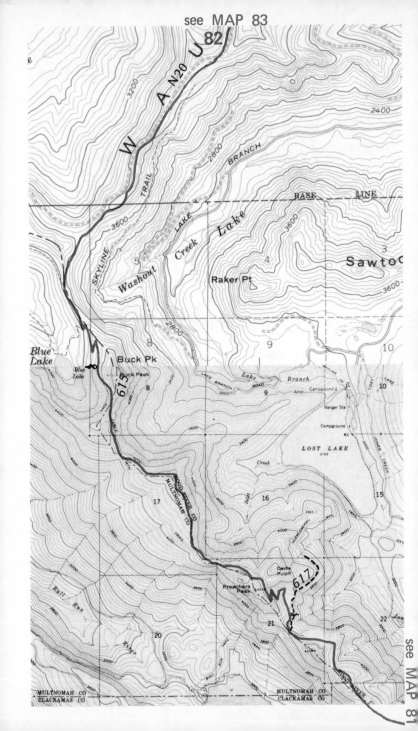

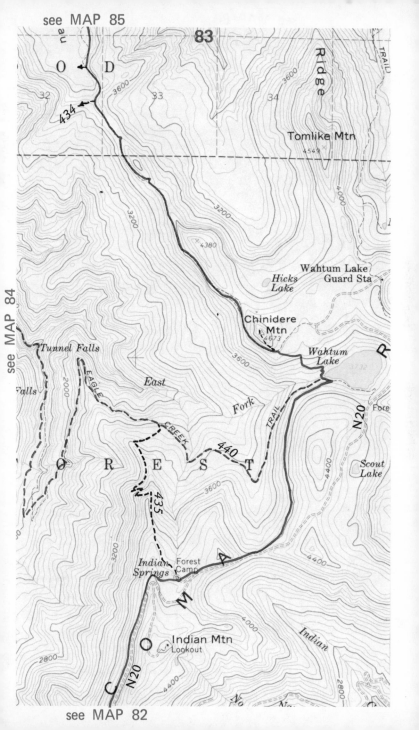

83

O   D

32

434

93

34

Ridge

3600

3600

Tomlike Mtn
4549 ×

3600

3200

3200

4000

4380

Wahtum Lake
Guard Sta

Hicks
Lake

Chinidere
Mtn
4673

Wahtum
Lake

R

N20   Fore

Tunnel Falls

EAGLE

2000

East

Fork

3600

TRAIL

4732

Falls

CREEK

440

S   T

N20

Scout
Lake

4400

O   R   E

3600

435

4400

3200

Indian
Springs

Forest
Camp

A

M

4400

2800

O

Indian Mtn
Lookout

4000

Indian

N20

4400

C

2800

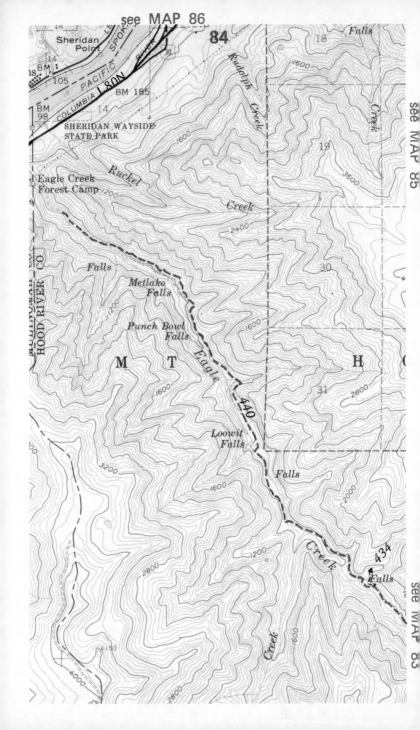

84

Sheridan Point

BM 105

BM 185

BM 98

SHERIDAN WAYSIDE STATE PARK

Eagle Creek Forest Camp

HOOD RIVER CO

Ruckel

Creek

Rudolph Creek

Creek

Falls

Metlako Falls

Punch Bowl Falls

Eagle

M T H

Loowit Falls

Falls

Creek

Falls

Creek

Falls

440

434

18

19

3600

30

31

2800

2000

1600

1200

2400

1200

1600

1600

1600

3200

2800

4000

4150

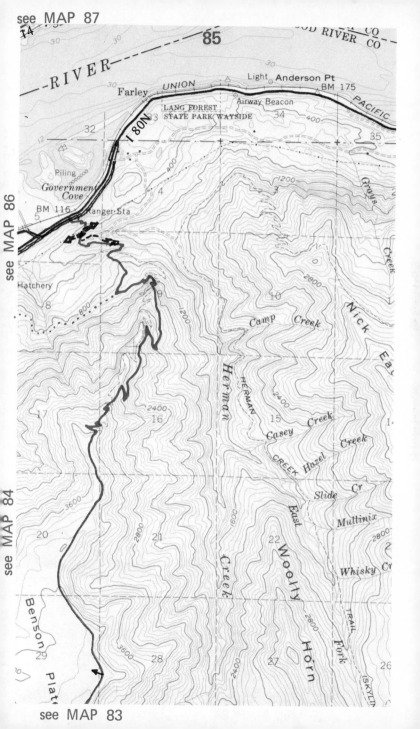

see MAP 87

85

COLUMBIA RIVER CO

RIVER

Farley UNION

Light Anderson Pt
BM 175

Airway Beacon

LANG FOREST
STATE PARK WAYSIDE

PACIFIC

180N 33 34 400 35

32

12

Piling

Government
Cove

400

4

3 1200

Grey's

Creek

see MAP 86

BM 116 Ranger Sta

5

2900

Hatchery 800

8 1200

Camp Creek

10

Nick Ea

17 2400

16

Herman

HERMAN

2400

15

Casey Creek

Creek

14

CREEK Hazel Creek

see MAP 84

3600 Slide Cr

East

Muttinix

2800

20

2800

21

22

Woolly

Whisky Cr

2800

TRAIL

29

Benson
Plate

3600 28

2800

27

Horn

Fork

2400

26

SKYLIN

see MAP 83

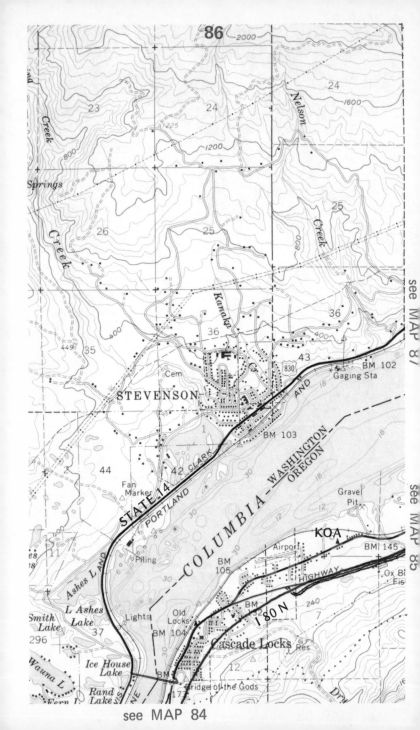

see MAP 87

see MAP 85

23

24

24

_1600_

Nelson

Creek

_225_

_1200_

_800_

26

25

25

Creek

Springs

Creek

_800_

36

_400_

Kanaka

400

_449_

35

36

43

BM 102

Cem

830

Gaging Sta

STEVENSON

18

1

BM 103

COLUMBIA

WASHINGTON

OREGON

44

42

CLARK

30

18

Fan Marker

STATE 14

PORTLAND

30

Gravel Pit

KOA

12

Airport

BM 145

11

8

Piling

BM 105

HIGHWAY

Ox B

Fis

Ashes L

6

30

240

L Ashes Lake

30

BM 132

I 80 N

7

Smith Lake

296

37

Lights

Old Locks

BM 104

BM

Cascade Locks

Res

Ice House Lake

BM

12

Wauna L

Rand Lake

Bridge of the Gods

17

Fern

see MAP 84

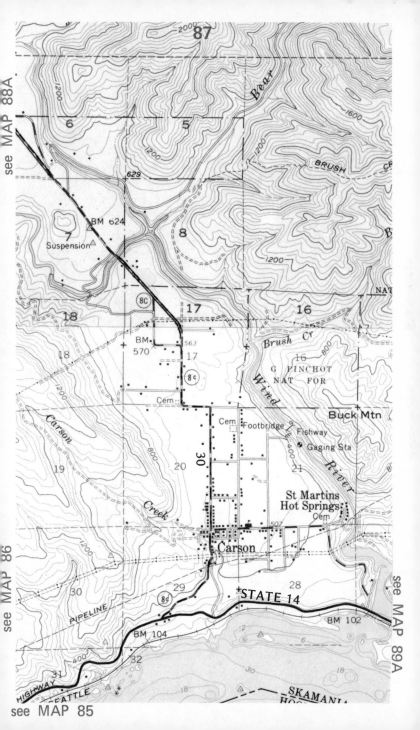

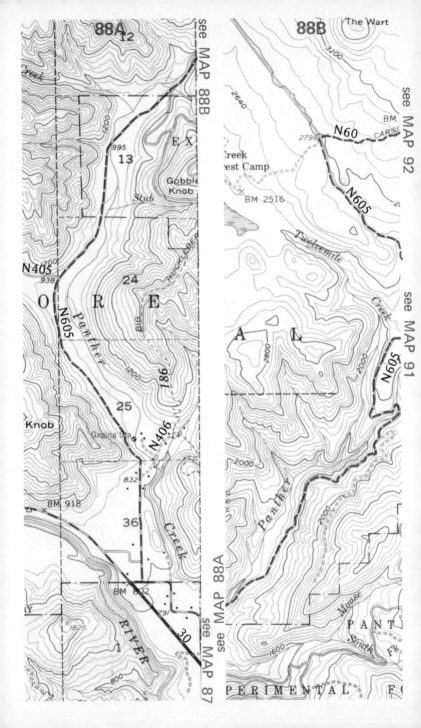

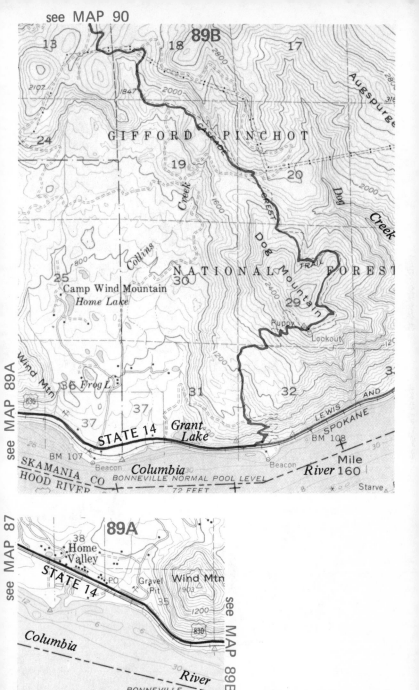

see MAP 90

89B

13 18 17

2107

1847

2000

GIFFORD PINCHOT

24

Augspurge

2800

Creek

19 20

CASCADE

2000

Creek

2000

1600

Collins

800

Dog

Creek

25 30 NATIONAL FOREST

TRAIL

Camp Wind Mountain

Home Lake

CREST

2400

Mountain

29

Puppy

Lookout

see MAP 89A

Wind Mtn

830

36 Frog L.

37

31

32

37

LEWIS AND SPOKANE

BM 108

STATE 14

Grant Lake

BM 107

Beacon

SKAMANIA CO.

HOOD RIVER

Columbia

Beacon

Mile

River 160

BONNEVILLE NORMAL POOL LEVEL

72 FEET

Starve

89A

see MAP 87

38

Home Valley

STATE 14

PO

Gravel Pit

Wind Mtn

1903

35

1200

see MAP 89B

830

Columbia

River

30

BONNEVILLE

NORMAL POOL LEVEL 72 FEET

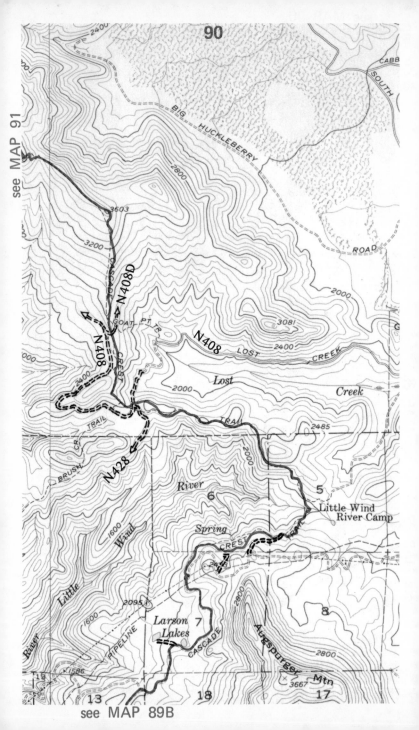

see MAP 91

CABB

SOUTH

BIG HUCKLEBERRY

ROAD

3603

3200

N 408D

GOAT PT 78

N 408

2400

CREST

N 408 LOST CREEK

3081

2400

Lost

2000

Creek

2485

BRUSH CR TRAIL

TRAIL

N 428

2000

River

6

5

Little Wind River Camp

Spring

CREST

TRAIL

2400

1600

Little Wind

2095

Larson Lakes 7

PIPELINE

CASCADE

2800

Augspurger

8

2800

1586

2800

Mtn

3667

13

18

17

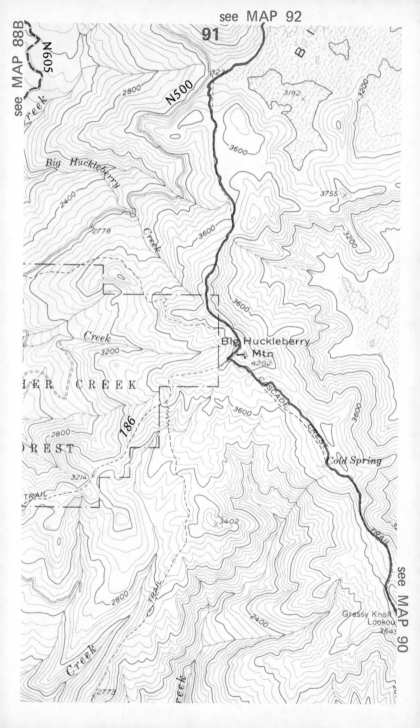

N605

N500

Creek

2800

Big Huckleberry

2400

2778

Creek

3600

3600

3200

3182

3600

3755

3200

3600

Creek

3200

Big Huckleberry

Mtn

4202

ER CREEK

186

CASCADE CREST

3600

3600

CREEK

Cold Spring

OREST

3214

2800

TRAIL

3402

TRAIL

TRAIL

2800

2400

Creek

eek

2773

Grassy Knoll
Lookout
3649

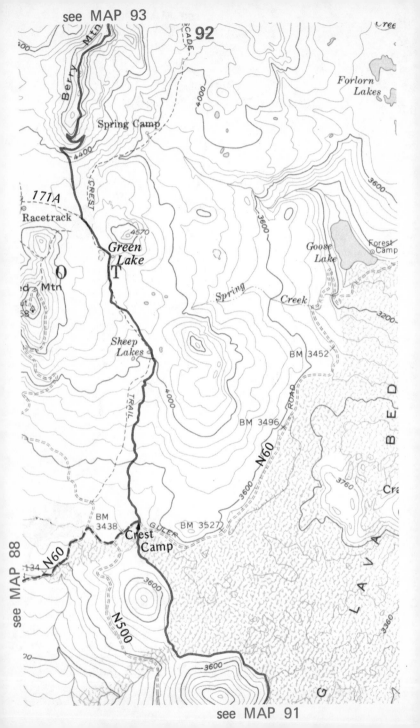

see MAP 93

92

Forlorn
Lakes

Berry Mtn

Spring Camp

CASCADE

4000

4400

3600

CREST

4000

3600

_171A_

Racetrack

4570

_Green
Lake_
T

Goose
Lake

Forest
Camp

O

d Mtn

Spring   _Creek_

3200

_Sheep
Lakes_

BM 3452

TRAIL

4000

BM 3496

N60

ROAD

3760

B
E
D

Cra

3600

BM
3438

GULER

BM 3527

N60

_Crest
Camp_

134

3600

N500

L
A
V
A

3760

3600

3600

G

see MAP 91

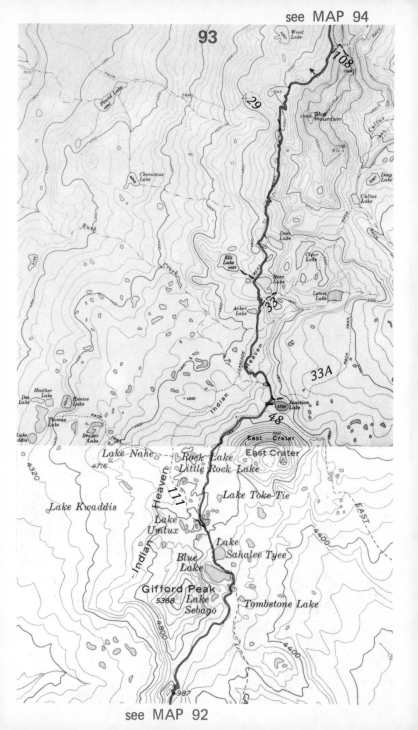

93

Wood
Lake

108

29

Bird
Mountain

Flood Lake

Chenamus
Lake

Deer
Lake

Clear
Lake

Cultus
Lake

Deep
Lake

Rush

Creek

Elk Lake
4685

Bear
Lake

33

Acker
Lake

Lemei
Lake

33A

Heaven

Dee
Lake

Heather
Lake

Bunice
Lake

Indian

Junction
Lake
4730

Thomas
Lake

Brader
Lake

48

Lake ddis

East Crater

Lake Nahe
4716

Rock Lake
Little Rock Lake

East Crater

4320

Lake Kwaddis

Heaven

111

Lake Toke Tie

Lake
Umtux

Indian

Lake
Sahalee Tyee

Blue
Lake

Gifford Peak
5368

Lake
Sebago

Tombstone Lake

4800

4400

4987

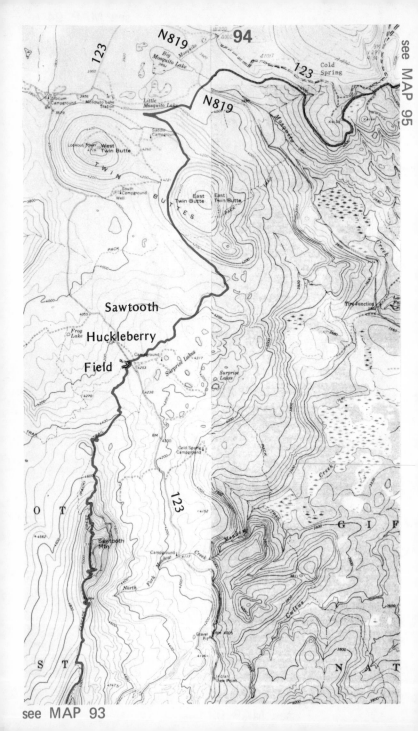

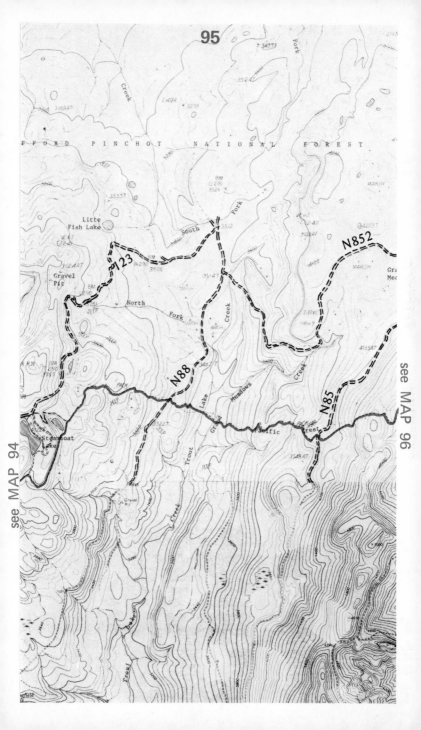

GIFFORD PINCHOT NATIONAL FOREST

Little
Fish Lake

South Fork

N852

Gravel
Pit

123

North Fork

N88

Grab
Mea

MARSH

N85

Grand
Lake

Trout
Creek

Meadows

Creek

Pacific Crest

Steamboat
Lake

see MAP 94

see MAP 96

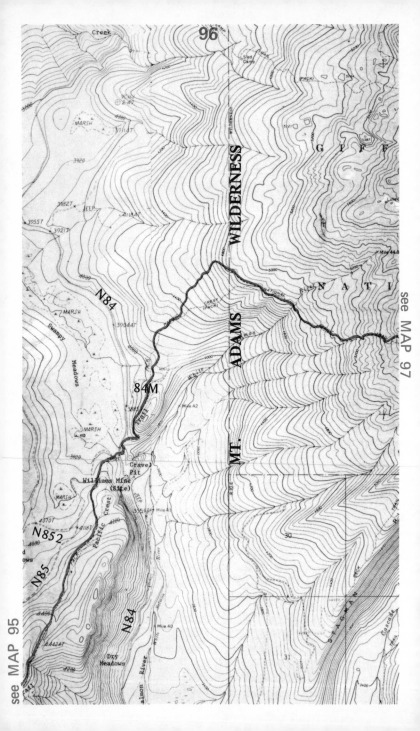

see MAP 95

see MAP 97

Creek

WILDERNESS

MT. ADAMS

GIFF

NATI

N84

84M

N852

N85

N84

Williams Mine
(Site)

Gravel
Pit

Pacific Crest

Swampy
Meadows

MARSH

MARSH

MARSH

MARSH

Dry
Meadows

White Salmon River

Mile 42

Mile 41

Mile 40

30

31

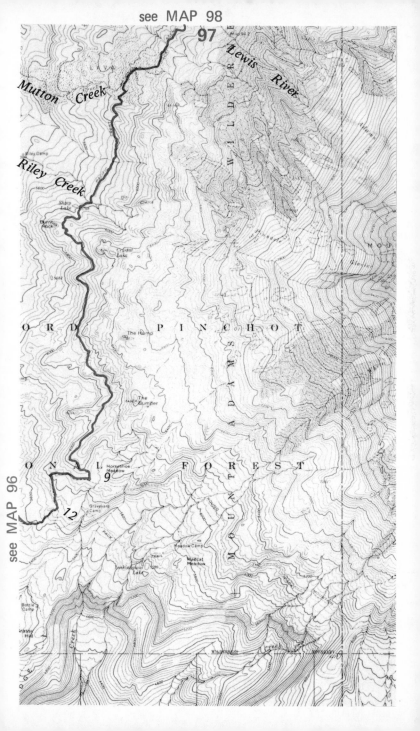

Lewis River

Mutton Creek

Riley Creek

Riley Camp

Shiko Lake

Burnt Rock

Crystal Lake

O R D   P I N C H O T

The Hump

The Bumper

O N A L   F O R E S T

Horseshoe Meadow

9

Graveyard Camp

12

Meadow Camp

Madcat Meadow

Junkinshu Lake

Bottle Camp

Grassy Hill

M O U N T   A D A M S   W I L D E R N E S S

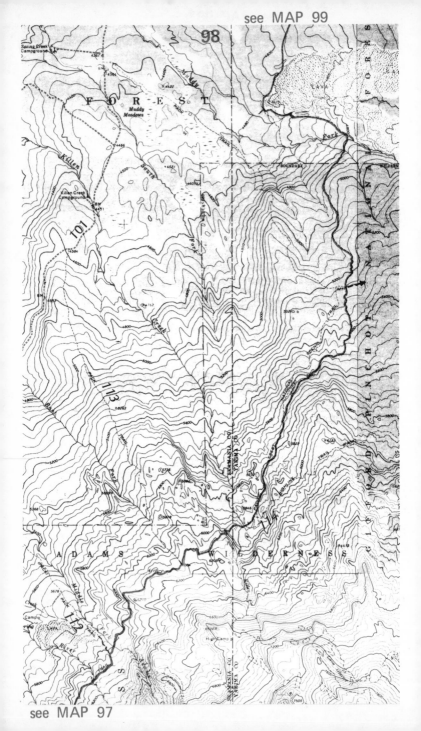

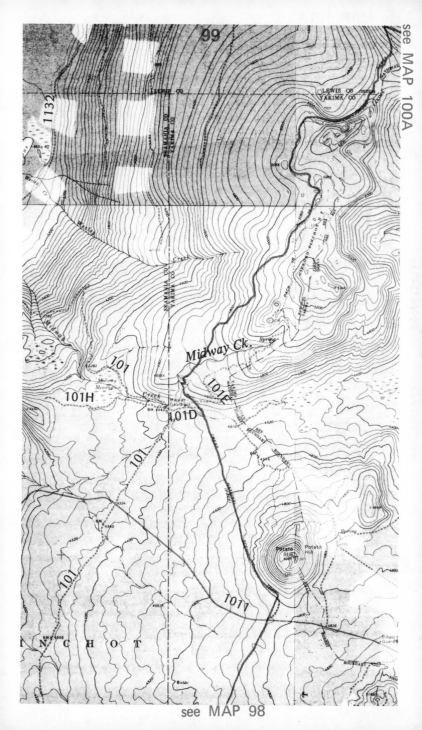

99

1132

LEWIS CO
YAKIMA CO

Midway Ck.

Spring

101

101H

101E

101D

BM 4447

101

101

Potato
Hill

1011

N C H O T

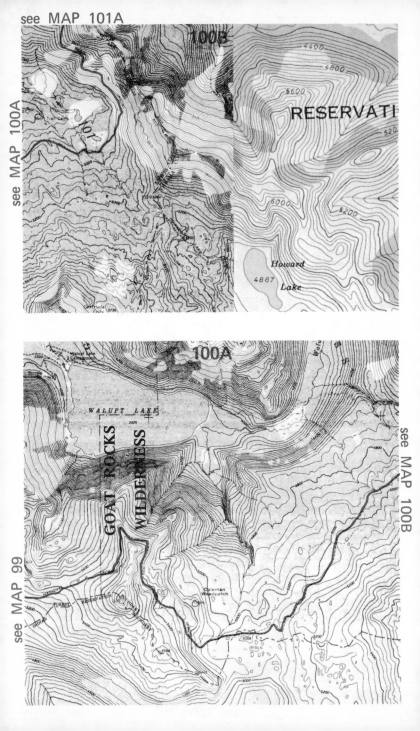

see MAP 101A

100B

see MAP 100A

101

4400
4800
5600
RESERVATI
520
5000
5200
6000
Howard
Lake
4887

100A

Walupt Lake Campground

WALUPT LAKE 2826

GOAT ROCKS
WILDERNESS

see MAP 100B

see MAP 99

Coleman
Weedpatch

FOREST
RESERVATION

INDIAN

5056

see MAP 102

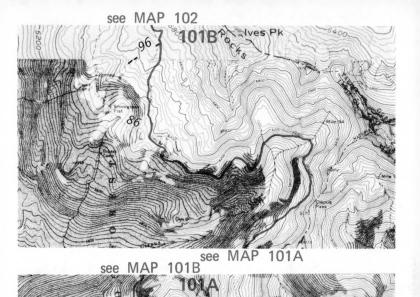

see MAP 101A

see MAP 101B

see MAP 100B

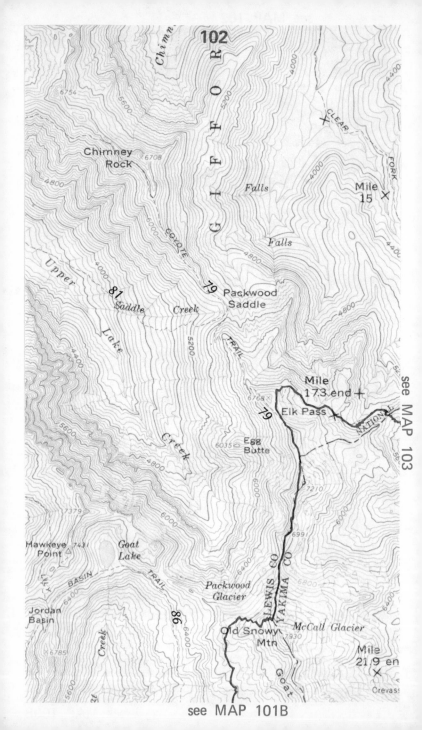

102

GIFFOR

Chimney Rock
6708

6754

Upper

Saddle

Lake

COYOTE

81

Creek

79

Packwood
Saddle

Falls

Falls

Clear

Mile
15

FORK

TRAIL

79

Mile
17.3 end
Elk Pass

NATION

see MAP 103

Egg
Butte
6035

6768

7210

Creek

Hawkeye
Point 7431

Goat
Lake

7379

LICK BASIN

Jordan
Basin

6400

6785

Creek

TRAIL

86

Packwood
Glacier

Old Snowy
Mtn
7930

6991

6800

McCall Glacier

LEWIS CO
YAKIMA CO

Goat

Mile
21.9 en

Crevass

see MAP 101B

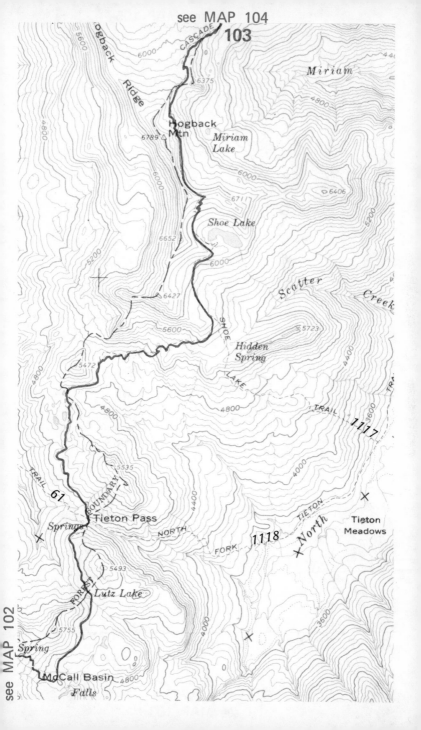

see MAP 104

103

CASCADE

6000

Hogback Ridge

6375

Miriam

4400

5600

6789 △ Hogback Mtn

Miriam Lake

4800

6000

6000

6711

6406

5200

Shoe Lake

6652

6000

Scatter

Creek

6427

5723

5200

5600

Hidden Spring

SHOE

5472

4800

LAKE

TRAIL

4400

1117

4800

4800

4000

5600

5535

TRAIL 61

BOUNDARY

Tieton Pass

Springs

NORTH

TIETON

4400

FORK

1118

North

Tieton Meadows

✕

4000

5493

FOREST

Lutz Lake

5755

4000

3600

Spring

✕

see MAP 102

McCall Basin

4800

Falls

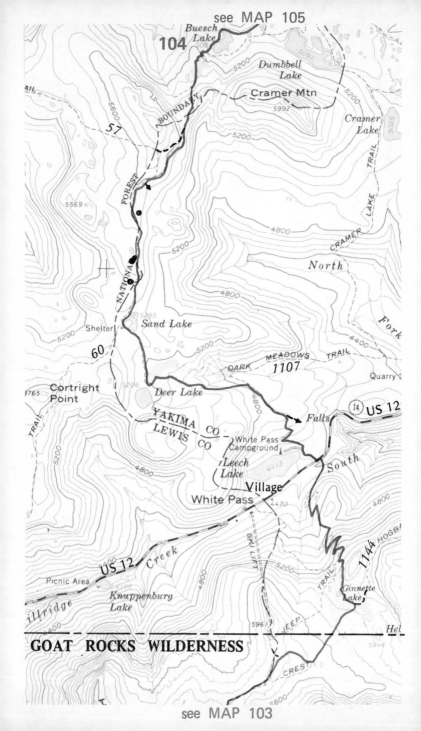

see MAP 105

104

Buesch Lake

Dumbbell Lake

Cramer Mtn

5992

Cramer Lake

57

BOUNDARY

FOREST

5200

5569 x

NATIONAL

North

Fork

CRAMER LAKE TRAIL

4800

5200

Sand Lake

5395

Shelter

60

5200

5296

Cortright Point

5765

Deer Lake

YAKIMA CO
LEWIS CO

TRAIL

5200

MEADOWS TRAIL

DARK

1107

4400

Quarry

4800

Falls

14 US 12

White Pass Campground

Leech Lake

4412

Village

White Pass

South

4800

4470

US 12

Creek

illridge

Picnic Area

Knuppenburg Lake

4800

SKI LIFT

5260

TRAIL

5969

JEEP

1144 HOGBA

Ginnette Lake

Hel

5849

4400

GOAT ROCKS WILDERNESS

CREST

5600

see MAP 103

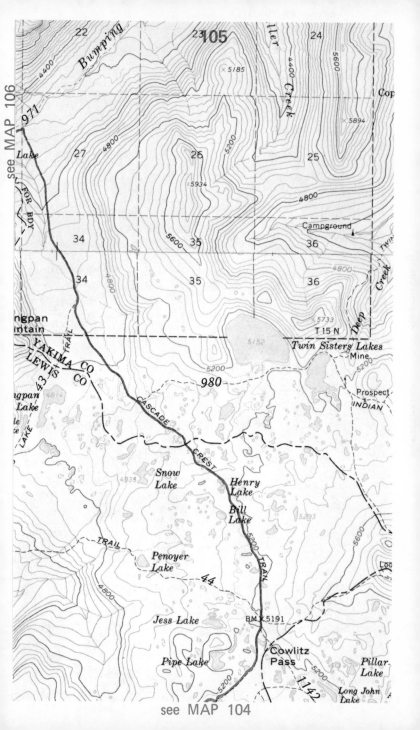

see MAP 106

see MAP 104

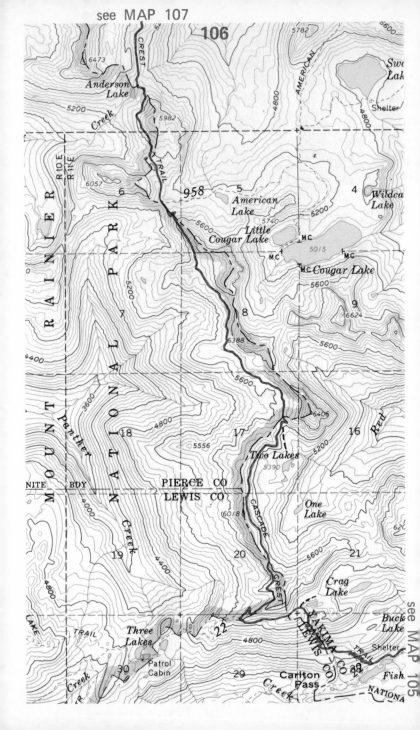

see MAP 105

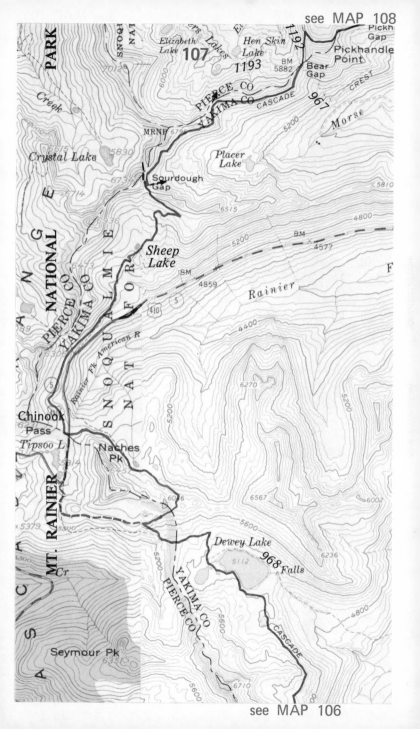

see MAP 108

PARK

Pickh
Gap

Elizabeth
Lake **107**

Hen Skin
Lake

1193

1192

Pickhandle
Point

BM
5882

Bear
Gap

RANGE

Creek

PIERCE CO
YAKIMA CO

CREST

967

CASCADE

Morse

Crystal Lake

5830

MRNP 6796

Placer
Lake

5810

6735

Sourdough
Gap

6714

6936

5200

6515

4800

BM
4577

NATIONAL

6173

*Sheep
Lake*

SNOQUALMIE FOR

5200

Rainier

PIERCE CO
YAKIMA CO

BM
4859

5

Rainier

410

4400

Rainier Fk American R

NAT

6270

5200

5

5

Chinook
Pass

Tipsoo L

Naches
Pk

5814

6257

6046

6567

6002

5600

Dewey Lake

6236

MT. RAINIER

5379

5800

5112

968 Falls

Cr

5200

YAKIMA CO
PIERCE CO

4800

CASCADE

Seymour Pk

6351

5600

6710

A S C

see MAP 106

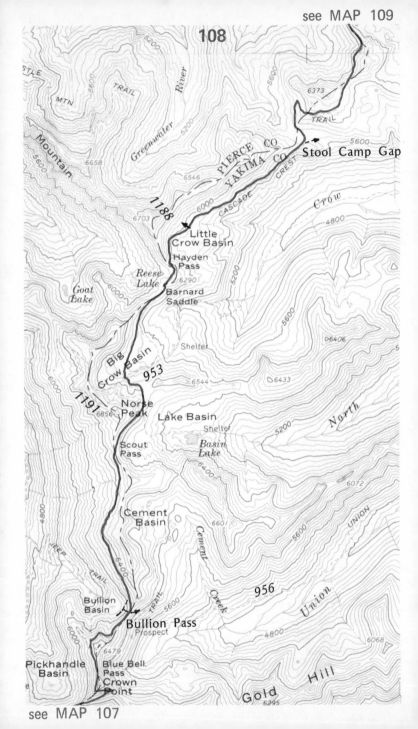

see MAP 109

108

Greenwater River

CASTLE MTN

TRAIL

Mountain

6658

PIERCE CO

YAKIMA CO

CASCADE

CREST

Stool Camp Gap

6373

TRAIL

6546

6000

1188

6703

Little
Crow Basin

Crow

4800

Hayden
Pass

Reese
Lake

6290

Barnard
Saddle

Goat
Lake

6000

5200

5600

6406

Shelter

Big

Crow Basin

953

6544

6433

North

1191

6856

Norse
Peak

Lake Basin

Shelter

Basin
Lake

5200

Scout
Pass

6400

6072

Cement
Basin

6601

UNION

JEEP

4800

TRAIL

6400

Cement

956

Creek

Union

Bullion
Basin

TRAIL

5600

Bullion Pass

Prospect

4800

6068

Pickhandle
Basin

6479

Blue Bell
Pass

6000

Crown
Point

Gold

Hill

6295

see MAP 107

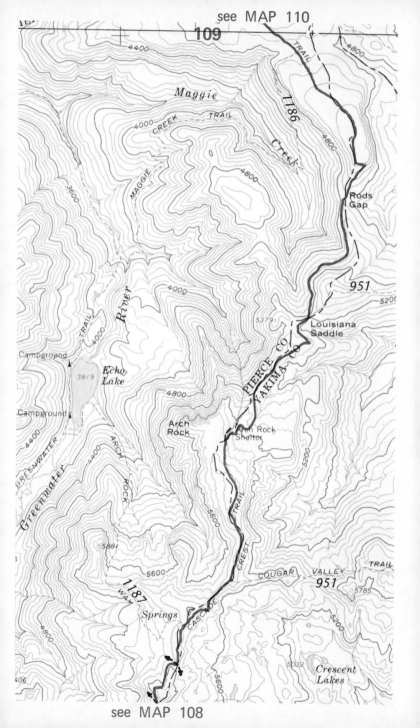

4400

4800

Maggie

CREEK   TRAIL

1186

4000

CREEK

Creek

4800

MAGGIE

0

4800

Rods
Gap

3600

951

5200

River

4000

5379

Louisiana
Saddle

Campground

4000

PIERCE CO

YAKIMA CO

Echo
Lake

3819

4800

Campground

Arch
Rock

Arch Rock
Shelter

GREENWATER

ARCH

4400

5200

Greenwater

ROCK

5600

TRAIL

CREST

4400

5881

VALLEY   TRAIL

5600

COUGAR

951

1187

5785

5200

WAY

Springs

CASCADE

5032

4800

Crescent
Lakes

406

5600

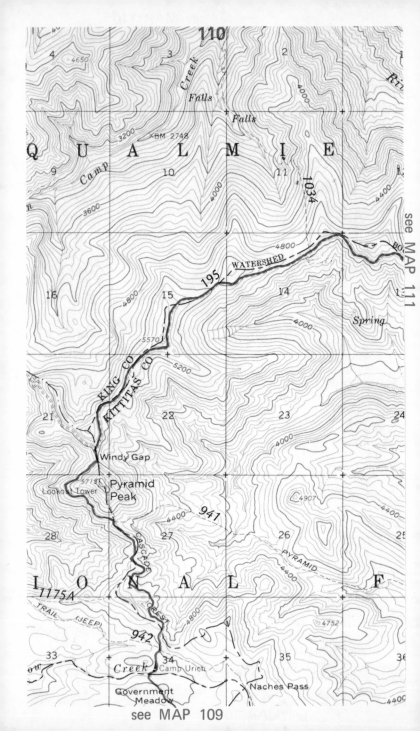

see MAP 111

see MAP 109

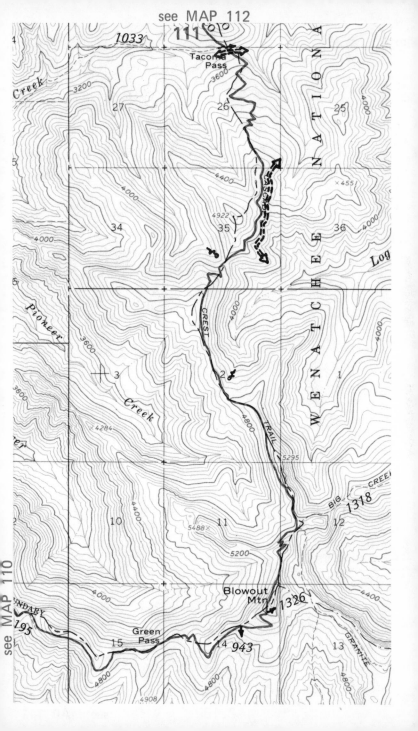

111

Tacoma
Pass

Creek

1033

3200

3600

27

26

25

4000

4400

×4551

4000

4000

34

35

4922

36

Log

CREST

4000

Pioneer

3600

3600

3

Creek

2

4800

1

4000

4284

TRAIL

5295

BIG CREEK

1318

10

11

12

5488

5200

4000

4400

Blowout
Mtn.

1326

195

Green
Pass

15

14

943

13

GRANITE

4800

4800

4908

see MAP 110

WENATCHEE NATIONAL

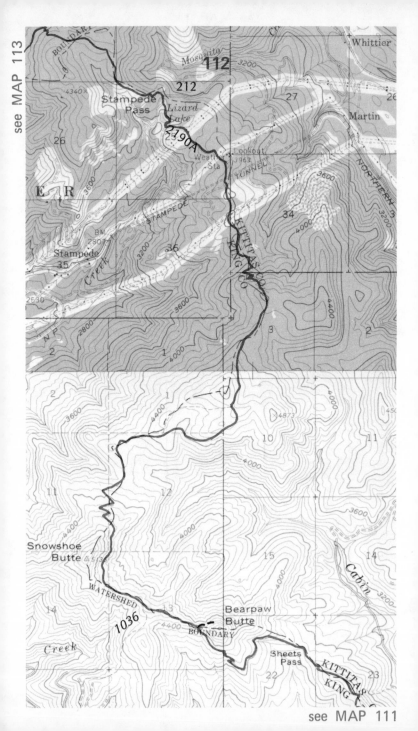

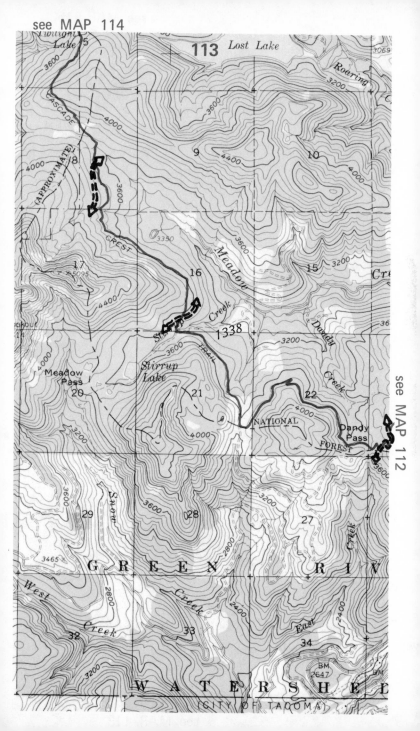

see MAP 114

113 Lost Lake

see MAP 112

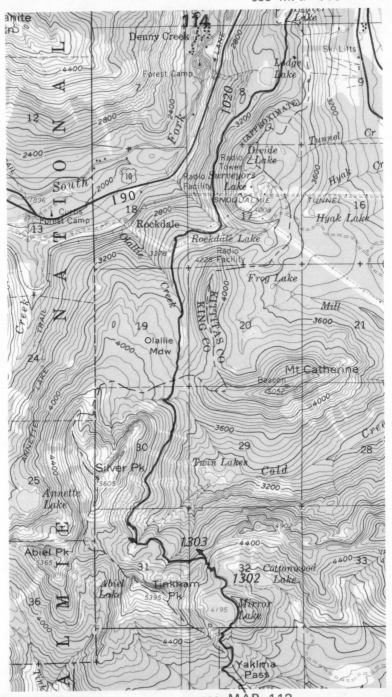

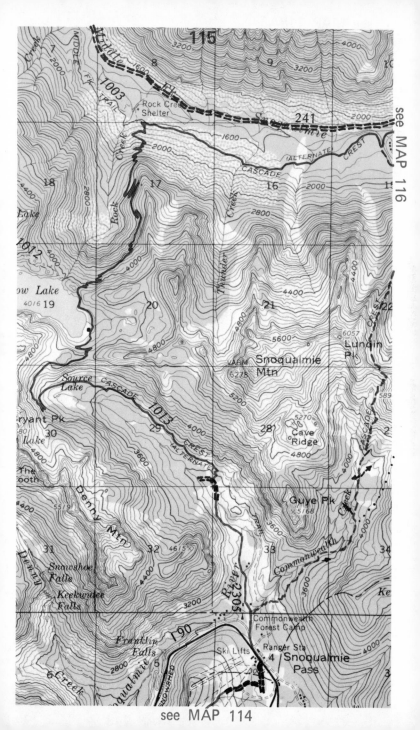

see MAP 116

see MAP 114

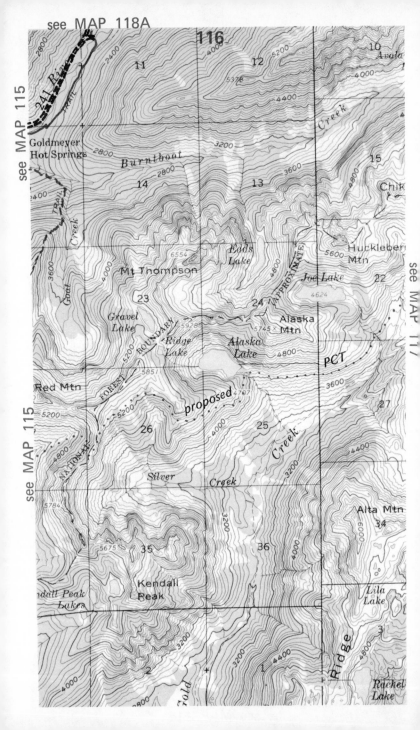

116

see MAP 115

see MAP 115

see MAP 117

241 Rd

TRAIL

Goldmeyer
Hot Springs

Burntboat

TRAIL

Goat Creek

10

Avala

11

12

15

Chik

14

13

Eads
Lake

Huckleber
Mtn

Mt Thompson

6554

Joe Lake

22

23

Gravel
Lake

Ridge
Lake

24

Alaska
Mtn

5745

Alaska
Lake

Joe Lake

4624

4800

PCT

Red Mtn

BOUNDARY

FOREST

5851

proposed

4797

3600

26

NATIONAL

25

Creek

27

Silver

Creek

Alta Mtn

5784

5675

35

36

34

Kendall
Peak

Lila
Lake

dall Peak
Lakes

2

Gold

1

Ridge

3

Rachel
Lake

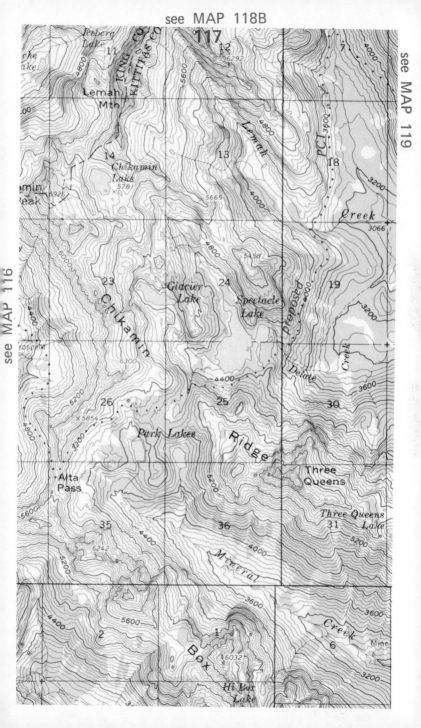

see MAP 119

see MAP 116

117

Iceberg Lake

che ake

11

12

7

KING CO
KITTITAS CO

Leman Mtn

Leman

14

Chikamin Lake

5781

13

18

min eak

8925

5665

Creek

3066

4800

4800

4000

4000

3600

3200

PCT

5458

23

Glacier Lake

24

Spectacle Lake

19

Chikamin

6300

Proposed

3200

Delate

Creek

3600

26

x 5854

25

30

Ridge

Park Lakes

Prospect

Alta Pass

Three Queens

35

36

31

Three Queens Lake

6242

Mineral

5200

3600

Creek

6

Mine

2

Box

1

6032

Hi Box Lake

3600

3200

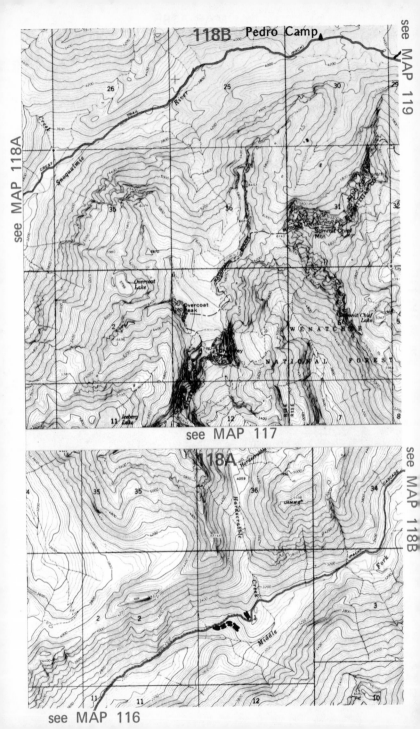

118B

Pedro Camp

WENATCHEE

NATIONAL FOREST

Overcoat
Lake

Overcoat
Peak

Summit Chief
Mtn

Iswoot Chief
Lake

Iceberg
Lake

118A

Hardscrabble

Middle
Fork

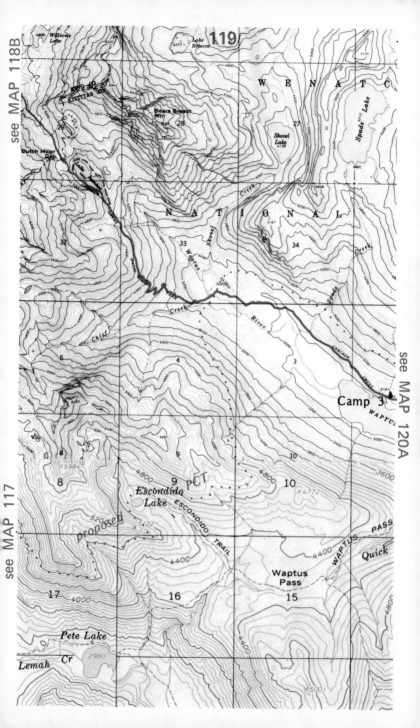

Williams Lake

Lake Rebecca

W E N A T C

Bears Breast Mtn

Shovel Lake

Spade Lake

Burch Miller Gap

N A T I O N A L

Shovel Creek

Spade Creek

Chief Creek

Waptus Creek

Creek

River

Cascade Creek

Camp 3

WAPTUS

Escondido Lake

PCT

ESCONDIDO TRAIL

proposed

Waptus Pass

WAPTUS PASS

Quick

Pete Lake

Lemah Cr

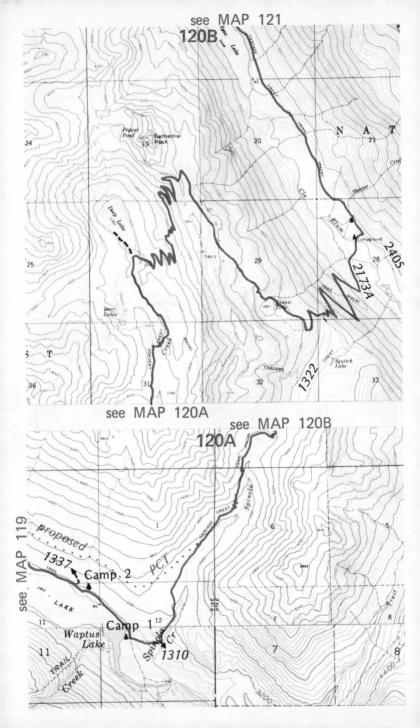

see MAP 121

120B

see MAP 120A

see MAP 120B

120A

see MAP 119

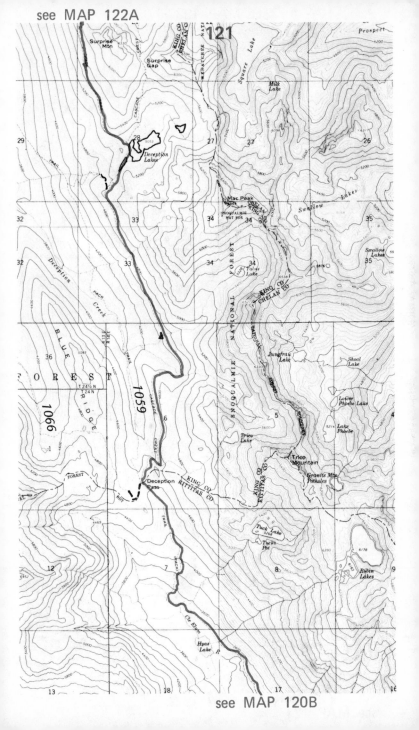

Prospect

Surprise Mtn

Surprise Gap

Square Lake

Milk Lake

Deception Lake

Swallow Lake

Mac Peak

SNOQUALMIE NAT FOR

Swallow Lakes

Deception Creek

Tullis Lake

KING CO
CHELAN CO

BLUE RIDGE

Jungfrau Lake

Shoal Lake

FOREST

Trico Lake

Lower Phoebe Lake

Lake Phoebe

Trico Mountain

Granite Mtn Potholes

FOREST

Deception Pass

KING CO
KITTITAS CO

Tuck Lake

Tucks Pot

Robin Lakes

Cle Elum

Hyas Lake

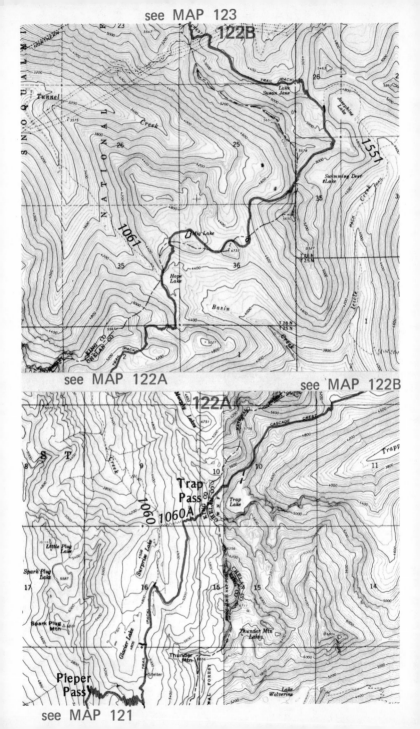

see MAP 123

122B

Lake
Susan Jane

1551

Swimming Deer
Lake

Big Lake

Hope
Lake

Basin

see MAP 122A

see MAP 122B

122A

CASCADE CREST

Trapp

Trap
Pass

1060A

Trap
Lake

1060

Little Plug
Lake

Surprise Lake

Spark Plug
Lake

Glacier Lake

Spark Plug
Mtn

Thunder Mtn
Lakes

Thunder
Mtn

Lake
Wolverine

Pieper
Pass

see MAP 121

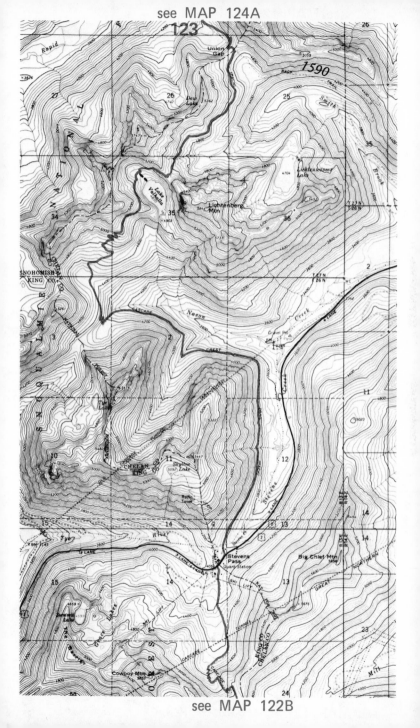

123

1590

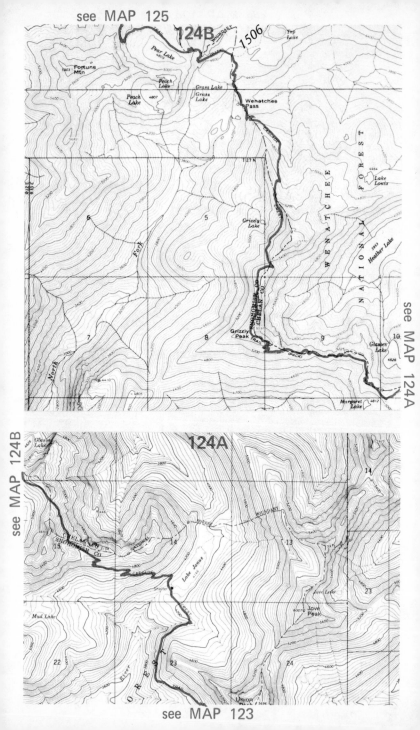

see MAP 125

124B

1506

see MAP 124A

see MAP 124B

124A

see MAP 123

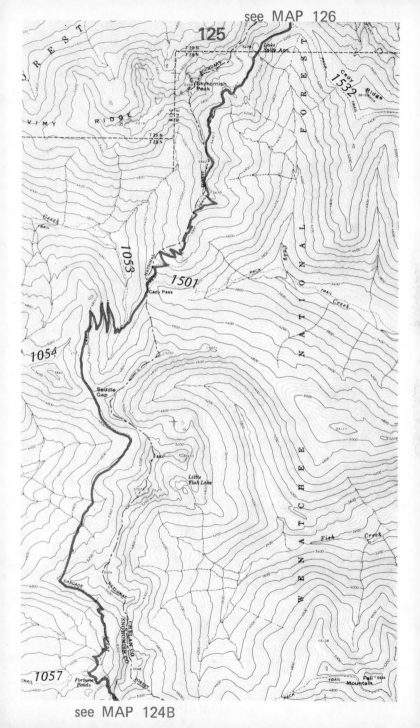

see MAP 126

125

FOREST

T 29 N
T 28 N

Lake
Sally Ann

Cady
Ridge

1532

Skykomish
Peak

BOUNDARY

VIMY   RIDGE

NATIONAL

T 29 N
T 28 N

Creek
TRAIL

1053

PACK

Pass

TRAIL Creek

1501

Cady Pass

5230

1054

Saddle
Gap

WENATCHEE

Little
Fish Lake

Fish   Creek

CASCADE

NATIONAL

CHELAN CO
SNOHOMISH CO

FOREST

1057

Fortune
Bowls

TRAIL

PACK

TRAIL

Fell
Mountain

see MAP 124B

Red Pass

126

White Mt n

VABM 7030

6000

5500

BM × 5135

649

5500

BM 5904
White
Pass

GLACIER

3574

3500

4500

Sauk

River

6203

4500

6113

5000

4500

PEAK

Reflection Pond

Lower
White
Pass

BM 5378

945

4000

N

PACIFIC

1507

CHELAN CO.

SNOHOMISH CO.

Kid Pond

4500

5703

5000

WILDERNESS

MT BAKER
NATIONAL FOREST

GLACIER PEAK

Johnson
Mtn

5800

PACK

WILDERNESS

Blue
Lake
5625

North Fork

5000

5500

Indian
Pass

1502

SNOHOMISH CO
CHELAN CO

Kodak
Peak

1524

TRAIL

PACK

NATIONAL FOREST

Little
Blue Lake

TRAIL

WILDERNESS

650

BOUNDARY

TRAIL

CREST

1525

PACK TRAIL

Meander
Meadow

Meander
Meadow

5400

CASCADE

CREST

5500

Dishpan Gap

CHELAN CO
SNOHOMISH CO

TRAIL

5905

Wenatchee River

Wards
Pass

4400

4200

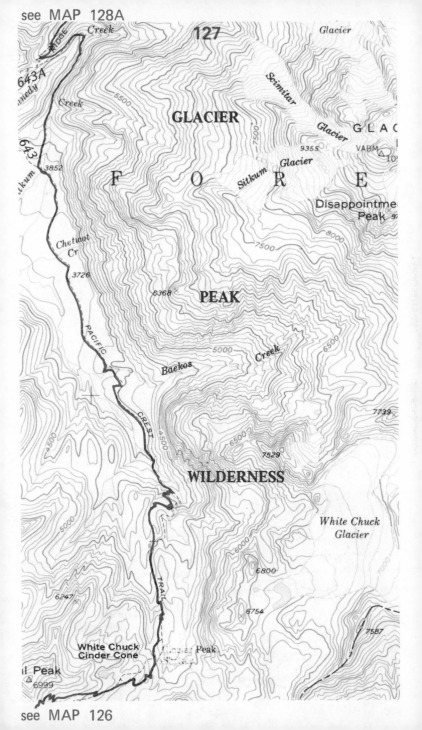

127

Creek

RIDGE

643A

Kennedy

Creek

5500

GLACIER

Scimitar

Glacier

7500

9355

VABM
10

GLAC

643

Sitkum

Glacier

F   O   R   E

3852

Kum

Disappointme
Peak

Chetwot
Cr

8000

3726

7500

6368

PEAK

PACIFIC

5000

Creek

6500

Baekos

CREST

4500

4500

5000

6500

7739

6500

7529

WILDERNESS

White Chuck
Glacier

4500

6000

5000

TRAIL

6800

6247

6754

7587

White Chuck
Cinder Cone

Peak

l Peak

6999

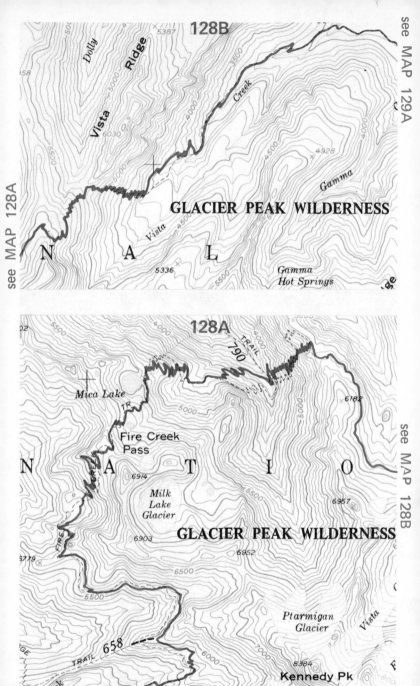

see MAP 129A

see MAP 128A

128B

Dolly

Vista Ridge

6030

Creek

4928

Gamma

GLACIER PEAK WILDERNESS

N A L

Vista

5336

Gamma
Hot Springs

128A

TRAIL
790

Mica Lake

TR

Fire Creek
Pass

N A T I O

6914

Milk
Lake
Glacier

6903

6952

GLACIER PEAK WILDERNESS

6500

5500

FIRE

CREEK

3779

6957

6182

see MAP 128B

Ptarmigan
Glacier

Vista

8384
Kennedy Pk

658

TRAIL

6000

Creek

TRAIL

Kennedu

see MAP 127

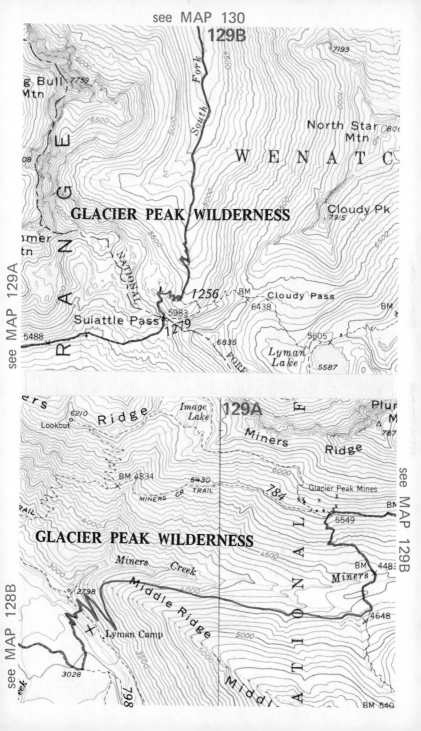

130

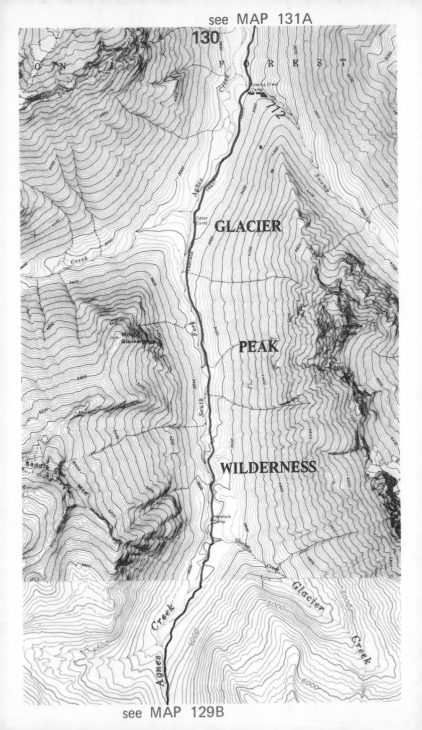

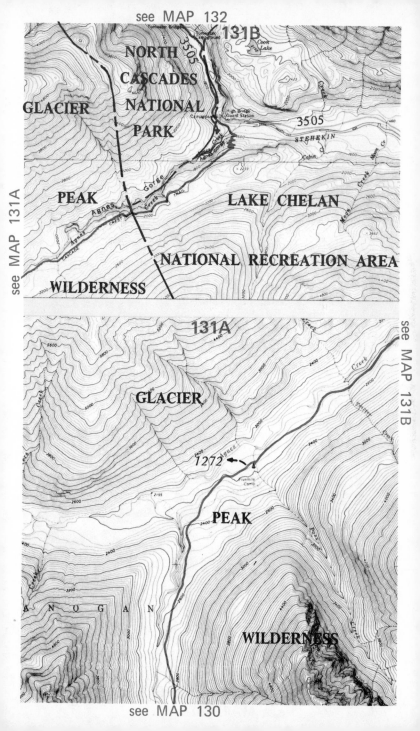

see MAP 132

131B

NORTH

CASCADES

NATIONAL

PARK

GLACIER

3505

High Bridge
Guard Station

3505

STEHEKIN

Cabin

see MAP 131A

PEAK

Gorge

LAKE CHELAN

Agnes

Creek

CREEK

CASCADE

NATIONAL RECREATION AREA

WILDERNESS

131A

see MAP 131B

GLACIER

1272

Agnes

Fivemile
Camp

2155

PEAK

O N O G A N

WILDERNESS

see MAP 130

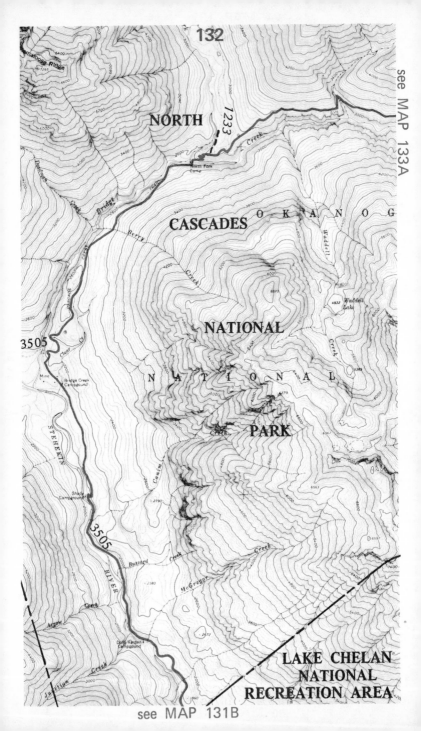

see MAP 133A

1233

NORTH

North Fork
Camp

CASCADES O K A N O G

Waddell

NATIONAL

Waddell
Lake

Bridge

Berry Creek

N A T I O N A L

3505

Creek Cr.

Mine

Bridge Creek Campground

PARK

Canim

Creek

STEHEKIN

Snahi
Campground

3505

Creek

Buzzard Creek

McGregor Creek

RIVER

Arpon Creek

Cott. Vaxdan's
Campground

Creek

**LAKE CHELAN
NATIONAL
RECREATION AREA**

see MAP 131B

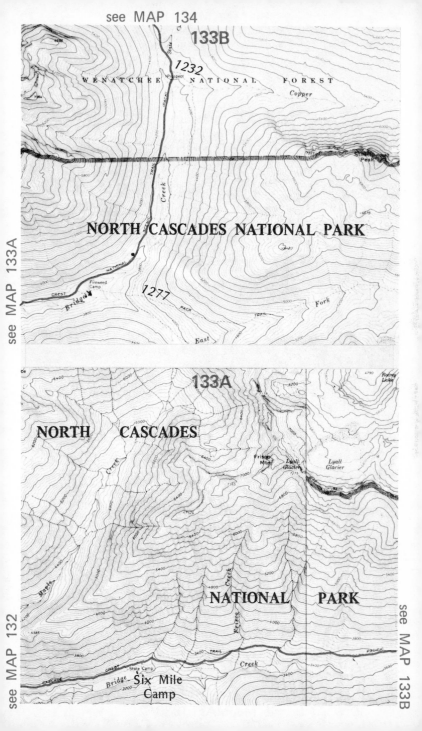

see MAP 134

133B

WENATCHEE NATIONAL FOREST

1232

Copper

NORTH CASCADES NATIONAL PARK

Fireweed Camp

Bridge

1277

Fork

East

see MAP 133A

133A

NORTH CASCADES

Frisco Mtn

Lyall Glacier

NATIONAL PARK

Bridge

Six Mile Camp

State Camp

see MAP 132

see MAP 133B

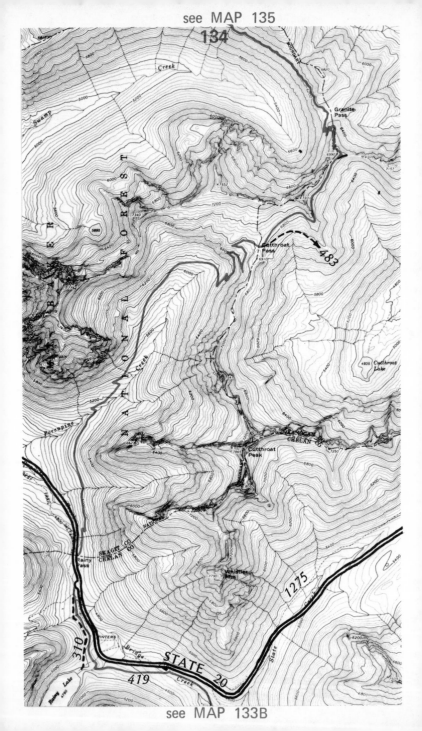

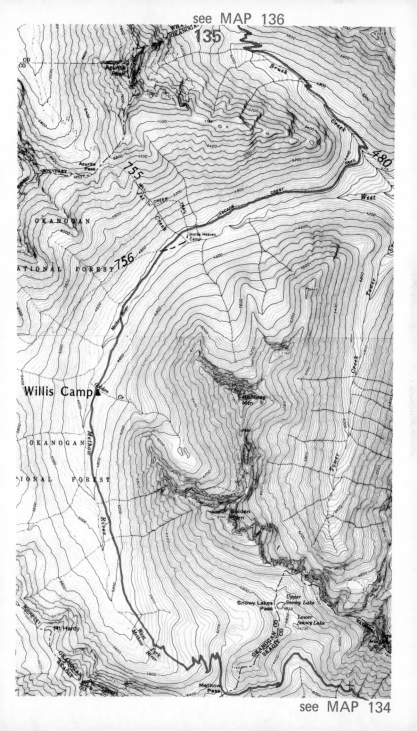

135

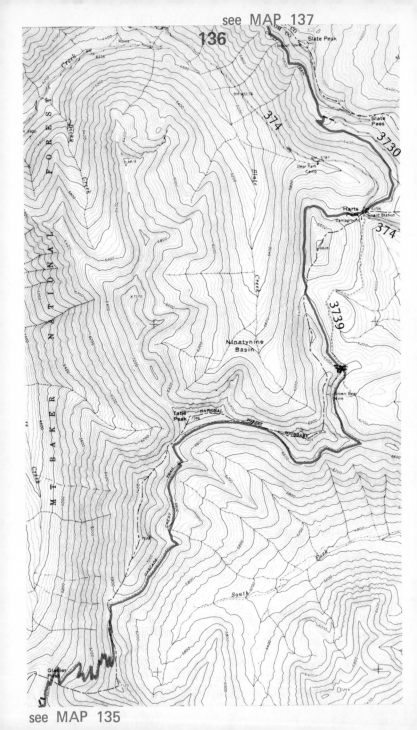

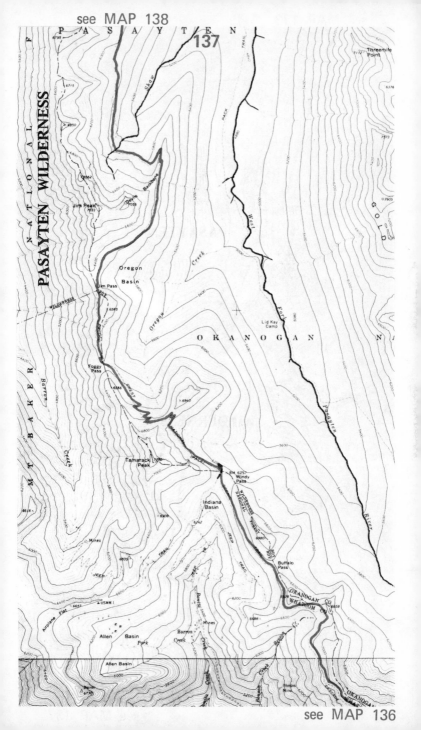

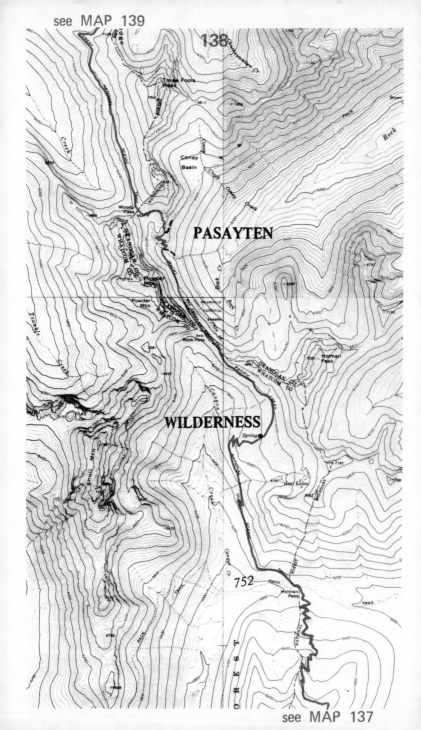

see MAP 139

138

PASAYTEN

WILDERNESS

752

see MAP 137

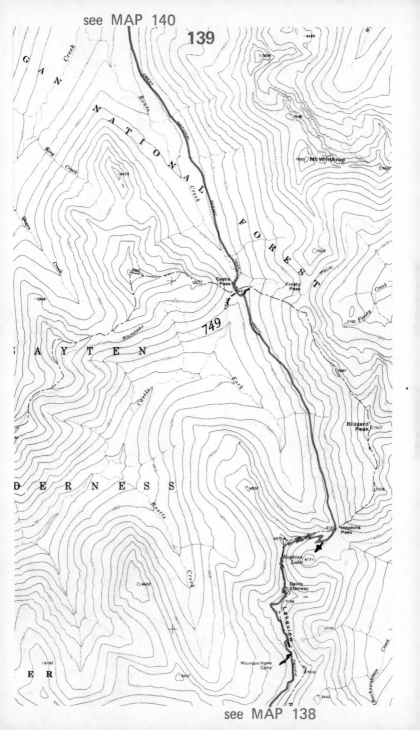

see MAP 140

139

see MAP 138

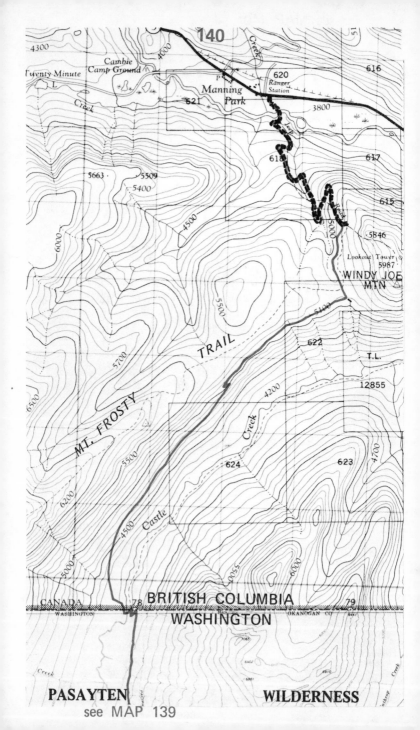

4300

Twenty Minute

Cambie
Camp Ground

Manning
Park

521

620
Ranger
Station

616

3800

617

615

5663

5509
5400

618

5000

5846

5500

TRAIL

Lookout Tower
5987

WINDY JOE
MTN

5700

622

T.L.

5100

12855

4200

MT. FROSTY

Creek

624

623

4700

5500

6500

6200

Castle

5000

4500

6000

CANADA

78

BRITISH COLUMBIA

79

WASHINGTON

WASHINGTON

OKANOGAN CO

Creek

PASAYTEN

WILDERNESS

see MAP 139

Index

Italic numerals refer to map numbers

Index

345